It's Your Money

Fifth Edition

The Authors

Brian E. Anderson (right) and J. Christopher Snyder have several things in common. Both were raised in small Ontario towns — Brian in Kirkland Lake and Chris in Collingwood. Both spent a lot of time on skates in their younger years — Chris as a comedy skater in amateur ice shows and Brian as a hockey player, which included trying out with the Montreal Canadiens back in the days of the six-team league. Both men are graduates of the University of Toronto and share extensive experience in the life insurance business — Brian was a multi-line agent for Travelers and Director of Education for the Life Underwriters Association of Canada, and Chris was a manager with Great-West Life. Brian and Chris are co-editors of the ECC Group's monthly *Personal Financial Planning Letter*.

Brian does personal financial planning for public company executives, and also deals with problems facing owner-managers of private companies as well as with executive compensation. He has also authored the book *The Joy of Tax Reduction* (Toronto: Hilborn/ECC).

Chris is well known for his book on RRSPs and related tax-deferral vehicles, *How To Be Sure You Have The Right RRSP* (Toronto: Financial Post/Gage Publishing), which has been a consistent best seller in Canada for many years, *How To Teach Your Children About Money* (Toronto: Macmillan; Reading, MA: Addison-Wesley), and *Financial Planning for the International Executive*. In his everyday consulting practice, Chris specializes in executive compensation and financial planning, with emphasis on financial planning for senior executives, retirement planning, and relocation counselling.

A final common bond between Messrs Anderson and Snyder is that they live in the Toronto area, Brian in downtown Toronto and Chris in Mississauga. Each is married — Brian to Diva and Chris to Pat — and has three children.

When they're not writing books, Brian is Director of Personal Financial Management Services for Deloitte Haskins & Sells, Chartered Accountants, while Chris is President of the nationally based ECC Financial Planning Group.

It's Your Money

Fifth Edition

Canada's bestselling guide
to personal financial planning

Brian E. Anderson
and J. Christopher Snyder

Methuen

Toronto New York London
Sydney Auckland

Canadian Cataloguing in Publication Data

Anderson, Brian E., 1935-
It's your money

Includes index.
ISBN 0-458-99750-1

1. Finance, Personal. I. Snyder, J. Christopher (John Christopher), 1941- . II. Title.

HG179.A52 1986 332.024 C86-093608-2

Printed and bound in Canada

1 2 3 4 5 86 91 90 89 88 87

Contents

Acknowledgments

For their help — emotional and spiritual as well as technical — we have many people to thank: Fred Thompson, F.S.A., F.C.I.A., for his actuarial input, the computer tables, and his specific contribution to the chapter on retirement; Phil Waters and Dave Gilliland, for their assistance in updating and editing the sections on estate planning, wills, and international transfers; Harry Pergantes, former President of our ECC Insurance Agency subsidiary, whose thirty years' experience in the life insurance business tested the accuracy and wisdom of our comments on the subject; Jim Fraser, who performed a similar function in relation to general insurance; John Rosebush, C.A., ECC Vice President, whose experience on taxes was utilized throughout the book on tax-related matters; Catherine Munro, an ECC Consultant who helped with the research and editing, and Don Wilson who with the other consultants continued to generate revenue, allowing us to work on this update; Muriel Gilbert, who kept the office running smoothly despite our attempts to sabotage its efficiency and tranquillity. Our thanks go also to Bob Copland of the ECC Kitchener office; Paul Boeda and Russ Popham, ECC Calgary; and Armel Bouchard at Le Groupe ECC in Montreal. Thanks, too, to Eva Keith, Cathy Robinson, Elaine Smith, Cathy Osborne, Catherine Munro, Muriel Gilbert, Monica Nickle, and Nicole Kapadia who assisted in many ways and whose comments on the chapter "Women and Financial Planning" helped to ensure that this chapter was not just another male creation. Cathy Osborne was also our typist who toiled through illegible longhand and cheerfully put up with fickle last-minute changes. Thanks, too, to the members of the ECC Advisory Board: Doug Young, retired Chairman of Hay & Associates, whose general assistance and encouragement is always appreciated; David Carlisle, President of Carlisle Videotex Consultants, whose knowledge of technology is helping us create a better financial planning product; and Jim Stewart, President of Triarch, whose knowledge of finance has been invaluable to us.

Over the years there are many who have made contributions to this book, and at the risk of missing some, these include: our wives, Pat Snyder and Diva Anderson; Eric Barton and his staff at Thorne, Stevenson

& Kellogg, for their input on termination; Paul Slan, Bob Simpson, Bill Scott, Gord Stovel, Jim Duckworth, Francois Mayrand, Michel David, Bob Paterson, David Condor, Mark Braganollo, Fred Meredith, Nancy Thompson, Mark Shilling, Jim Gibson, and Jim Hilborn, the Publisher of the Personal Financial Planning Letter. The monthly discipline of writing a Newsletter forces us to keep up to date on new events.

Our clients, too, deserve thanks — they keep us on our toes and inspire us to be creative.

A host of other people in many organizations and institutions were most helpful, and although they are too numerous to mention individually, they all know who they are; to them we extend a collective, hearty "thank you."

Preface

We all want to get to heaven, but no one wants to die to get there. We all want financial success with an inner sense of peace and the admiration of our peers, yet few of us are willing to pay the price in time, effort, and discipline to have even a fighting chance of accomplishing these goals.

Everyone knows the problem: the government takes away too much in the form of taxes, and inflation erodes the purchasing power of what is left.

At this point, you may find yourself much like Cleopatra in the arms of Mark Antony floating down the Nile on her barge — not prone to argue, but impatient to find dramatic and instant solutions. If so, you may be disappointed — this book offers neither. What it does offer, we sincerely believe, is hard data and soft wisdom to give you that fighting chance to handle your personal financial planning effectively, so that you may reach most of your reasonable financial objectives.

We know from our day-to-day practice as personal financial counsellors that all the information, conventional widsom, and good intentions in the world will not yield concrete results without the determination to succeed by persisting in doing at least a few things right and following through. A word of caution: don't take financial planning, or this or any other book on the subject, too seriously. It is only one aspect of your existence — your health, your family, your career, and your recreations are at least as important. Sound financial planning can enhance your total enjoyment of life but it should not distort your perspective to the point where you become a successful miser or a miserable misanthrope.

And when the going gets rough, remember that even those apparent wizards of finance whose faces appear on television and whose newsletters you are encouraged to buy had their share of problems when they started out. They too fall short of perfection.

Besides, even the most perfect financial plan won't get you into heaven — at least that's what the experts tell us. Something about a camel and the eye of a needle . . .

Introduction

Most authors dedicate their books to someone who had a significant influence on their lives and on their work. Our book is dedicated to the governments of Canada, from Robert Borden's Conservatives — who first introduced income tax in Canada in 1915 — to successive governments both Liberal and Conservative who since then have not only introduced increasingly complex tax and social legislation, but have also contributed more than their fair share to inflation. Without their combined efforts, it is questionable whether a book such as this would even be needed.

Interest in financial planning has never been greater than it is today, with people trying to fight the double-barrelled problems of inflation and high taxation. Inflation in the '80s has not been the threat it was in the '70s; but the severe recession of '81 and '82 made Canadians more conscious of financial security than ever before. In fact, financial planning has become a virtual necessity for everybody from the middle-aged executive who moans, "I earn more money than I ever dreamed I would, but we have less to spend than when we were just starting out," to the young first-time homeowners who suddenly are forced to do a budget for the first time.

In recent years a parade of so-called crisis investing experts have counselled us on what to buy — from old licence plates to gold bullion. These prophets of doom trade on people's fears and fantasies rather than deal with real-life financial problems. If you are looking for a book full of apocalyptic advice, stop reading, return this book to where you bought it, and ask for a refund. *It's Your Money* is not that kind of book. Instead, it takes a practical approach to most of the issues and questions that affect all Canadians day to day. How do I borrow money? How much insurance should I carry? What is the right kind to have? How do I budget? What do I do if I lose my job, become widowed or divorced, or change my place of residence? How do I refinance my mortgage? Should I invest in gold or buy an RRSP, or should I pay off my mortgage first? Should I invest in a tax shelter or a mutual fund? What should I include in my will?

It's Your Money is also designed to:

- help you define your personal financial objectives and priorities
- give you some basic practical concepts and rules of financial planning
- provide you with information and recommendations based on current financial products and the most recent Canadian tax and social legislation
- help you make better decisions and take more effective action to make your money go further during these uncertain times.

You may find that we deal with only one or two areas that concern you personally. If that is the case, use this book as a handy reference guide. But we recommend you read it from cover to cover if you want to know more about financial planning. Read the whole book, then return to the chapters you find of most interest. After that you will be able to make decisions as they apply to you and act on our recommendations with discretion. A fact-finding questionnaire at the back of the book will help you work out the specifics of your financial situation and save you valuable time and money, especially when you are dealing with professional advisers.

Good luck, and always remember — it's *your* money we are talking about!

CHAPTER 1

The Gentle Art of Financial Planning

Money can buy almost anything. It can't make us happy, perhaps, but it shouldn't make us unhappy either. Unfortunately, money often does bring unhappiness, even to people who are quite well off.

Some people earning $100,000 a year have trouble making ends meet; others make $20,000 and routinely save and invest a good percentage of that sum. These lower-income people manage to build up a cushion for themselves because they have no options. Too many of us fail to realize that a financial cushion is something we all need.

WHY PLAN?

Inflation

Many of us think we don't need to plan. We even use inflation, a factor that makes financial planning more urgent, to convince ourselves that we can keep putting it off.

How much money did you make five years ago? It probably seemed like a lot then, didn't it? And every year since then your income has gone up, hasn't it? So, if things are a little tight right now, what the heck? Next year's raise will take care of it. Never mind that the real purchasing power of next year's raise will be eroded by inflation even before you get it, even though inflation has gone down in recent years. Those annual increases will still seem like a lot of money, you'll still feel as if you are getting richer, and you'll believe your problems will sort themselves out.

By using that kind of rationalization, each year more and more Canadians fail to get ahead of the money game. Yet they keep making more, spending more, borrowing more, and even investing more. They also find themselves worrying more. Rational financial planning begins when you stop worrying about money and start doing something about it.

If anyone had told you ten years ago that it would take $113,000 to buy a respectable but unspectacular three-bedroom house in Toronto, you would have told them they were crazy. If anyone had told you that a gross income of $25,000 would mean tough times for a family of four in most big Canadian cities, you would have laughed.

When most of us were starting out, we set our financial objectives, vague as they might have been, in terms of dollars. Let's look at David, a writer. In 1976, when he turned twenty-one, he decided he wanted to make $35,000 a year by the time he was thirty. He now makes his $35,000, but because of inflation it doesn't translate into the kind of lifestyle he thought he would have. Instead of the vacations in Europe and the expensive sports cars he'd counted on, he drives a Ford and his family stays at a friend's summer cottage for ten days every August.

But David is lucky compared to people living in retirement. He can at least keep on working and increasing his income.

Okay, then, what is ahead? Table 1.1 shows you how much income you'll have to generate for each $1,000 you need now *just to break even* at various levels of inflation over the next twenty-five years.

Table 1.1
Inflation Equivalents of $1,000

Years	*Annual Inflation Rate*				
	3%	5%	7½%	10%	12%
1	$1,030	$1,050	$1,075	$ 1,100	$ 1,120
5	1,159	1,276	1,435	1,610	1,762
10	1,344	1,629	2,061	2,593	3,105
15	1,558	2,079	2,958	4,177	5,473
20	1,806	2,653	4,247	6,727	9,646
25	2,094	3,386	6,098	10,834	17,000

It's pretty staggering, isn't it? What it means is this: if we assume that the average rate of inflation over the next twenty years is going to be 5% (and that's lower than it's been most years in Canada during the last ten years), anyone with an income of $30,000 today will need an annual income of $79,590 ($30 × 2,653) in twenty years' time—just to break even (without allowing for taxes).

One of the most common responses to inflation is the "To hell with it, let's borrow, buy now, and pay later with inflated dollars" syndrome. Over the past few years this attitude has proven successful with such items as homes, whose value has increased faster than inflation; however, it has led to disaster with depreciating items such as big cars.

Government and Corporate Benefits

Inflation can be frightening, but there are some compensations. Benefits such as the Canada Pension Plan, the Quebec Pension Plan, and Old Age Security are available to all Canadians. Along with corporate benefits they have grown to help protect us from financial disasters. The costs of medical care will not bankrupt you today in Canada. Your employer or your provincial government probably provides you with basic protection that you can build on with private arrangements. But the complexity of these benefits may have left you confused. If, furthermore, you have not been doing any planning, you are probably wasting some money through duplication of benefits. You may also be wasting money by purchasing the wrong Registered Retirement Savings Plan or owning the wrong kind of life insurance for your needs.

Taxes

Did you know that in 1915 a "temporary" income tax of 3% was imposed? Did you know that if you now earn $40,000 a year your marginal tax rate is over 40% in most provinces? Do you like the way the government is spending your money? Do you like paying taxes? Would you like to take advantage of some of the so-called "tax breaks" so that you can keep more of what you earn for yourself?

If you answered no to all these questions except the last one, you had better do some financial planning. There are still a number of ways you can defer and minimize your taxes and help yourself to meet your financial objectives.

WHO SHOULD BE INVOLVED?

Financial planning should be a family matter. Studies have shown that financial pressures are the most common single cause of marriage failure in North America. If spouses share financial information from day to day, there's less chance of these kinds of pressures wrecking a marriage.

It's common sense: if a husband has no idea what groceries really cost and he's the only one working, it's pretty easy for him to start assuming his wife is a bad manager when she says she needs more money to run the house. If a wife knows nothing about income tax rates in Canada, she can very easily start to believe her husband's a tightwad when he refuses to buy a new washer and dryer.

Women at home who are not producing income often feel as if they are continually asking their husbands for handouts and feel totally reliant upon their husbands for their financial upkeep. Some men want to keep it that way and, unfortunately, try to keep their wives in the dark about finances.

Not only is this a throwback to the nineteenth century, but it is also extremely shortsighted. Women should be involved not only in discussions about family finances but in managing the money as well. In fact, we find many women do a much better job at running family finances than their husbands do. One system that works well is for the non-working spouse to manage the money and pay all the bills, while the breadwinner receives an allowance or "walking-around money" for personal expenditures such as lunches, haircuts, and small clothing items.

It probably doesn't matter who writes the cheques as long as it has been decided in advance. The system breaks down when both people write cheques and don't advise the other partner. This practice often comes home to roost when an NSF cheque arrives unexpectedly.

When both spouses are working and generating income, it's even more important to communicate financial information. If one or the other starts to feel as if he or she is carrying an unfair share of the family's total financial burden, it won't take long for arguments to begin about money and all sorts of other things.

The couples who get into trouble are those who do not talk about what to do with two incomes. Unfortunately, attitudes such as "I made it and I can spend it any way I want" have destroyed more than one marriage. This attitude is increasingly common among women who have just reentered the workforce and who feel "At last I'm being useful; the income I earn is a measure of that. And since I earned it, I want a say on how it is spent. Besides, I have some catching up to do." Feelings like these should be discussed openly with your husband.

One back-to-work woman overcame this problem after a lengthy discussion with her husband. Now she uses the money she earns to buy her clothes and pay for maintenance and redecorating of their home.

Another woman took pride in knowing that her income was being used specifically to finance her daughter's private-school education and, therefore, she could identify with a specific expense instead of just throwing it into the general pot.

This approach can also create problems; for example, if one spouse provides all the luxuries and the other looks after the basics, disputes can arise.

Wives who earn more than their husbands are becoming more commonplace. We know women who hide some of their income from their husbands in order not to undermine the man's traditional role of being the breadwinner.

Our suggestion: talk about it. Review your financial objectives together and decide how you want to spend your money and do your investing in the most tax-effective manner.

When it comes to the actual management of the money, write down all the jobs to be done and divide up the responsibilities. Tell each other what you are doing and rotate responsibilities regularly.

Communication also means communicating with your children, at least making sure they understand the financial goals and realities of the family. Too many parents alternate between "Do you think I'm made of money?" and "You just pick out the one you want, Johnny." Children should be included in financial discussions at regular family meeetings every few months from the time they are around ten years of age. It's good training for them.

Planning should not be limited to families but should be done by everyone, rich or poor, young or old, male or female.

HOW TO PLAN

Many people are intimidated by the whole idea of financial planning. However, following a few basic steps will make it easier and more enjoyable.

Step 1: Sit Down and Assess Your Situation

What is happening to you? Are you gaining ground? Are you wondering why your neighbours are taking a trip every year and you can't afford it? Are you going nowhere in your job? Do you anticipate a career shift? Are you nearing retirement? These are only a few of the possible questions to ask yourself. Take some time and think about your position, then discuss it with your spouse. Filling in the Personal Financial Profile at the back of the book will help. Complete the Personal Balance Sheet and Cash Flow worksheets to see exactly where you stand.

Step 2: Set Your Objectives, Both Long and Short Term

Goal setting is the cornerstone of the whole planning process. If you write down your objectives it may help you clarify them. Above all, they should be specific. For example, "I want to be rich some day" is a daydream, but "I want to have a net worth of $1,000,000 by the time I am forty" is a specific goal and therefore attainable. Often your financial goals will have a social or human reason behind them. For example, "We want to have a summer place by the time the children are in school" is a goal in which money becomes merely a way of acquiring a place where the whole family can have fun.

In setting goals, make conscious decisions about what you want to do as it relates to your *family security, financial independence, vacations, savings and investments, the type of home you want to live in, the general lifestyle you want for yourself and your family, career, and retirement*. You also will have to establish priorities and, above all else, be honest with yourself and realistic about your ambitions.

Step 3: Develop a Plan of Attack and Carry It Out

To start, take each individual objective and decide how to implement it. For example, if you have decided your main goal for the year is to clear off $3,000 in debt, you must decide how to come up with that $3,000. Do you go without a holiday or can you work harder to increase your earnings?

At this stage your first priority must be to develop a budget. Without it you won't know how much money you can actually put toward your goals. The budget is so important that Chapter 2 is devoted to it. Decide whether or not you will seek professional assistance to help you design and implement your plan.

At this time you must also develop a spending strategy, including a process for comparing prices on major purchases, especially luxury goods. These prices can vary as much as 30% or even 50% depending on where and when you buy such major items.

We're not suggesting you drive all over town to save 5¢ here and 10¢ there on groceries — that's nonsense. But when it comes to bigger purchases, real savings can be made, and you should plan to take advantage of them. One family we know developed a simple tactic to cut 20% from their annual cost of buying Christmas presents. They purchased items on sale during the course of the year. Not only did they save money but they also avoided a lot of hassle in December. Another person we know found the prices on a pair of skis ranged from $180 to $360 simply by making some telephone calls.

Make a quick review of your major expenses over the whole year by date and category. Probably you will find ways to change your buying strategy, and save considerable amounts of money by knowing when various sales are on in your area, by being sure about the items you wish to purchase, and by using the telephone to determine in advance where you can obtain the best price. Following these procedures will get you closer to things you really want to do. To prevent blowing your money on items you don't really want or need, keep in mind what you are planning for and what you really want. For more ideas, see Chapter 4, "How To Be a Smart Consumer."

For most of us designing a financial plan is easier than making it work. We start to rationalize, "Oh well, next year's automatic increase will take care of my problems." Here self-discipline is the key to success. If you have set your objectives carefully and really have the desire to reach your goals, you will activate your plan and not procrastinate any longer. You might start by calling a financial adviser, or by purchasing the Registered Retirement Savings Plan you have been thinking about for the past three years, or selling your cottage because the carrying charges for two months' use are prohibitive. *The biggest mistake you can make is to do nothing.*

Step 4: Evaluate the Results

At least once a year sit down and see what has happened over the course of the past twelve months. Companies do this every year and, when you think of it, you are your own company. An updated personal net worth statement at this stage will help you see how things have gone for you (a sample is included in the appendix). This statement will provide you with an opportunity to reflect on the past year and plan ahead for the future. Once you have evaluated the results, return full circle to Step 1 and repeat the process.

Successful companies know that all work and no play makes for bad business. At your year-end, celebrate a little. Take your spouse or friends out for dinner, or take a weekend away from the children. You deserve it!

What Financial Planning Can and Cannot Do for You

Financial planning is by no means a panacea for all your financial woes. In fact, you can expect financial concerns of one sort or another to be with you the rest of your life. But if it does nothing else, financial planning will tell you where you are now and give you some control over where you are going. In doing that, it should remove much of the anxiety you may feel about money matters in general.

DO'S AND DON'TS

Do Start planning early in life and remember it is valuable to men and women in all occupations and on all income levels.

Do Reflect on your specific personal goals — education, vacations, career, retirement, savings, investments, home, security, day-to-day expenses, and financial independence.

Do Establish an order of priorities.

Do Put down your goals in writing.

Do Develop a budget.

Do Update your plan every year.

Don't Exclude other members of your family from your planning.

Don't Procrastinate or let your ego get you off the track.

Don't Hesitate to seek professional help.

Don't Expect your plan to make you millions overnight, but have the discipline and patience to make it work.

Don't Get discouraged if you aren't 100% successful the first time. Replacing bad habits with good ones is never easy.

CHAPTER 2

Budgeting: What It Can and Cannot Do for You

"How much money have I made in total over the past ten years? If I had saved even 5% of it, and if today I invested that amount at 10% interest, what would my interest income be for the next year?"

When most Canadians look at how much they've earned over the past ten years, and consider the good position in which they'd be today if they'd saved even a small percentage of that total, they shake their heads and say things like, "Yeah . . . well . . . I've got some equity in my house."

The fact is that beyond forced and semi-forced saving – the equity we accumulate in our houses, the money we accumulate in company pension plans, the increasing value of an RRSP – most of us aren't very successful savers, mainly because we don't manage our money very well.

How much money did you make last month that you can't account for? Most of us lose track of at least 10% of our incomes – that is, if we're making enough to *have* 10% left over after covering basic necessities. And that "lost" money is what motivates many people to sit down and draw up a personal budget.

Most people, however, hate drawing up a budget. Many are afraid to find out where the money actually goes – they anticipate arguments and, as a result, don't budget. Budgeting can and should be a pleasant exercise, particularly if you view it as a guide to how you want to spend your money, not a purgatory demanding constant self-denial.

Drawing up your budget then, is the first step toward acquiring reasonable control of your income. Here are some rules to help you.

THE RULES OF BUDGETING

Rule 1: A Personal Budget Is Not a Method of Character Reformation

A short case history will illustrate this.

Alvin Anxious found himself getting short of money, even though he was earning a good income. He had trouble meeting payments on his car, he had made only partial payments on his bank credit card for the past three months, and the financial pressure was starting to affect his work and his marriage.

Alvin decided to turn over a new leaf. He drew up a budget and decided to correct many aspects of his lifestyle.

He was smoking too much, up to two packs on a busy day. He'd been talking about cutting down for years, so, when he drew up his budget, he allowed for only one pack of cigarettes per day, not necessarily to save money, but for health reasons.

He often had a drink or two at lunch. He knew it made him less effective in the early part of the afternoon and he'd been planning to do something about that too. He therefore allowed for lunches that cost about $3.00 less.

He also noticed that he simply couldn't account for about 20% of his monthly income. He decided he must have been wasting that money and consequently allowed only 5% of his total budget for miscellaneous expenses.

Alvin's new life lasted only two weeks. Why? Because he violated the cardinal rule of personal budgeting by trying to use a budget to reform his character instead of realistically basing it on his way of living. Alvin's budget had become a straitjacket — and straitjackets get uncomfortable.

Budgets are no more than a means of dealing with your money. When you're trying to get out of financial trouble you may be in for some pretty extreme cutbacks in certain areas; remember that major changes in your lifestyle resulting from your budget should be based strictly on financial considerations, not moral ones.

Rule 2: When You're Budgeting to Get Out of Financial Trouble, You Have to See a Light at the End of the Tunnel

The people at Alcoholics Anonymous will tell you that anyone who starts off saying, "I'll never have another drink" is going to have a tough time staying dry. What does work is getting up every day and saying, "I won't have anything to drink today."

The same principle applies when you're designing a budget to help you get out of financial trouble. Don't say, "I'm going to cut back on my standard of living." Say, "I am going to cut back on my standard of living for six months, then I'll have this thing licked." Like the people who go to AA, you'll find that the latter approach works much better. And, like the people who go to AA, you'll probably find yourself being tempted to make grandiose statements of intent. The reason's the same in both cases — guilt. Like people who've been drinking their lives away, people who've painted themselves into financial corners feel guilty about it. If you set up a budget with the idea of working off that guilt by punishing yourself, it probably won't work.

Rule 3: The First 10% of Your Income Belongs to You

Plan to save 10% of your take-home income. Take that 10% off the top, before you start calculating how much you have available to spend on other things. Often people will protest, "I don't have 10% to spare," but that is simply not true for most of us.

Let's start by making it clear that when we talk about saving we include paying off debts — not mortgages, but debts. Reducing indebtedness increases financial elbow room, just as buying bonds does.

There's a simple way to prove to yourself that you really do have spare money. Calculate how much cash you normally carry, then carry 25% less for a week. You'll find yourself spending less. It might be irritating occasionally, but before the week is up you'll be making financial judgments before spending, instead of just taking it for granted that you have the cash in your pocket.

Let's assume you start putting away 10% of your income when you start to work, that your initial income is $15,000, and that this commences when you are twenty-two. If your salary increases by 10% per year and you earn 10% on your money, you will have more than $3,500,000 by the time you are sixty-five. To bring this into today's dollars, assume this 10% represents a real gain of 3% (salary increase minus inflation), and your salary gain over inflation is 3%. This will represent $223,000 in 1986 dollars — not bad when you consider you probably wouldn't even miss the money along the way.

If you still don't think this "10% off the top" rule is worth a little effort, go back and answer the first two questions at the start of this chapter.

Rule 4: Interest Is Something You Should Collect, Not Something You Pay

A lot of people think that using other people's money is smart. There are many reasons for that kind of attitude.

Most of us assume that next year we'll be making more money than we made this year. We believe that this "extra income" will make the repayment of debts less demanding. That increase in earnings may have been a fact for most of us, but it's going to be less true as we near our peak earning years.

Because a business can do very well on borrowed money if the interest paid is lower than the return gained by using or investing the money, many people believe that they can repeat the process in their personal budgeting. They know that inflation is cancelling out part of the interest cost.

Unfortunately, these assumptions usually don't apply to personal finance. It is true that inflation does cancel out part of the real interest cost you have to bear on borrowed money, if your income reflects the general rate of inflation. But it's just as true that the people who lend money—banks, finance companies, credit card companies—know all about that, and increase the rates they charge as inflation increases. You'll pay 11% or more on money you borrow from the bank and 1.5% each month on your credit card balance (that works out to about 18.6% a year). And this does not include new user fees introduced by some of the credit card companies.

You can't build profits while paying interest on money you're using for consumption. If you're investing money at 10%, but at the same time you're paying 18% interest on an overdue balance on each of five credit cards, the interest differential is working against you.

The biggest problem with using other people's money, however, is that it restricts your financial freedom. In the short run it may give you more cash to spend or to invest. But in the long run it ties up an ever-increasing portion of your total earnings in debt repayment. Unless you borrow even more, you'll have less cash to use for your own purposes.

We're not suggesting that you shouldn't ever borrow money. There are many good reasons for borrowing. Remember, however, that if you use other people's money it usually will cost you money; if other people are using yours, you'll earn money.

DRAWING UP YOUR BUDGET

This process begins with the setting of some general objectives. Why are you working and earning money anyway? Most of us work to finance the lifestyle we want for ourselves and our families—the house and furniture we own or want to own, the transportation we use, the clothing we wear, the vacations we enjoy, the quality of education our children get. We work to buy the freedom to acquire these things without having to be too concerned about money.

HOW TO USE A MULTI-ACCOUNT SYSTEM

Your budget should make it possible for you to spend *less* time and effort worrying about money and *more* time enjoying the choices you've made about your lifestyle. A Multi-Account System can help you do this.

Start by calculating your *net family income*. Include both spouses' incomes, but subtract from your gross incomes what you have to pay in income taxes, Canada Pension Plan contributions, Unemployment Insurance premiums, health care premiums, deductions for your pension plans and so on. This is an important step. Confusing gross with net is a great way to get into financial trouble.

Calculating your real net income doesn't end when you've taken into account these direct deductions. Let's take, as an example, a family where both spouses work. The husband is a fairly successful salaried sales representative. His net income after all his deductions works out to $30,000 a year. The wife teaches elementary school and after deductions her take-home pay is $19,000 a year.

Between them, they appear to have a total net income of $49,000 available to purchase the kind of lifestyle they want for themselves and their children. But having both people work costs money—money that should be subtracted from that take-home amount to arrive at the true net income at their disposal. Are the children in day-care? Does someone come in to make them lunch? What about a house cleaner? What about the out-of-pocket expenses of a sales rep for things such as clothing? Although the tax people don't recognize this as a cost of doing business, try selling to business people while wearing jeans and see how far you get. The wife also needs more and different clothing when she goes out to teach than if she were staying home. Also, there's depreciation on and operating costs of the family car. Although many of these expenses are not deductible from income tax or recoverable for expense-account purposes, they're often essential when both spouses work.

All those costs necessary for earning your income should be calculated, because only then can you get an accurate picture of your real financial position. Taking care of the costs of earning your income becomes the central purpose for the first account in your Multi-Account System.

Account #1: The Business Account

This should be a joint current or personal chequing account into which the total incomes of both spouses are deposited. All the costs of earning this income should be paid directly out of this account—including a contribution toward a "sinking fund" to replace the family car. The balance remaining after those essential costs have been paid will be transferred to other accounts to help you meet your financial objectives.

Account #2: True Savings Capital Account

This is where you put that 10% of your take-home income that you're "paying" yourself. This is money that you're saving to buy capital goods—a summer cottage, ski chalet, or investments. If you're going to get rich, this is the money that's going to do it for you: 10% of your take-home pay every month. It's an invaluable habit to acquire.

And the allowance you're making in your Business Account for replacement of your car, the "sinking fund" we talked about, should be held in this account where it will earn interest for you.

Account #3: The Family Living Account

Each month, a set amount should be transferred from your Business Account into your Family Living Account to cover basic necessities—mortgage payment or rent, groceries, utilities, insurance on your house and life, lunch money for the kids, money for clothing for the kids and for that part of the adults' clothing expenditure not counted as a business expense.

Make sure you calculate realistically to cover all these costs. Base the amount you're going to deposit into this account on your actual costs for the last few months and make an extra allowance for seasonal expenses such as new winter boots for the kids. Use a daily interest chequing account for this purpose. Ideally, it should pay a competitive interest rate and return your cancelled cheques to you at the end of each month. You may, however, have to compromise on the interest rate in order to receive the cancelled cheques for your records.

Account #4: "Walking-Around" Money

In this system, we're talking about combining incomes, but the fact is that both spouses — whether they are working or not — should have some money of their own.

It should be paid into each partner's personal account out of the Business Account. Payment should be automatic and the amounts should be set. Neither spouse need then ask the other for money — and that's worth avoiding. The account permits both spouses to buy a few things on whim: a drink after work, gifts for each other or for the children, or a totally unjustifiable piece of clothing. It also preserves a little financial privacy, and that's important too. The amounts involved don't have to be (and shouldn't be) very big. All the necessities will be taken care of by the joint Business and Family Living Accounts; but this private money should be there every month.

We're calling this an account, but each partner should make whatever arrangement he or she considers most convenient. For example, one may prefer to take this walking-around money in cash at regular intervals; another may want a monthly transfer to a personal chequing account or a daily interest savings account. The point is, after having paid the costs of earning the income and providing the necessities, walking-around money is the next priority.

Account #5: True Savings Consumption Account

This is the money you're saving toward the purchase of non-capital goods or services, where you'll save for your Christmas presents and for your vacation. It will help you cure the "fly now, pay later" syndrome.

The concept's simple enough: calculate how much whatever you're saving for is going to cost you, decide how soon you want to have the money saved, and you'll know how much you should put into this account every month.

If it's long-term, it may be worthwhile to have the money accumulate in the name of the lower-income spouse, as the gain will be taxed at a lower rate.

Let's go back to our sample family and see how this Multi-Account System works for them.

1. Net Revenue Deposited to Account #1	$ 49,000.00
Allocation	
Cost of earning income	
Lunch for children ($18 × 50 weeks)	$ 900.00
Sinking fund for car ($250 × 12 mos.)	3,000.00
Non-recoverable business expenses ($200 × 12 mos.)	2,400.00
	$ 6,300.00
Net revenue available for other purposes	$ 42,700.00

So far, it's pretty clear. After allowing for the real costs of earning that total income of $49,000, our sample family has only $42,700 available to spend as they like.

The next step is to take 10% off the top and deposit it into Account #2.

2. Deposit to Account #2 for savings (or debt reduction) 10% of net income ($355/mo.)	$ 4,270.00

Then allow for planned contributions to Account #5 to save for a vacation.

3. Deposit to Account #5 for vacation fund (total cost $3,600; monthly contributions of $300	$ 3,600.00

The principle of taking the money you "owe" yourself right off the top of your income is sound, and most of us really can spare it. Remember how much of your last month's earnings you couldn't account for? Not all of it was just frittered away, but part of it certainly was. The test we suggested – reducing the amount of cash you carry by 25% and seeing how it reduced your casual expenditures – helps to prove the point.

After you've put the money into your two savings accounts, you'll find it doesn't make much difference to the total income you have available. Let's look at our sample family again.

Balance of Revenue	$ 34,830.00

The next step is to calculate the amount you'll need for family living costs. Remember to be realistic. Your calculation may prove that you have to cut back on your vacation plans. You may have to plan right now to keep your car for an extra year so that you can reduce the contributions to your sinking fund. It's better to make these kinds of adjustments now than to try to scrape along on less money than it really costs you to live. If you attempt that, there's a good chance that you'll abandon the whole system as unworkable, or you'll start scrimping on your basic capital savings. Neither course of action makes any sense.

Let's see how our sample family would work out their living costs. (Please note: a more detailed budget is given in the appendix.)

Family Living Costs (monthly)	
Mortgage payment	$ 800.00
Groceries	$ 500.00
Home maintenance repairs	$ 150.00
Clothing	$ 250.00
Entertainment	$ 180.00
Furniture (new and replacements)	$ 230.00
Utilities	$ 140.00
Car (operating and repair)	$ 240.00
Miscellaneous and insurance	$ 250.00
	$ 2,740.00

Now let's incorporate that figure into the account system.

4. Deposit Account #3 (12 × $2,740.00)	$ 32,880.00
Balance Available For Account #4	$ 1,950.00

That's only $162.50 per month for two people, probably not enough, but it clearly puts the choices before our sample family. They can cut back on their vacation plans, take less walking-around money, purchase fewer pieces of furniture or clothing. At least they can see more clearly just what financial choices they do have. And that's the purpose of the system. It lets you set your own priorities; it lets *you* make your own decisions, instead of having them made for you by your financial circumstances and your creditors.

AN ALTERNATE METHOD

You may want to streamline the multi-account system. It requires more discipline, and you will likely earn less interest, but instead of several accounts, you can get by with as few as two—a Daily Interest Savings Account (DISA) in one person's name and a joint personal chequing account. Here is how it works:

Have your paycheque deposited directly into a DISA, then transfer enough money each month to your joint personal chequing account to handle your expenses.

Try to write the cheques only once or twice a month. This way you will minimize the administration and you can keep your money in your DISA, earning interest longer. Money in a DISA pays you interest every day on a minimum amount in the account on that day.

With this system, you will not have specific amounts set aside for purchases in separate accounts as you did in the Multi-Account System, and discipline may be required not to spend the money in the account. You will have to keep track of the amounts which are in there for the specific purposes; furthermore, the interest paid on a DISA will be slightly less than in a true savings account. It is possible to have DISAs on a joint basis; however, we feel for tax reasons it is better to have separate DISAs.

Remember, neither of these systems is intended to be a strait-jacket. Neither is any other financial management plan worthy of the name. It merely provides you with a clear picture of your real financial position so that *you* can make the decisions.

BUDGETING TO GET OUT OF FINANCIAL TROUBLE

The same basic system works whether you're budgeting to improve your financial position or to get out of serious financial difficulties, except that when you're budgeting to get out of trouble you'll apply 10% to debt reduction. You'll probably want to build in some short-term sacrifices as well.

Design your getting-out-of-trouble program so that the biggest sacrifices are made early. Build in short-term goals and rewards. As you get closer to the point where your affairs are back under control, you should be able to make fewer sacrifices. That's the light at the end of the tunnel that can make financial sacrificing easier.

Let's take our sample family again, this time assuming they are about $10,000 in debt. They owe $1,500 on their bank credit cards at 1¾% per month interest; $700 to a department store at 1¾% per month; $2,300 in back income taxes; and the rest on two bank loans at 12% a year each — a recent one for $2,000 and an older one with $4,500 still outstanding that has been refinanced twice.

The first step is to decide which debts to clear first. There are two factors to consider: the cost of the loan, and the effect slow repayment will have on your credit rating.

On both tests the credit card and department store debts get first claim. They're expensive, and failure to make at least the minimum payments required can have quick and dramatic effects on the couple's ability to get credit anywhere.

The loans come next. Bank loans are not cheap, especially in the case of an insured personal loan. Whenever possible the borrower should have a demand note with regular principal payments and the right to make extra payments. If the bank wishes to have the loan secured by insurance, then use a current personal policy or arrange for a new term insurance policy at competitive rates.

The principle behind the system is that if you pay off debts, more usable dollars are available and progress can be readily measured. The principle is sensible and easy to understand. Extreme sacrifices aren't too hard to make if you know you're making them only for a short period of time. They make the lesser sacrifices to follow seem easier to handle, and they let you see tangible signs of your progress.

KEEPING SCORE—YOUR PERSONAL CASH FLOW

Some people are content to work out a budget and use the budget as a guide to how they will spend their money. Others want to be a little more precise and estimate what the expenses will be each month. No two months' expenditures are exactly the same, and sometimes a forgotten expense can create undue anxiety. A monthly cash flow will help you determine where you will be every month.

To complete your cash flow, go to page 223 in the appendix. Use a pencil to fill in the monthly income you expect, less source deductions. If you expect an increase in income, make a reasonable estimate. To obtain current income figures, use your pay slips. Don't forget to include both incomes. Once completed, turn to page 224 to list your estimated expenses for the next year and when they will occur.

Some items such as debt repayment, food, housing costs, and transportation will be fairly consistent. Others such as insurance premiums, club dues, entertainment, and vacation costs are a little more sporadic. Try to make your expenses as uniform as possible. For example, with vacations, set up a separate vacation account to which you contribute monthly.

To help you estimate, go to your last-year records and this year's budget. Try to come up with an estimate of when the expenses will occur. Then, at the end of each month when you have paid the bills, tally up the figures.

If you don't balance, don't worry about it. A few dollars either way won't make much difference.

Doing this will give you greater peace of mind and help you weather the tight months when they come.

As with most things, the first time through will be the most difficult; however, if you make it a habit once a month, the rewards will be yours.

YOUR FAMILY NET WORTH STATEMENT

The Multi-Account System makes available to you all the information about your income, allowing you to make reasonable decisions as to how you want to spend your money. A provision for saving is also built into the system. The Family Net Worth Statement lets you and your family see your progress.

Financial pressures can be hard on family relationships. We therefore recommend that you draw up a statement and discuss it with your family. Knowing that Dad and Mom are saving for a vacation the whole family will enjoy may make it easier for the kids to accept bicycles that are less expensive than those of their friends. Besides, teaching your children how to manage money is one of the most valuable lessons you can give them.

FAMILY NET WORTH STATEMENT

Assets	Jan. '85	Jan. '86	*Liabilities*	Jan. '85	Jan. '86
House	$75,000	$ 78,000	Mortgage	$37,800	$ 36,200
Car depreciated value	5,500	3,500	Bank loan	550	Nil
RRSP	7,200	9,000	Credit Card	260	Nil
Savings account	420	700	Loan from parent	1,000	500
Canada Savings Bonds	1,000	1,500			
Value of furniture, etc.	8,700	9,600			
Funds in allocated accounts	1,600	4,000	Net worth	$59,310	$ 69,600
Totals	$98,920	$106,300		$98,920	$106,300

Net Worth Jan. '86 $106,300 less $36,700	$69,600
Net Worth Jan. '85 $98,920 less $39,610	$59,310
Net Worth Increase (profit for year)	$10,290

Let's take a closer look at the sample Family Net Worth Statement above. (A more detailed format is provided in the appendix.)

This fictional statement doesn't allow for depreciation of furniture. Nor does it allow for the increased value of either spouse's pension plan at work. It shows high amounts in the allocated accounts (car sinking fund, vacation fund) because the family hasn't bought a car or taken a vacation that year.

It also shows that simply by paying off debts the family was able to build their asset base in exactly the same way they could have done by saving. And it provides a system for assessing, once a year, what their financial program is providing for them.

No system of financial management is as much fun as having so much money that you never have to worry about it. Unfortunately, most of us will never be in that position. This method of budgeting is designed to minimize the amount of time and effort you have to spend on money. It's designed to help you make sensible decisions.

That's the core of any effort to improve your financial standing. You must deal with realistic information and make positive decisions, rather than wait for financial circumstances to make them for you.

DO'S AND DON'TS

Do View budgeting as an outline of how you plan to spend your money.

Do Be realistic about how much things cost; don't underestimate.

Do Pay yourself first; the rule of 10% does work.

Do Pay off the debts with the highest interest cost first.

Do Remember interest should be something you collect, not something you pay.

Do Establish a Multi-Account System to suit your needs.

Do Keep track of your expenditures using the Cash Flow Statement.

Do Draw up a Net Worth Statement.

Don't Finance purchases on a charge card unless you intend to pay the full amount (no interest) on the date due.

Don't Confuse your gross income with your real income, after tax and cost of earning money.

Don't Worry: let the system work for you.

Don't Use your budget to reform your character.

Don't Put yourself in a financial straitjacket.

CHAPTER 3

Credit: Just Another Word for Debt?

In recent years, many Canadians discovered how costly misuse and overuse of credit can be, as interest rates went sky-high, and they did not have the means to carry their loans. The heartbreaking result for thousands was the forced sale of hard-won assets at bargain-basement prices.

In fact, a good case can be made that the most fundamental cause of recent double-digit inflation, followed by the sharp recession in the early '80s, was overspending by individuals, companies, and governments alike. All had to borrow initially to pay for their overspending, and ultimately to cover the carrying charges on previous borrowing. The government had two alternatives: print more money and increase inflation, or shut down the printing presses, make money scarce, and force up the cost of money by raising interest rates. We all know they chose the latter course and what happened to interest rates as a result.

In reality, credit can be more than just another word for debt. By using credit creatively and prudently, we can acquire assets sooner and in larger amounts than we otherwise might. And, if we use credit properly, we can save hundreds of dollars in interest costs.

Many Canadians, however, overuse their credit, assuming debts for things they could have paid for just as easily in cash. Since some forms of credit, typically the most expensive forms, are so convenient, most of us don't even stop to think whether or not the debt is justified when we use our credit.

People who grant credit — banks, trust companies, finance companies, credit unions, department stores — determine how much credit they'll give you by looking at your total earnings and your ability to repay the loan. They are also interested in what other debts you have. But they are *not*, and cannot take the time to be, interested in your overall financial objectives. They assume that, if you have to, you can make a large portion of your total earnings available to pay back your debts. That's fine for them, but it could be all wrong for you.

SETTING YOUR OWN CREDIT LIMITS

When setting your own credit limits, remember that debt is a substitute for savings, not earnings. The money you use to pay back debts, like the money you save, is money you take out of current earnings. Instead of using it immediately, you put it aside to pay for things in the future (in the case of savings) or to pay for things you bought in the past (in the case of debt).

If you want to buy something, your two obvious alternatives are to borrow and incur a debt or to save the money needed for the purchase. Unless the circumstances are exceptional — such as when you are purchasing a home or contributing to a Registered Retirement Savings Plan or another income-producing asset — saving always makes better financial sense.

The problem is, you may find there are many "exceptional" circumstances, many times when you want to use credit, whether you need to or not.

That's fine, as long as you begin by setting your own credit limit. How much money can you afford to take out of current consumption to pay back debts without hindering your ability to meet other financial commitments and objectives? The answer to this question gives you your own personal credit limit — and it should include that all-important 10% for yourself we talked about in the previous chapter.

THE RIGHT AND WRONG WAY TO USE CREDIT CARDS

Credit cards are useful. They can help you over the last few days before payday if you are short of cash. They make it unnecessary for you to carry large amounts of cash when you travel. When you are on an expense account or self-employed, they provide you with a clear record of your expenses. If you pay the balance as soon as it's billed, they even provide you with *free* credit — unless there is a service charge on your card.

Generally, the people who give you the cards don't want you to use them intelligently. The common bank cards, Visa and Mastercharge, charge high rates of interest: as much as 18% or more per year. They'll offer you high credit limits: if you are above the poverty line they'll give you a limit of $250; if you are making an average income, your limit should be at least $2,000. They want you to build up large debts. And they want you to pay them off, not all at once — in which case you get free credit — but in small amounts over the year. That gives them a chance to charge you those high rates of interest and make a lot of money on your card.

The right way to use credit cards is to have as few of them as possible. Some people make the mistake of assuming that having five, seven, or ten of them in their wallet is a sign that they have really arrived. This is actually a recipe for financial chaos. So, if you want to use your credit cards properly, the first thing to do is to edit your collection. Select two or three that you really need, and destroy the others.

The second thing to do is to define the kind of purchase where it makes sense to use your credit card. There's only one kind: use it *only* when you can pay for your purchases during the interest-free period permitted by the credit-card people. Any other purchase you won't be able to pay for in the next month can be financed more cheaply with a normal consumer loan from your bank.

BANK LOANS

If It Will Take You More Than a Month To Pay Off Your Loan, Don't Use a Credit Card

Most of us don't realize how credit-worthy our lending institutions think we are. Literally thousands of Canadians run unnecessarily high balances on their credit card accounts when they could get the same amount of credit more cheaply with a consumer loan from their bank. Hundreds of us take loans from finance companies. Their effective interest rates can be as much as double those charged by the banks.

The banks are in the business of lending money. They want to rent you some because they make a profit doing so. It's up to you to make sure you are not paying any more into their coffers than you really have to. The best way to do that is to shop around for a loan. If your banker doesn't want your business badly enough to be competitive, get a new banker.

When you walk into your bank to ask for a loan, chances are you'll be offered a standard consumer loan. The interest rate could be in the neighbourhood of 12% or more. There may be other charges involved — administrative costs, life insurance costs, legal fees on property you are offering as security, and so on.

Don't just sign the loan form the banker pushes across his desk at you. Ask for a low interest rate. If the loan is relatively small and there can be no doubt about your ability to pay it, you should be able to get a loan at a few points above prime. That's about the cheapest loan you will get without collateral.

You should be able to qualify for an even better rate if you can put up collateral for the loan. Do you have savings bonds? Do you have deposit certificates or cash value life insurance? If you're borrowing a large sum, particularly if it's for an investment purpose, it could even make sense to offer a collateral mortgage against your equity in your home. If you have any financial product that you can pledge as security for the loan, the rate should come down even closer to prime.

If your banker isn't willing to discuss rates lower than the normal consumer interest rate, take your loan request and your banking business to another bank. Don't be afraid to shop around. It is just like buying a car — look for the best buy.

The Best Time To Negotiate Credit with Your Bank is Before You Need It

If you have already written the cheque to the car dealer, you really don't have much time to shop around for a loan, and you'll end up paying the highest rate. That's the wrong way to take a bank loan. The right way is pretty simple. Talk to the appropriate person in the branch where you do business. It may be the manager; it may be a loans officer. Establish your ability to borrow from that bank and find out the interest rate they will charge you *before* you want to make a loan. They'll clearly explain the circumstances under which you will qualify for an interest rate below the normal consumer interest rate.

While you're there, get an understanding from them that your cheques will *never* be bounced. Returning cheques NSF is a fairly automatic procedure in most banks, unless you make it unautomatic.

If you are not in the habit of spending more money than you have in the bank, you should have no difficulty getting them to agree to a reasonable *line of credit*. If you have a job and a good credit rating, you should qualify for a line of $3,000 or more, at rates competitive with regular consumer lending rates at the institution.

Make sure you're getting a line of credit as opposed to *overdraft protection*. You may want overdraft protection as well, to prevent the embarrassment and cost of an NSF cheque if you ever exceed your account balance and your credit line. But remember that overdraft protection will cost you 18% or more, and avoid using it if at all possible.

If you have arranged your loan in advance, all you have to do to get the money is telephone the bank and tell them you want it. Sign the note the next time you're in and you should have no trouble. You'll be a lot more relaxed, and in a better frame of mind to drive a hard bargain for whatever you're buying.

When You Take Out a Loan, Be Sure You Can Make the Monthly Payments

One of the best ways to have the cost of your loan accelerated is to miss a payment or two. The financial institution will charge you a penalty, then they will charge you interest on that penalty until the total amount is paid off. If you really can't manage a loan repayment amount, arrange a longer-term loan with smaller monthly payments. Although total interest cost might end up being higher, at least you will be sure you can meet the payment every month. And there's always the possibility of paying off the loan earlier if you find yourself with some extra dollars.

Shopping for a Loan: Watch for the Hidden Costs

A 12% loan doesn't necessarily cost 12%. Extra charges for insurance are often a requirement. Interest "bonuses" are often added by finance companies, and search or legal fees may be charged on some collateral mortgage loans. All these add to the basic cost of a loan.

Fortunately, it's easier these days to determine the true cost of a loan, because consumer protection legislation requires that lenders disclose not only interest rates, but also all other costs associated with the loan.

Insuring Your Loan

If a bank loan can seriously jeopardize your estate, consider insuring it. Often, loans that can be paid off easily while you are alive are not as simple to get rid of after your death. To avoid placing hardships on your family, insure the loan now so that at your death the loan at the bank or the mortgage on your home can be eliminated. This is especially desirable in cases where debts are incurred for investments that are not liquid and therefore cannot readily be sold. This extra insurance can prevent "estate sales" at sharply discounted prices. If the amount of the loan is small, i.e., below $25,000, the least expensive method is to insure it through the bank where you get your loan. If the amount is larger, get a competitive price from your insurance agent. If the purpose of the loan is to produce income, it may be possible to deduct the cost of the insurance for tax purposes. However, the bank must give you a letter indicating that it requires the insurance as security for the loan.

Protect Your Prepayment Privileges

Before you accept a loan with regular payment and/or a term of more than one year, get in writing from the lender exactly what your prepayment privileges are – how much, how often, on what notice and at what cost?

The computer makes possible daily interest calculations on our loans as well as our savings. So, there's no reason you should be locked into a rigid payment schedule and pay more interest than is necessary.

If you want to let the lender know you're a knowledgeable borrower, ask for assurance that the Rule of 78 will not be applied on prepayments of principal. It's a formula which builds in an element of "front end loading" of interest charges. Even if your lender has never heard of it, he or she should be impressed!

MORTGAGES

Yes, a Mortgage Really Is a Debt

In 1981, when housing prices were escalating rapidly, the parents of a client of ours found a very good buy on a house. Because they paid substantially less than market value ($80,000 for a house that was worth $100,000), they could have sold the house for a profit almost immediately.

Our client was ecstatic at their good fortune, but when he asked his mother how she felt about it she said, "Well, it's not easy getting used to being $35,000 in debt."

Your mortgage is usually your largest debt; thus the consequences of getting bad terms can be disastrous. It's not enough to bargain hard for a competitive interest rate and monthly payments you can handle comfortably. Because it will typically take you ten years or more to pay off a mortgage, other questions become vital:

- For how long is your interest rate guaranteed?
- What will it cost you to renew your mortgage at the end of the current term?
- What prepayment privileges are available, and at what cost?

Shop Around for Your Mortgage

Many Canadians have mortgages that are more expensive than they should be for the simple reason that they don't make an effort to get a good deal. Since a mortgage is the biggest loan most of us are ever going to take, it makes sense to shop around. Check with several sources. A difference as small as .25% in your interest rate for a twenty-five-year $50,000 mortgage can cost you as much as $2,600.

The sources for mortgage funds include banks, trust companies, credit unions, life insurance companies, and mortgage brokers. Look for the best interest rate. Choose an amortization period that will allow you to make sensible monthly payments without personal hardship. Make sure the term for which the interest rate is guaranteed is adequate and that renewal privileges are built into it. Make sure you are taking into account how much it is going to cost you to get the mortgage. There will be search fees, lawyers' fees, and possibly finders' fees. Take all of this into account. Make sure the lender allows you to prepay the mortgage at any time without such penalties as three months' interest. Most lenders allow an annual prepayment privilege of up to 10% of the original mortgage balance. If you want a totally open loan, you'll have to pay a somewhat higher interest rate to get it. So make sure you really can use a total prepayment privilege before you pay extra to get it.

A note on mortgage renewal—it will likely be less expensive to renew a mortgage through the same lender, because it is necessary to pay fees to discharge your old mortgage, as well as new legal and appraisal fees for a new mortgage.

A Mortgage from Relatives May Be One of Your Best Sources

One possible source for a mortgage is your family. Many parents would prefer to see their children use their money rather than money belonging to a bank or trust company.

Parents who don't need the money often lend it at 0% on a demand note basis and forgive a portion of the debt every year as a gift.

Words of caution: first, make sure you take their loan as a second mortgage, not a first, if you need additional funding. Otherwise the lending institution that holds the balance of the mortgage will charge you a higher interest rate. Second, make sure every transaction is properly documented—and make sure your payments are on time!

LEASING

In some situations, to acquire possessions you really need, it may make more sense to lease than to incur a debt. Leasing is used most by Canadians for cars. These leases often cost more than borrowing the money, because the leasing company has to borrow the money, administer the lease, and make a profit. But there may still be some advantages to leasing.

For one thing, leasing may preserve your capacity to borrow from financial institutions if you ever really need to borrow. For salespeople, professionals, or self-employed persons, leasing may offer tax advantages. If you've got a bad personal credit rating, the interest rates you may have to pay for a loan could actually be higher than the rates charged by a leasing company.

If you are going to lease a car, make certain you are aware of the terms of the agreement. Look especially at mileage limits and the cost of exceeding them. Take a look at the purchasing privileges at the end of the lease. You can reduce lease payments during the lease term, but only at the cost of a higher buy-out figure at the end of the term. Make sure you know what the cancellation costs of the lease are. And make sure you know what repairs may cost you when you return the car at the end of the lease.

BORROWING AGAINST INSURANCE POLICIES

One of the greatest benefits of permanent life insurance is that you can borrow money against the cash value of your policy, often at rates below the market. If you have had the policy long enough, it's possible that the dividends paid into the policy will themselves help pay off interest costs and could even retire the loan for you. Outstanding loans against the policy will, however, diminish the amount of money your family would receive if you died. They may also affect the use of an automatic premium loan if you are late in paying the premium. A solution is to leave sufficient cash values to pay one year's premiums. But, if you do need money, make sure you shop around and consider your insurance policies as one source of credit among many alternatives.

DO'S AND DON'TS

Do Set your own credit limit and stick to it.

Do Base your credit limit on how much debt you can repay, not how much lenders and sellers are prepared to advance you.

Do Use your credit cards effectively, for small purchases which you can pay off currently.

Do Arrange your credit needs well in advance of requiring a loan.

Do Shop around for the best terms for a loan.

Do Investigate your house mortgage thoroughly. It will be one of your largest debts. Remember that it can affect your monthly costs, your ability to resell the house, and the eventual selling price.

Do Try to negotiate a mortgage that allows you to prepay significant amounts without penalty.

Do Try to make your loan interest tax deductible by borrowing for purposes that allow the interest expense as a deduction against your taxable income; for example, stocks, bonds, real estate, business loans, or car loan if you use the car for your work.

Do Start with the cheapest sources first when you need to borrow — relatives, insurance policy, banks, credit union, trust company, etc.

Do Pay off loans first where the interest is not tax deductible. Never pay off loans for an investment when you have a mortgage on your house unless your after-tax cost is less.

Loan	*Rate*	*Marginal Tax Rate**	*After-Tax Rate***	*After-Tax Saving by Paying Off Loan*
Mortgage	12%	44%	12%	12%
Investment	13%	44%	7.84%	7.84%

*Marginal tax rate — the highest rate of income tax you pay.

**Gross interest rate minus marginal tax rate.

Don't Use credit cards for impulse buying.

Don't Use revolving credit — ever.

Don't Hesitate to communicate with a lender if you are going to have trouble making a payment.

Don't Think it's disloyal to shop around for credit.

CHAPTER 4

How To Be a Smart Consumer

Living expenses take a large bite out of our paycheques, however hard we try to fight it. This chapter is dedicated to minimizing that bite in the marketplace, where talk about spending becomes reality.

Merchants set their prices to protect their profit margins, especially against increases in their own costs. In a free enterprise economy this is legal and fair. But it is equally legal, fair, and very important for you, the consumer, to challenge their prices and get the best value for your money.

For example, one woman we know entered a store to price broadloom. It was marked at $22.95 per square metre. The salesman told her that because it was their last roll she could have it for $18.95. Thrilled to get a 20% discount off the regular price, she called her husband, who also thought it was a good deal. A few minutes later her husband, in casual conversation, mentioned the discount to a friend, a local contractor.

"Hold it," said the friend, "let me call the store for you." He introduced himself to the salesman on the telephone, saying, "I am the contractor for Mrs. B., who was just in your store looking at some broadloom. You offered her a price of $18.95 per square metre. What price can I buy it for?" The salesman paused for a moment and then replied, "I could let it go for $14.95."

"No, much too high," said the contractor. "Unless I can get it for $12.00, it's no deal." Another pause. "OK," said the salesman, "it's a deal."

This story dramatizes two market realities: the margins some stores are getting and the savings you can gain by challenging high prices and haggling over them.

The key to "being a smart consumer" is being well informed, determined to obtain value for your money, and thick-skinned about how you do it. Here are some rules to help you:

Rule 1: Work from a Buying Plan

If you have prepared a shopping list, you will know what you are going to buy and approximately how much each item should cost. If properly drawn, your list will help you decide in advance exactly what you want, what you want the item to do for you, and how long it should last. For example, if you need new tires for your car but your car has only 10,000 miles of life left in it, it is probably a waste of money to buy an expensive set of steel-belted radials. A set of cheaper tires will do the job just as well.

Planning your shopping also saves time and helps you resist impulse buying. While some impulse buying is fun, it can play havoc with your budget. Stick to your plan and likely you will end up with a better quality product at a lower price, instead of with things you don't really need or want.

Mary and Charlie were out for a stroll. They wandered into a rug store where they saw a beautiful, small Oriental rug. It had a big sale sticker on it and a price tag of $800. "Wouldn't that look great in our living room!" exclaimed Mary. Charlie agreed, and within minutes they were walking out of the store, Charlie carrying their new rug on his shoulder. Now, Mary and Charlie had not been in the market for an Oriental rug: a few moments of weakness would now erode their savings, or restrict their cash flow over the next few months.

Credit cards make impulse buying easy. It used to be that if you didn't have the money in your bank account or in your pocket, you didn't buy. All you have to do now is flash a piece of plastic and the goods become yours instantly. If you can't pay for them in full within the 31 days normally allowed to settle your account, the cost of the item you have acquired goes up 1½–2% each month you don't pay for it. This doesn't sound like much over one or two months, but in the course of a full year it can add up to 18 to 24%.

To resist the temptation to buy on impulse, ask yourself, "Is this item on my list of wants, is it something I really need, and will I be miserable if I don't have it?" Better still, before you walk into a store, make a pact with yourself to buy only those things that are on your list, and put a ceiling on your spending on the total list.

Rule 2: Use Credit Cards Wisely

Use your credit cards to purchase only what you can pay for within 31 days. Misuse of credit cards is a major source of consumer anxiety, caused by overspending. Merchants know this. They know consumers with credit cards buy more than those without them. If you don't believe us, take out your credit card, cut it up and begin to list your expenditures over the next six months. Compare that list with your expenditures for non-essential items in the previous six months. In fact, unless you need your credit cards for record-keeping, cut them up and see how long you can last without them. They are easy to replace if your withdrawal symptoms become unbearable.

Rule 3: Consider Alternatives

Sometimes it's better to use another product, defer buying, or go without altogether.

For instance, Harry, one of our clients, recently walked into a hardware store to price a stepladder. "How much?" he asked the sales clerk.

The clerk replied, "One hundred and five dollars." Harry thought for a moment. "Well, at that price I think I'll borrow my neighbour's for a little longer. Thank you very much," he said, and left the store.

Don't hesitate. Walk away if goods are not worth the price. However, make sure you let the store owner or the salesperson know you are unhappy with the price and unwilling to pay it. You may be surprised at how willing he or she is to make some concessions to keep you happy. Another solution might be to share such items as lawnmowers, wheelbarrows, and similar possessions with neighbours. Just make sure it's a reciprocal arrangement lest you end up a smart consumer known as the neighbourhood mooch.

Charlene likes to wear designer fashions but finds the cost prohibitive. A skilled seamstress, she has discovered she can buy designer patterns and make these same clothes for about one-sixth the retail price. Stick to your self-imposed guidelines regarding price and alternatives will likely turn up.

Rule 4: Comparison Shop

Planning determines the product you need; research determines the brand you buy. Real savings come when you are buying big items such as furniture and appliances. Decide what you want the product to do for you. Find out how long different brands are under warranty, how long they are expected to last, how much upkeep they require and the cost of the upkeep. Compare this information with what you want the product to do for you. Talk to people who have used the product, read advertisements carefully, and talk to salespeople. Of course, what the ads say and what the salespeople tell you should be treated with caution. Both are programmed to sell products and always stress the good things about them.

Ask yourself:

- Is the price competitive?
- Can I return the item if it isn't suitable?
- What is the reputation of the manufacturer?
- Are the materials high quality?
- Is it guaranteed? By whom? For how long?
- Will it be difficult or expensive to take care of?
- Will the retailer give me service if it doesn't work?
- Is the store conveniently located?
- What is the attitude of the sales staff?

Comparison shoppers must weigh the relative merits of convenience as well as price, quality, and service. It makes no sense to drive ten miles each way to save 20¢ a pound on chicken. That's inconvenient and expensive. Similarly, if you're buying a car, get estimates from several dealers and use them as bargaining tools if you really want to buy from a dealer near your home or office. If you know the exact product and make you want, save time by checking prices and availability beforehand, over the phone. Let people know you are shopping around. This will encourage them to offer you a better price or lower interest rates on financing.

Here are some other ways to shop wisely:

Consumer's Report. For large purchases, it's worth consulting a Consumer's Report. One person we know was looking for a small, used car. He checked an old Consumer's Report at the library, which told him that the 1978 Datsun had scored well in most categories except that the heater didn't start quickly and was noisy, and that riding in the back seat was uncomfortable. Reflecting on his needs, our friend concluded that the car he needed was primarily for short-distance commuting. The fact that the heater didn't work particularly well and that the back seat ride was not the best in the world was of little consequence to him. As a result, he bought a Datsun and saved money — and a lot of shopping time and effort.

Packaging. Look beyond the package that is used to sell you the product. Bacon in a plain wrapper may not look as tempting as a higher-priced brand in a fancy package, but it may be just as tasty, and you'll have saved money.

Sales. Plan your major buying around sale times. The following list compiled for our Personal Financial Planning Letter indicates the best times of the year to buy certain goods:

January: Bicycles, blankets, books, china, Christmas items, furs, home appliances, furniture, jewellery, linens, lingerie, sportswear, stereos, toys, winter clothes, men's suits, storm windows.

February: Bedding, cars (used), china, drapes, furniture, radios, men's shirts, silverware, toys, air conditioners, towels, rugs, lamps.

March: Luggage, winter sports equipment, spring clothing, appliances, winter coats.

April: Dresses, children's clothes, stoves, appliances, women's and children's coats, men's suits.

May: Blankets, linens, lingerie, rugs, tires, towels, TV sets.

June: Building materials, dresses, furniture, housecoats, summer clothes and fabrics, TV sets.

July: Bathing suits, children's clothes, handbags, home appliances, men's shirts, rugs, carpets, shoes, sportswear and equipment, stereos, summer clothes and fabrics, radios.

August: Air conditioners, bathing suits, bedding, bicycles, camping equipment, carriages, cars (new), furs, garden equipment, hardware, furniture, men's clothes, paint, school clothes, rugs, fans.

September: Batteries and mufflers, bicycles, children's clothes, dishes, rugs, lamps.

October: Bicycles, fishing equipment, school clothes, silver.

November: Bicycles, blankets, cars (used), children's clothes, dresses, men's clothes, shoes.

December: Cars (used), shoes, women's and children's coats.

Before you buy, make sure the sale price is genuine. Just because an item is "on sale" doesn't mean it's a bargain, especially if you don't really need it. Comparison shopping of sale merchandise is still important. And remember — often there is no exchange or refund on sale items.

Discount houses. Discount houses often have great bargains because they buy in volume and provide little in the way of service. If you need a lot of assistance from sales personnel, don't look for it at a discount store. These houses sell inexpensive clothing, cosmetics, records, etc. — items you can easily choose yourself. They usually have bargains in children's clothes — important if your kids are outgrowing theirs quickly. To pay $50 or more for a girl's blouse, for instance, at one of the "in" stores may inflate a parent's ego, but will surely deflate the pocketbook.

Pawn shops. Most of us know pawn shops exist, but would never think of shopping there because we associate them with people who are "down on their luck," unable to obtain money unless they "hock" some personal possessions. The pawn shop usually charges 2% per month interest, and the amount of the loan is normally 50% or less of the value. The item is left at the pawn shop as security for the loan. Things most frequently pledged are jewellery, electronic equipment, cameras, musical instruments, old medals, fur coats, and miscellaneous curios.

If the loan is not paid off in 13 months, the pawn shop has the right to sell the pledged item. In many cases you can find brand-name goods barely used and in good working order. Pawn shops also sell new equipment, and many of the owners are certified and knowledgeable appraisers. You can find real bargains, particularly if you haggle a little. Find out what guarantees they are willing to give you on equipment you buy, and know before you get to the store how it is priced elsewhere *with* a full guarantee.

Auctions. Auctions can be fun and a good source of bargains. Watching the give-and-take between the auctioneer and the bidders is an exciting experience, but to get the best chance at a bargain, be there before the bidding starts and preview the items to be sold. If you have done your research beforehand and know what you are looking for, you will spot good value. But beware of the impulse buying syndrome; it could get you into a lot of trouble.

Do-it-yourself. Amelda and John had several estimates done for landscaping, but the best price was $5,000, an amount well beyond their budget. They decided to do it themselves, bought a couple of handbooks, pored over them for many hours, spoke to friends, and also picked up ideas from local nurseries. Then they went to a country nursery to buy the shrubs and plants they wanted, paying less than they would have had to in the city. The final cost of landscaping their garden was $1,200 – a saving of $3,800 in after-tax dollars. In a 50% income tax bracket, that's equivalent to earning $7,600!

Do-it-yourself projects take time and patience, and unless you have both, they can turn into real horror stories. There's the one about Henry, whose house was in a turmoil for more than a year after he decided to paint it himself on weekends. And Perry, who had decided to repair the carburetor on his car, ended up having to buy a new one and pay someone else to install it. Such do-it-yourself projects often end up costing more than employing a professional. However, if you have the patience *and* the time, but do not possess the skill, take a course at your local high school or community college. With a little bit of basic know-how, doing things yourself can be fun and produce real savings.

The art of haggling and bartering. The highly taxed '80s are a good time to put to practical use the experience you gained as a child when you were trading baseball cards or comic books. People who sell services offer them at a price they hope and expect to get. The buyer, however, should not automatically accept these prices. While it is impractical and embarrassing to haggle in restaurants and department stores, do not hesitate to try your luck in smaller, owner-managed shops. Many people hesitate to haggle because they feel it makes them appear cheap or gives the impression they can't afford to pay the full price for an item. But money tied up in inventory can be very costly, and merchants may be more inclined to let goods go at a lower price and thereby reduce the amount of money they have to borrow from the bank. When negotiating a deal, know what the competition is charging. For example, if you have received one estimate of $5,000 for work to be done on your home and another one comes in at $8,000 and you feel the high-priced contractor will do a better job for you, don't be afraid to tell him that his competition has made you a lower offer. Ask if he can reduce his price. Chances are he will do so.

If life is really only cycles, the return to barter is a good case in point. The concept is very simple. You can trade your goods or services for another person's goods or services. For example, an accountant could offer to do an appliance dealer's income tax return in exchange for a new stove.

Many people barter on their own; however, great savings can be made by joining one of the barter clubs and skills exchanges springing up all over North America to coordinate such transactions. Whether you join one of these organizations or decide to make your own arrangements, be sure to nail down the specific terms beforehand. For example, if you are preparing someone's income tax return, make sure your trading partner clearly agrees to give you what *you* want in return. Furthermore, try to use his or her wholesale price when negotiating the transaction. (A caveat on barter: Don't try to beat the tax system with barter. You could end up faced with a charge of tax evasion.)

Second-hand goods. Modern advertising would have us believe we are simply not a success unless we buy everything new. Often, the opposite is true. Buying good quality items second-hand often can give you the same quality product for much less money.

One well-to-do businessman we know always buys cars six to twelve months old, with 10,000 or 15,000 kilometres on them. He drives them until they show approximately 100,000 kilometres. Many new car makes depreciate as much as 25–30% in the first year, but more slowly thereafter, yet the car will still give the owner a good deal of use well beyond the one year. It also makes sense to hand down and pass around children's clothes; these things usually are outgrown before they wear out.

The classified sections of your daily newspaper and special publications such as the Bargain Hunter Press carry advertisements offering second-hand items for sale. Great bargains are available at garage, lawn, and backyard sales; and don't forget about your own possessions that may be sitting in your attic. They can be converted into money and you will get the satisfaction of knowing that although they are things you no longer use, they can be of service to someone else.

Warranties and guarantees. Smart consumers will not ignore warranties and guarantees. If a purchase does not live up to expectations, don't be afraid to challenge the advertising or ultimately return the item. To be fair to the merchant, however, don't expect him to reimburse you for shoes or clothing after you've worn them several times.

DO'S AND DON'TS

Do Develop a plan and use it.
Do Buy only from a list you've prepared in advance.
Do Research major purchases before you buy.
Do Look for alternatives.
Do Look for value when you comparison shop, including service as well as price.
Do Take advantage of seasonal bargains.
Do Use consumer publications to help "shop" for major purchases.
Don't Hesitate to haggle on price.
Don't Be above buying second-hand.
Don't Use your credit card unless you can pay for your purchase within a month.

CHAPTER 5

Savings: Short Term, Long Term, Forced, Voluntary, Taxed, or Tax-Free?

Let's start with the simplest and most familiar definition of the word "savings": putting aside money regularly for some future use. Like most simple definitions, however, this one needs elaboration to be really useful.

One of our clients always pays cash for his clothes. He puts a little aside out of every paycheque and uses it to buy the suits and shirts and shoes he needs for work. That little bit of money he sets aside regularly is savings. If you total it all up, over a full year he saves more than $1,000. And everything he has to show for it hangs in his closet.

We hope the point is clear. Most of us, from time to time, do this kind of *saving for current expenses*. It's simply a means of organizing our money to accommodate the bulges in our expense patterns — buying new clothes, small items of furniture, or taking the odd vacation. It's an important money management skill. But it's not all there is to saving.

Another individual — a sales representative — never saved a dime until he discovered Registered Retirement Savings Plans. These plans allow him to defer paying taxes on part of his income — *if* he saves it. Since he has a strong aversion to paying taxes, he's put aside $3,500 a year for the past three years and he has saved $10,500 plus interest. But *none* of it is available to him for current expenses without first being taxed at the highest rate he pays. That's saving too. This kind of *long-term saving* is an equally important money-management skill.

A good savings program should include both kinds of saving — saving for current expenses and long-term saving.

Another client who was a highly paid advertising executive found himself looking for work when his company lost a big account. He sat down and calculated that he'd earned more than $500,000 over the previous ten years. The only savings he had was some money in an RRSP and the cash surrender values of four whole life insurance policies that he'd bought. He'd simply never been able to get around to saving. Because he was *forced* to pay the premiums on the life insurance policies, or lose them altogether, he had accumulated a few thousand dollars that were available to tide him over.

As it turned out, he didn't need to use the money. Over the same ten years his wife had voluntarily been banking a few dollars a week out of what she called her "housekeeping money." With the compound interest paid on the trust company account where she kept the money, it had grown into several thousand dollars.

Some people can save voluntarily; some people can't. A good savings program has to be based on an honest evaluation of whether or not you're the kind of person who will put money aside without being forced to.

Elsewhere in this book we deal with financial planning, budgeting, and investment. That's not what this chapter is about. It's about designing a savings program that will help you handle current expenses wisely, build up long-term wealth, maximize savings from taxes, and do this based on a realistic understanding of your own character.

DESIGNING YOUR OWN SAVINGS PROGRAM

The best way to design your own savings program is to ask yourself a series of questions.

Am I Saving for Current Expenses or for Long-Term Purposes? The Answer Should Be *Both*.

None of us really has equal expenses every month. Major purchases, clothing, vacations, that paint job we've been meaning to get on the car, all add up and make certain months more costly than others. A portion of the total amount we save should be earmarked for these kinds of expenses. This system has an added advantage because it lets you build in a series of rewards for yourself when you design your savings program. If you meet your total savings targets, you can afford that new suit — and this kind of thing is important. Money management is really self-management.

It is even more important that a large part of your savings be devoted to long-term financial purposes. Read the chapter on retirement. It will tell you how to set realistic goals for yourself. Remember that devoting the major part of your total savings to long-term goals has its own emotional rewards. It's a nice feeling to know that you have $100,000 or $200,000 squirreled away for the day when your paycheque stops.

How Much Do I Save Each Month?

A savings program works best if you save a set percentage of your total net income every month. A good place to start is at 10%. Make sure that the amount you save is put away *before* you start allocating the amounts you want to spend.

If you take a fixed percentage right off the top, you won't miss it, and saving will be less of a hardship. Because you're saving a percentage, the amounts you are putting aside will increase as your income increases.

Will I Save Voluntarily, or Will I Have to Force Myself?

Only you can answer this question. Some of us are simply not able to save; if we have money we spend it. Forced savings are simply programs that make sure we put the money away and never touch it. Naturally there are different degrees of force.

If you have your bank automatically take your savings percentage out of your chequing account every month and put it in a non-chequing savings account, that may be enough force for you. The money is simply less available than money sitting in your chequing account. There is no chance of your "accidentally" spending it.

If you take a hard look at the assets you already have accumulated, we think you will find that most of them have been built up through forced savings plans: payroll deduction plans, RRSPs, the premiums you have paid on whole life insurance policies, the payments you've made on your mortgage.

The key is to be realistic about your own ability to put money aside voluntarily. You may be able to set your savings objectives and meet them, with nothing more elaborate than a series of postdated cheques given to your trust company or credit union for deposit in your savings account there. On the other hand, you may need the discipline of a payroll deduction plan to purchase Canada Savings Bonds or company shares. You might also decide to invest in a mutual fund through automatic monthly deductions from your bank account.

Your answers to these three questions give you the "bones" of your savings plan—your reasons for saving, the amounts you're going to save, and the decision to do it voluntarily or by forcing yourself.

The amount you can accumulate by putting aside $100 a month is outlined in Table 5.1. Perhaps the amount will help motivate you.

Table 5.1
Amount to which $100/Month Invested at 8% Will Grow

End of Year	*Amount*
1	$ 1,243
2	2,586
3	4,036
4	5,602
5	7,294
10	18,012
20	56,900
30	140,855
40	322,108

WHAT TO DO WITH YOUR SAVINGS

The best thing to do with your savings is to put them where they will grow.

Bank Savings Accounts Are for Short-Term Savings Only

Too many people have too much money sitting in bank savings accounts. As a rule the interest paid by banks on savings accounts is low. They may call it 6% a year, but that figure means little. Is the interest calculated on the minimum daily, monthly, or semi-annual balance? For example, if it is on the semi-annual balance and if you make a deposit on the first of every month for six months, you will receive interest only on the first deposit you make.

Is the interest calculated, credited, and *compounded* monthly? Semi-annually? Annually?

Most banks and trust companies now have accounts that pay you interest based on the minimum daily balance. Terms vary significantly from company to company and from account to account, so shop around. And ask questions. Find out how often and when interest is paid. Remember that rates of trust companies or credit unions are usually higher than the banks. They are safe, too. The first $60,000 of your money with a trust company is insured under the Canadian Deposit Insurance Act; the same is true for some of the credit unions.

Chequing accounts, even those paying interest on the minimum daily balance, should be used for just that—chequing. Some accounts, however, will pay a competitive return if you maintain a minimum balance in your account. While it is a good idea to earn interest on small amounts in a chequing account between paydays and the time you write your cheques, use your savings accounts to accumulate money on an ongoing basis. Use a Daily Interest Savings Account when making deposits or withdrawals at different times during the month, even though the interest paid is slightly lower than on a True Savings Account; the flexibility usually is well worth it. True Savings Accounts are useful if you withdraw your money at the end of the month and make all deposits at the first of the month.

These accounts usually do not permit you to write cheques, and hence pay higher interest rates. Your savings for current expenses can build up in these accounts, earning a little interest and staying liquid (that means easy to get at); the money you are saving for a long term can stay there until there is enough accumulated to make other more profitable arrangements, such as term deposits for 30, 60, 90, 120, or 180 days, or treasury bills of the federal government.

Table 5.2 shows the importance of thinking about interest rates. It is based on the assumption that you save $1,000 a year, every year for

Table 5.2
Different Rates of Return on
$1,000 Savings/Year Compounded Annually

End of Year	Interest Rates 6%	8%	10%	11%	12%	14%	16%
1	$ 1,060	$ 1,080	$ 1,100	$ 1,110	$ 1,120	$ 1,140	$ 1,160
5	5,975	6,336	6,716	6,913	7,115	7,536	7,977
10	13,972	15,645	17,531	18,561	19,655	22,045	24,733
20	38,993	49,423	63,002	71,265	80,699	103,768	133,841
30	83,802	122,346	180,943	220,913	270,293	406,737	615,162
40	164,048	279,781	486,852	645,827	859,142	1,529,909	2,738,478

one year, five years, and so on up to forty years. You can see the difference a few interest points will make.

Taxable or Tax Deferred

If your taxable income (total income minus deductions and personal exemptions) is in excess of $36,000, your marginal tax rate—the tax rate that applies on the last dollar you make—is about 45%. This varies from province to province. That means you have to earn $18.20 to have $10.00 available to save.

But there are certain kinds of savings and certain kinds of income that are either not taxed or taxed on a deferred basis. It makes a great deal of sense to look for these when you're thinking about your long-term savings.

It's important to remember that you will be taxed on the income your savings earn for you, other than the first $1,000 of Canadian interest on taxable dividends. So, when you are planning your long-term savings program, look for savings vehicles where contributions are tax deductible or where earnings get exempt or tax-deferred treatment. One key objective of any savings or investment program should be to maximize your after-tax return.

Your First Savings Priority: An Emergency Fund

An important part of any savings plan is the emergency fund – liquid cash available in case of a personal or family emergency. These funds should be invested in the safest, most liquid investments. Each family must assess the size of its emergency fund, because needs can vary considerably in this area. Typical investments would be cash, Canada Savings Bonds, bank term deposits, or money market funds.

Canada Savings Bonds. Canada Savings Bonds are the safest and most liquid investment available in Canada today and a superb form of emergency fund. They pay interest rates high enough to offset inflation in most years, and they can be converted into cash easily and quickly.

If you're holding a few thousand dollars in your bank account, you could be better off to put them into Canada Savings Bonds at the next issue. The bonds are usually issued November 1, and you can purchase them until November 15 without paying any premium for the accrued interest. In the past as interest rates have increased, the government of Canada has increased the yield so people will not cash them in. However, be careful. There could be severe penalties for cashing the bonds early, such as loss of compound interest bonuses near maturity.

Treasury Bills. Treasury Bills are an excellent low-risk investment for short-term investors. Issued by the government of Canada in an auction to Canada's major financial institutions each Thursday, maturities are available for up to 182 days. Rates fluctuate weekly and can be quoted by banks and stockbrokers. As a rule of thumb, deposits of less than $50,000 can usually be placed at better rates elsewhere. For the more sophisticated investor with $100,000 or more in his or her emergency fund, an interesting new development is covered bond options. They combine the higher return of long-term bonds with the liquidity of 91-day maturities.

Money Market Funds. Money Market Funds are a viable and often preferred alternative to savings accounts. Money Market Funds usually pay about 2% more than bank savings accounts and are equally liquid. Some accounts, such as those offered by such investment firms as Merrill Lynch and Walwyn Stodgell through Citibank, even allow you to write cheques against them. Others just offer you a good place to obtain a reasonable interest rate on your funds. These are offered by some Mutual Fund companies. The underlying investment is usually in Treasury Bills and short term paper. While these are not covered by deposit insurance, the underlying investments, particularly Treasury Bills, are sound and liquid.

Another attractive feature of these funds is that you may buy units by automatic bank withdrawal. You simply authorize the bank to withdraw the amount you want to save on a regular basis, and have it deposited to your Money Market Fund.

The New Hybrid: T-Bill Passbook Savings. Early in 1986, at least two major trust companies increased the ante in the savings sweepstakes. They introduced a new savings account which, for a $10,000 minimum balance, offered interest rates close to the rate on 91-day Treasury Bills and 2–3% above the regular daily interest savings rate. No doubt the competition will continue to accelerate and produce more attractive alternatives, combining convenience and competitive returns.

Your Second Savings Priority: Elimination of Consumer Debt

The whole purpose of investing is to increase the amount of income you will have available later, and the best way for middle-income Canadians to do that is to pay off consumer debt, especially their residential mortgages, as quickly as possible.

Quicker repayment of your mortgage means less money spent on interest — and every dollar you save on mortgage interest is an after-tax dollar. For example, let's say you are paying 11% interest on your mortgage and are in the 45% tax bracket (taxable income as low as $36,000 will put you into this bracket). You would have to earn at least 20.2% before taxes on any other investment in order to approach the real dollar return you get from early payment of your mortgage.

Table 5.3 shows the interest savings you can realize by accelerating repayment of a $50,000 mortgage at 11%.

Table 5.3
Interest Paid on an 11% Mortgage

Monthly Payment	*Years to Pay Off*	*Total Interest Paid*
$490	25	$97,016
$516	20	$73,862
$543	17	$60,709
$568	15	$52,294
$604	13	$44,187
$655	11	$36,410

By spending $165 more on your mortgage every month, you not only save about $60,606 in interest charges — charges you would have to pay with after-tax dollars — but you are debt-free fourteen years sooner.

In effect, you will have freed the amount you are paying on your mortgage every month so you can add it to your truly disposable income.

You are getting the same asset — the house, which may increase in value every year (value that can be realized 100% tax-free) and which will return the constant dividend of providing you with shelter — for $60,606 less than you would otherwise be paying. The gain, of course, varies with the interest rate, but the principle is the same.

Yet, there are times when it may not be wise to pay off your mortgage, such as when your mortgage rate is less than the after-tax return you can receive on other investments. If, for example, you had an 8% mortgage, no interest income, and $5,000 to invest, you would be better off investing the money in a GIC, at say 10%, than putting it into your mortgage, as all of the income is tax free and your after-tax return is 10% versus 8% on your mortgage. If, on the other hand, you and other members of your family were earning $1,000 each of investment income

Figure 5.1
Median House Price vs. Average Income in Toronto

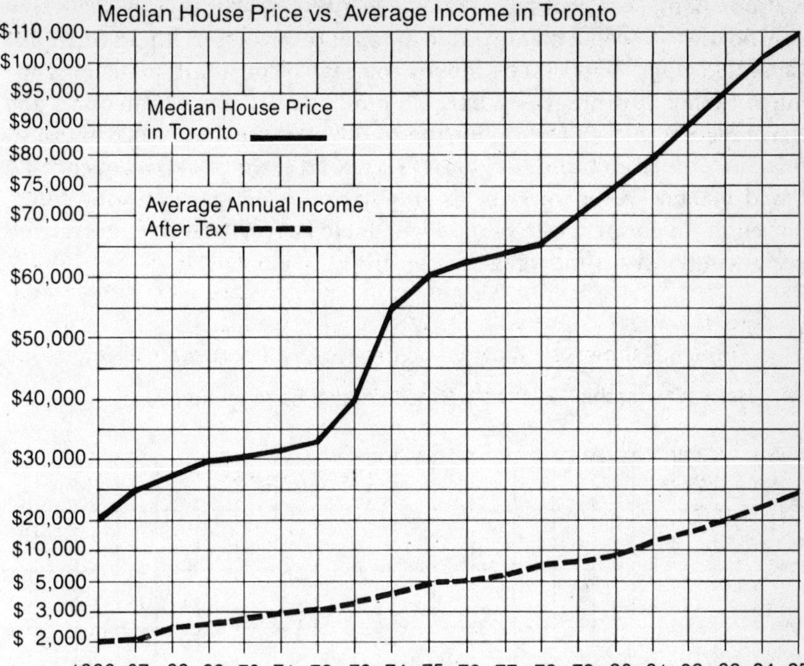

Your own home is a good investment. In Toronto since 1966, the median house price has increased 262%; the average annual income has increased 197%.

Note for 1984 the average house price was $102,350 and for 1985 the average house price was $109,000. Income is up about 5% for '84 and '85.

from taxable Canadian sources and you were in a 45% tax bracket you would have to earn 15% pre-tax on a guaranteed basis to better the return you would get from paying off an 8% mortgage on your home.

A word of caution, however. Don't use your last dollar of savings to prepay your mortgage. It's not a liquid investment — you'd have to sell the house or remortgage it to "get your prepayment back" in a hurry if you needed it for an emergency.

It may also be unwise to repay your mortgage just before selling your home, especially if you have a mortgage of, say 10¼% with a few years to run on it, and the going rate is 12%. Assuming the existing mortgage is transferable, a low mortgage rate can be a very attractive feature for the new buyer and could result in a much higher selling price for your home.

So always keep a comfortable amount of savings in liquid form like Canada Savings Bonds. The money you save by avoiding panic borrowing or taking advantage of a bargain purchase will more than offset any loss of regular interest return. Furthermore, since the first $1,000 of investment income from Canadian sources is tax-free, the tax effect of earning the $1,000 tax-free is the same as prepaying the mortgage on your home, although the interest rate earned will likely be less than the interest you are paying on your mortgage.

Figure 5.2
Home Ownership Costs as a Percentage of Family Income

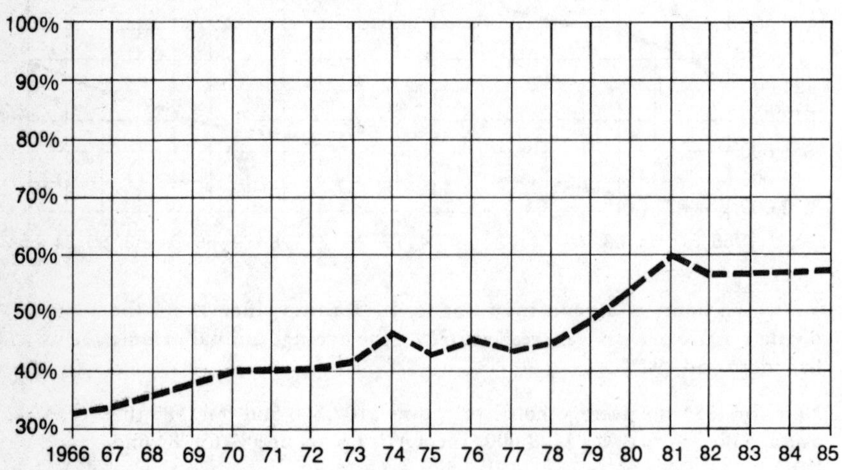

As a result of higher interest rates, the percentage of family income required to carry a home has increased considerably.

Your Third Savings Priority: RRSPs and Pension Contributions

If your taxable income is approximately $35,000 a year (after taking personal deductions and exemptions; see Chapter 8 for details), you will have to earn more than $1,800 to save $1,000, unless you hold your savings in one of the government-approved, tax deductible plans such as a Registered Retirement Savings Plan. They permit you to deduct the actual amount you contribute to the plan from your taxable income in the year you make the contribution. You don't pay tax until you withdraw the money.

These tax-deferred schemes are the first to consider when you are planning your medium- and long-term savings programs. If you can save your money and the government's share as well, you'll end up with a lot more dollars, even after tax, when you start taking your money out.

Your Fourth Savings Priority: Interest and Dividend Income

Your first $1,000 of interest income is tax free. Therefore, both you and your spouse should put your money into such things as true savings accounts, guaranteed investment certificates, mortgages, Canada Savings Bonds, and other interest-producing plans. Do this until both you and your spouse produce the $1,000 of income each year. If your spouse has no earned income, he or she can earn additional investment income of $500 to $600, without costing you a cent of your spousal exemption for him or her.

If you and your spouse are both earning income, both of you should save to generate $1,000 of investment income tax free. If there is additional income earned, plan to have it earned on savings by the lower income earner. Meanwhile, the higher earner should be paying most of the bills — an arrangement which requires faith as well as foresight!

DO'S AND DON'TS

Do Plan to create an emergency fund for irregular current expenses as well as save for long-term goals.

Do Save a fixed percentage of your take-home income every month. This will "index" your savings.

Do Be realistic about how much you really will save voluntarily and how much forced savings you should build into your program.

Do Use bank, trust company, or credit union savings accounts and money market funds to hold your savings for current expenses and for short-term goals.

Do Switch to higher-interest instruments for longer-term savings.

Do Build up $1,000 of investment income for you and your spouse, and for children age 18 or over.

Do Look for those programs such as RRSPs that allow you to save untaxed dollars. Then look for programs that permit you to get tax-deferred earnings on your savings.

Do Consider paying off your mortgage as quickly as possible. The savings in interest will likely give you a better guaranteed return than any other investment with after-tax dollars.

Don't Expect savings to just happen.

Don't Use bank accounts for long-term purposes.

Don't Confuse savings and investment. Save first; invest afterwards.

Table 5.4
Summary of Savings Plans

Plan	*Current Approximate Return**	*Recommended for*	*Tax Status*	*Remarks*
Bank, trust, or credit union savings accounts	6% on minimum monthly account compounded twice per year. Rates change regularly. Slightly less on minimum daily balance.	People holding money for emergencies and irregular current expenses.	Interest fully taxable.**	Deposit paycheque into daily interest account or have your bank automatically debit your chequing account every month or issue a series of post-dated cheques to transfer a fixed percentage of your take-home pay to a savings account. A trust company, credit union or money market fund will usually give a higher rate of return than a bank. Use for short-term accumulation only, then transfer to a higher-yielding plan.
Canada Savings Bonds	9–10% interest, payable monthly. Varies with issue.	People who want a good safe rate of return and instant liquidity.	Income fully taxable;** can be declared annually or every three years.	Good forced savings plan, especially if bought at work, but better return if bought with a lump sum. Good short-term plan. Very liquid. Usually extra return if kept to maturity. Rates sometimes increase after issue.

Money in banks, trust companies, credit unions, and broker accounts, for 30, 90, 180, 365 days.	7–9% Varies with money market.	People saving for the short term, but who are willing to tie the money up for certain periods of time.	Interest fully taxable.**	Usually a minimum amount required. Rates will vary considerably from time to time. Sometimes possible to negotiate special rates over $100,000 — not for long-term saving.
Guaranteed Investment Certificate	9–10%	People who are able to tie up money for one to five years.	Interest fully taxable.**	Normally the longer you hold the certificate the higher the rate, but the opposite has been true in recent years. Trust companies usually give best rates (particularly smaller trust companies). Be careful the amount with one trust company does not exceed $60,000. Good for producing income, not for accumulating money. Tax can be paid annually or every three years.
Life insurance	6–8% guaranteed for term of contract.	People who need permanent insurance or find it difficult to save in other ways.	Tax on growth may be deferred until surrendered;*** no tax in the event of death.	A good forced savings plan for the long term. Don't register as RRSP.

*Rates are subject to change at any time, although the relative rates should remain fairly constant.
**Taxable but qualifies for $1,000 of tax-free investment income from Canadian sources.
***See Chapter 10 for a detailed discussion of taxability of cash value increases in life insurance and deferred annuities.

CHAPTER 6

Investments: Using Today's Income To Increase Tomorrow's

Most middle-income Canadians don't take the steps necessary to ensure that the money they save today returns the greatest possible benefit to them in terms of tomorrow's income. They are *losing* money by not using it wisely.

THE BASIC LAW OF INVESTMENT

The one basic law of investment is that *the potential return on an investment should vary directly with the risk of loss and inversely with the safety and liquidity of the investment.**

If you want to make a fast bundle on an investment, you'll have to risk losing all or part of what you put into it. On the other hand, if you want to guarantee at least the return of the money you invest, you will have to settle for a less spectacular return on your money.

If you are concerned about liquidity — the ease with which you can turn your investment back into cash — you will usually have to settle for a lower rate of return than if you are willing to tie up the money for long periods of time. In other words, fortunes can be made and lost overnight on common shares in Consolidated Moose Pasture; fortunes are never made, nor lost, by investing in Canada Savings Bonds.

The factors you have to balance as you put your money to work for you are: (1) return on investments (just how much can you expect to make on the investments you are selecting?); (2) risk (how likely are you to lose all or part of the money you are investing?); and (3) liquidity (how easy is it to turn your investments into cash if you need to?).

TWO BASIC INVESTMENT RECOMMENDATIONS

First, *be realistic about risk.* Unless you have the time, energy, and experience to evaluate high-risk investments and the guts to live with them,

---

*We have dealt separately, in Chapter 9, with tax shelters, but the reader should recognize that all tax-shelter decisions involve investment decisions as well. Chapters 6 and 9 should be read in conjunction with one another.

stay away from them or give them low priority. The returns from relatively safe investments are high enough that for most of us the chance of extra profit from something risky is simply not justified.

Second, *be realistic about liquidity*. Most Canadians like having money in a bank savings account where it is easily available. But because it is so easy to draw the money out, the bank pays relatively low rates of interest — often not enough to keep up with inflation. Do not keep more money in the bank than you need for convenience, emergencies, and buying opportunities. Nowadays you can't afford to!

INVESTMENT PRIORITIES

Forearmed with our one basic law and two basic recommendations, let's turn to a more specific review of various investment vehicles. And let's start where your investment considerations should start — by reviewing the levels of risk involved in various investment vehicles.

Pyramid Power

The pyramid below combines basic financial planning and investment portfolio structuring. The lower levels must be constructed initially to form a solid financial base on which you can move toward the higher-risk investments. It's absolutely vital that you avoid the temptation to scale the top of the pyramid in one jump. You may be a hero in a hot market, but a turnaround could wipe you out.

If you build from the bottom, you'll enjoy the twin advantages of emotional security and financial staying power. In building your financial structure, remember that discipline is indispensable and patience really is a virtue.

Commodities
Options Tax Shelters
Gold Silver
Common Stocks Mutual Funds Real Estate
GICs Bonds Preferred Shares Mortgages
RRSP Canada Savings Bonds T-Bills Term Deposits
Debt Elimination Emergency Fund Home

Most of the items in the lowest two levels of the pyramid have been dealt with in the previous chapter. Let's look now at the higher levels, where the returns get more interesting, but the element of risk becomes a factor.

DEBT INSTRUMENT INVESTMENTS

We have already seen that Canada Savings Bonds and government Treasury Bills make excellent emergency fund investments because they are safe and liquid and pay a respectable rate of interest.

Longer-term debt-type investments lack the liquidity to be considered as emergency funds; however, they are favoured by many investors, who consider them safer than common-stock investments. Let's look at some popular ones.

GUARANTEED INVESTMENT CERTIFICATES OR CERTIFICATES OF DEPOSIT

Trust companies and banks sell Guaranteed Investment Certificates (GICs) or Certificates of Deposit which yield a guaranteed rate of interest over a set period of time. For instance, a typical "bonus" savings account may pay 6%,* but a five-year GIC could pay up to 9½%.*

You get that extra interest because you agree to give up a little liquidity. These certificates are insured up to $60,000, and banks and trust companies are not likely to have any trouble meeting their obligations. If an unexpected cash pinch does arise, you can usually sell them through an investment dealer, cash them in at a discount, or pledge them as security on a loan.

A good alternative to a savings account is a term deposit whose term can be anywhere from 30 to 365 days. Most institutions require a minimum of $5,000 to purchase a term deposit, but the interest return will be significantly higher, especially at maturities of 270 to 365 days.

LONG-TERM BONDS: THE INTEREST RATE TEETER-TOTTER

In addition to the well-known Canada Savings Bonds, bonds are issued by the different levels of government as well as by corporations. They pay various rates of interest, generally based on the security as appraised by one of the big bond-rating houses such as Moody's or Standard and Poors in New York.

As a bondholder, you know you will be paid the interest specified on your bond (e.g., 9% or 11%) every year until the bond matures in one, five, ten, or twenty-five years. At maturity, you will receive the full face value, usually $1,000.

A bond ranks ahead of preferred shares in terms of quality of investment, and preferred shares rank ahead of common. If a company goes into bankruptcy, the assets will be distributed to the bondholders first, the preferred shareholders second and the common shareholders last.

When you buy a bond, you are effectively lending the government or company money. They are agreeing to pay you interest on the loan at specified intervals (quarterly, annually), and then repay the principal at maturity.

---

*Interest rates used in this chapter reflect levels current at press time. These will vary over time but the relationship between rates should remain consistent.

There are huge and highly organized secondary markets where bonds may be bought and sold, thus providing investors with a degree of liquidity not generally available in GICs.

Bond price fluctuations may be described most simply by the analogy of a teeter-totter. When interest rates at one end go up, bond prices on the other go down. When interest rates go down, bond prices go up.

Figure 6.1
Prime Rate vs. Bond Price

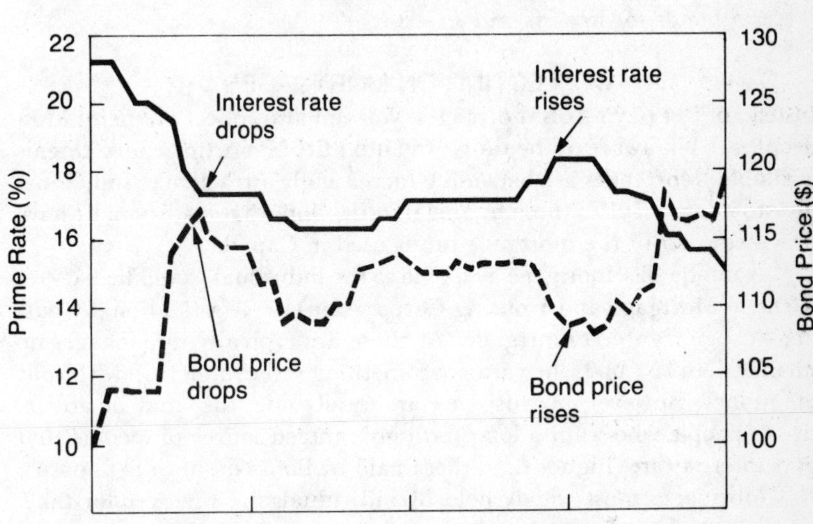

Illustration of Bond Coupons, Prices, and Yields

$10,000 bond with 11% coupon is issued and sells at par value. Interest: $1,100.

A. Interest rates decrease by 10%
   Market equivalent of 11% is 11 × 9/10 = 9.9%
   Capital value of $1,100 interest @ 9.9% = $1,100/.099 = $11,111
   We could expect the bond to trade around $11,000 to $11,200, depending on whether speculation was for further decreases or a "correction" to higher interest rates.

B. Interest rates increase 40%
   Market equivalent of 11% is 11 × 140/10 = 15.4%
   Capital value of $1,100 interest @ 15.4% = $1,100/.154 = $7,143
   We could expect the bond to trade around $7,000 to $7,200.

An analysis such as this makes it easy to understand the devastation caused to the bond market by the explosive increase in interest rates in 1981 and 1982, and why they rebounded so strongly when interest rates started into a free fall in the latter half of 1982 and early 1983 and have continued to decrease right up to the present.

Bonds are typically used by investors to meet three objectives:

1. As an alternative to GICs in a tax-sheltered investment; i.e., RRSP.
2. As a total return (interest and capital gain) vehicle in time of declining interest rates.
3. As a safe, relatively high income-bearing instrument, especially short-term bonds for low tax rate investors.

COLLECTING ON MORTGAGES

Instead of just paying off mortgages, you can also collect on them. Most people are not aware of the range and quantity of mortgage investments available. Mortgages are becoming increasingly attractive to individual investors, as well as to those financial institutions that traditionally have provided most of the mortgage funds used in Canada.

A top-quality mortgage available to the individual would be a CMHC (Central Mortgage and Housing Corporation) or NHA (National Housing Act) guaranteed mortgage. As these are typically in packages no smaller than $50,000, they are not something you can pick up with your pin money. However, because they are totally safe, they may be attractive to people who want a long-term guaranteed source of income that pays interest rates higher than those paid by banks on normal deposits.

Mortgages most widely held by individuals are the "vendor-take-back" type, where the person selling a house agrees to take back a mortgage — often a second or even a third, frequently at below-market interest rates — to facilitate the sale of the house. Typically, if the holder of a low-interest vendor-take-back mortgage has to turn it into cash, he or she will have to sell it at a substantial discount to bring the effective interest rate up to market for the buyer. If a vendor-take-back mortgage is sold below face value, the seller experiences a capital loss. The buyer earns a bonus (the difference between the face value and the buying price), a capital gain.

As mortgages become more attractive and better known, mortgage brokers are becoming more important. They operate on various scales, from very big players who put together packages of investors' money to finance large commercial projects, to real estate lawyers who run small-to-medium residential second mortgage operations.

If you are interested in mortgages but do not have a great deal of money available to invest, you might ask your lawyer to recommend someone who is organizing a money pool. But remember, mortgages normally are not very liquid investments. Since principal is paid back gradually in relatively small amounts, reinvestment becomes a problem. Still, at interest rates of 14% and up, second mortgages provide a relatively safe and attractive savings alternative—*if* the cash you are putting up really is surplus to your short term needs.

THE STOCK MARKET

Most people who have tried the stock market once and had an unpleasant experience started off with expectations that no broker could possibly live up to. Few people get rich on the stock market. For everyone who runs a few dollars' worth of penny mining stock into a fortune, literally hundreds of people lose money.

If you start off realistically and don't try to get rich too fast, it is possible to make money on the market. The Investment Dealers' Association states that a return of about 11% is a good long-term average for equity investments.

Don't be misled by some of the big gains that have been made in the last few years. If you want to do well in the market, here are a few pointers.

Pick your adviser carefully, get to know both the broker and his or her firm, and make sure he or she knows what kind of person you are. If you're just putting up a few dollars, knowing you're bucking the odds, say so. If you're interested in moderate capital gains, tell your adviser that too, or that you are just looking for income. Look at the whole market. It may be unwise to go against the trend; however, there are worthwhile buys in both good and bad markets, so look for the broker or adviser who can show you individual companies with exceptional values. These may be companies that have had a couple of bad years that caused their shares to be undervalued. Under new management, however, it's expected that the company's profits will turn upward.

Selecting companies with exceptional values allows many successful money managers to ring up returns averaging 15%-20% compounded annually—but they are prepared to wait. John Templeton, the manager of the extraordinarily successful Templeton Fund, holds stocks an average of five years.

Take the same patient attitude with your brokers.

Remember, the broker is a salesperson. It is you who makes the final decision on the stocks to buy and/or sell. To do well, you will need time to study stocks in order to make a wise decision. If you do not have the time, knowledge, or interest, and still wish to invest in the stock market, you'll be better off in a mutual fund where stock selections are made for you.

Don't commit money you are going to need for other purposes in the near future. Staying power in the stock market can be very important.

Cut your losses and don't be afraid to take a profit. This is the opposite of human nature; there seems to be a suicidal urge to hold onto a stock until it reaches its absolute peak, or to hang on to a turkey waiting for it to come back. The rising stock could pass its peak if held too long, and the turkey might stay a turkey. You could have that money working for you elsewhere in the meantime.

If you are seeking good income and some growth you might consider high-quality common stocks or convertible preferreds.

PREFERRED SHARES: HALFWAY HOUSE BETWEEN BONDS AND COMMON STOCKS

Preferred shares rank ahead of common stocks and behind bonds in terms of safety of investment. Income is in the form of dividends and therefore receives favourable tax treatment where the issuer is a Canadian-controlled corporation.

The market action of preferred shares is very similar to that of bonds. Rising interest rates affect preferred share prices negatively and vice-versa.

Recent years have seen the introduction of many new kinds of preferred shares. Investors wishing to convert interest income to dividend income for tax purposes, but seeking a high degree of *safety*, may choose a *retractable* preferred share. Retractable refers to the shareholder's right to sell the shares back to the issuing company at a time and price set at the time of issue.

CONVERTIBLE PREFERRED SHARES

Certain preferred shares have a feature which allows investors to exchange preferred shares for common shares of the same company. This feature offers the investor greater flexibility, since it allows secure income from the preferred to be combined with the capital gain potential of the common stock.

If you are thinking of investing in preferred shares, check closely the features outlined in the prospectus when the shares were originally issued. Many pitfalls await careless investors who do not check the details of preferred shares when purchasing them. As a guide to investors who wish to avoid these pitfalls, the *Financial Post* publishes a rating service called "Can-Pref," which is a worthwhile investment if you are seriously interested in preferred shares.

OPTIONS

In property transactions or other business dealings, an option contract is bought to reserve the right to buy or sell a product at a fixed price within a specified period of time.

The advantages of trading stock and bond options are:

1. Options cost less than the underlying security and therefore allow a smaller investment.

2. The potential gains and losses are greater than holding the stock itself. This is known as "leverage." Since the price of an option is a fraction of the price of the stock itself, a relatively small change in the stock price can produce a relatively large increase in the value of the option, and therefore the profit or return on investment is proportionately greater.

However, the option can also expire worthless, with the total investment lost, whereas a security seldom goes to zero.

Trading in options is obviously a more speculative form of investment and should be undertaken only by those able to risk the loss of the capital involved.

Covered options offer a way to reduce risk. Let's look at an example. You buy 100 shares at $33 per share. At the same time you sell to someone an option to buy your stock some time in the future for a predetermined price—let's assume $35 per share. If the buyer pays you $2 a share for this, your cost is reduced from $33 to $31 per share. If the stock goes up to or beyond the $35 you must give up your stock at $35, but you have made a gain of $4 ($2 plus $2 you have already received). If the price remains the same your profit is the $2 received. If the stock goes down you would lose no money unless it goes below $31.

Anyone considering the option market should work closely with a qualified broker.

Investors wishing to learn about options should inquire about educational seminars conducted by investment dealers (stockbrokers). Many new types of options have been developed in the past few years—including covered bond options mentioned earlier—and information about such options can be obtained at these seminars.

Whether you're in stocks, bonds, or options, diversify sensibly. Don't try to keep track of too many stocks. Having more than five stocks in a portfolio under $10,000 just creates confusion and extra commission expense.

COMMODITIES

Commodities are the most speculative investments available because of the high degree of leverage. You should not speculate in contracts to purchase commodities such as base metals, bonds, stocks, pork bellies, lumber, and heating oil unless you are a seasoned, well-heeled investor who can handle the volatility of such markets.

Buying and holding precious metals is quite another type of investing. Let's look at what it has to offer as an investment strategy.

GOLD AND SILVER

Gold has been called the ultimate storehouse of value because it is indestructible. Of all the gold ever mined, it has been estimated that 97% is in current use in one form or another. Gold is the ultimate retreat when confidence in other values dwindles.

Increases in the value of gold do not occur in an orderly fashion; they respond to crises in world political, fiscal, and monetary situations. As to new production, gold comes from two basic sources: South Africa and the Soviet Union. Each year a portion of the world supply is transformed into non-monetary gold in the form of jewellery. This transmutation is currently less than the gross production from these two sources, but if supply were to cease from either source it would have a major effect on world prices.

In the past few years the price of gold has made front-page news. When gold and silver prices were exploding in 1979 and early 1980, the lineups outside institutions selling gold were several blocks long. People wanted to cash in on a bonanza, but many of the buyers found the price of gold had increased several times before they got to the front of the line.

As you will see from Figure 6.2, the gold bubble did burst, although not as spectacularly as the silver bubble.

Figure 6.2
Gold and Silver Prices $US/oz.

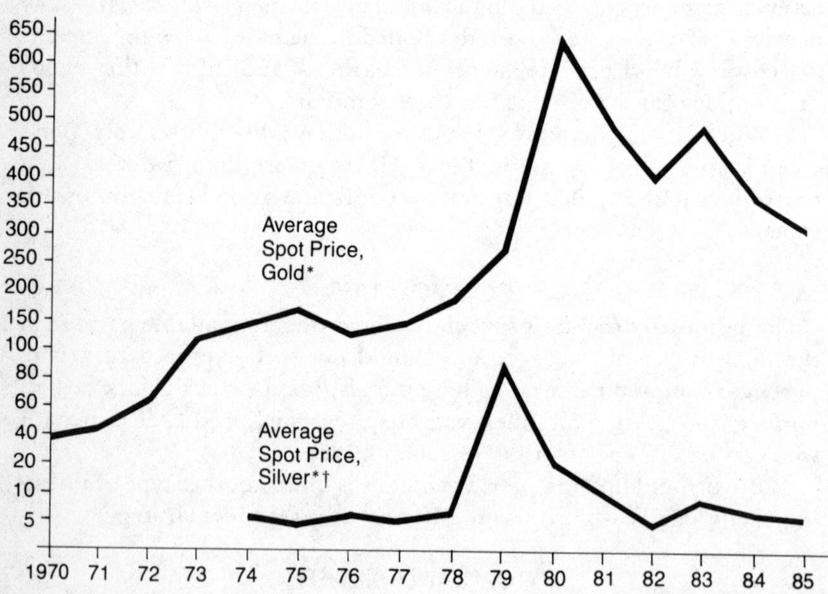

*Figures supplied by Deak Perera Canada, Inc.

†Silver prices not available prior to 1974.

The fabulously wealthy Hunt family in the United States, whose personal assets were reported to be in the billions, tried to corner the world silver market. In 1980 they found themselves overextended, and the price of silver came tumbling down. Many experts believe there is a "normal" relationship between the price of gold and silver, with gold usually selling for 16 to 18 times the price of silver. This ratio is not always maintained: in June 1981 it was about 40:1.

Table 6.1 shows you the many ways to buy gold and silver.

Table 6.1
Types of Investments in Gold and Silver

Type	*Charges*	*Minimum*	*Security*	*Remarks*
Bullion	$5.50/bar charge & storage charge	5 grams	Stored in bank inside or outside the country	Can buy from bank or precious metal dealer
Jewellery	Sales tax plus premium of up to 40% plus insurance costs	—	Store at home or in safety deposit box	Has decorative value as well
Certificate	1% to 3% on purchase and sale depending on size	$2,500	Can retain certificate	Most convenient way to hold for most people. Can be bought from bank or precious metal dealer
Coins	Dealer receives premium of as much as 40%; charge hidden	1 coin	Store in safety deposit box	Can also have value as an antique or collector's item
Stock	Depends on size of transaction. Ranges from 1% to 3% on purchase and sale	1 share	Certificate can be retained at broker's or stored in safety deposit box	Price may not reflect changes in price of gold. Buy from investment dealer

In our view, gold and silver could be good long-term investments. We suggest, however, you invest no more than 10% of your total holdings in these precious metals. As noted earlier, if you want to trade seriously in gold and silver, you must be extremely knowledgeable. If you are merely looking for entertainment, stick to the racetrack; you'll have more fun and get some fresh air!

You can choose whether a gain or loss in value on the sale of gold or any similar commodity will be taxed as capital gain or loss or an income gain or loss; however, once you have made that choice, you must stick with it on all transactions. If you are buying gold as a long-term investment, you will be best to opt for capital gains treatment, especially with the capital gains exemption in effect.

REAL ESTATE MAKES REAL MONEY

Real property—land and buildings—has proved to be an excellent long-term inflation hedge. Its value has generally risen at least as much as the general price level over a period of five years or more.

The rent-control programs in most provinces in Canada now make investment in residential real property less attractive, but this disadvantage has been somewhat offset by tax-shelter incentive programs.

In 1974, in response to the shortage of new low-cost apartments, the government started a number of programs to increase investment in specified areas. Known as Class 31 (or MURB) investments, they are still available on a resale basis. The rules allow an investor to claim losses (true losses as well as paper losses) through capital cost allowance or depreciation against other taxable income, not just from rental income—a big potential advantage if investments are selected carefully. Further details are spelled out in the chapter on Tax Shelters.

These days it is easier for the small investor to gain access to real commercial property. Lawyers and developers now are assembling deals in which the small investor can put his or her money into a syndicate with other small investors. He or she also will get professional advice on buying and managing properties such as office buildings, shopping plazas, or industrial park developments. It is possible to invest in a syndicated real estate deal with as little as $2,500.

The Real Property Trust, now Royal Lepage, was the first to make purchases of this size possible, and now other institutions such as Investors Syndicate, Counsel Trust, and First City Trust have come out with similar funds. An investment in commercial real estate through one of these vehicles can be used for your RRSP or can come from after-tax funds. Income on after-tax funds, which otherwise might be taxable, can be sheltered through write-offs for capital cost allowance ("depreciation"). When fund units are cashed by an after-tax investor, tax is levied on 100% of your deemed share of the capital cost allowance "recaptured" on sale. Any capital gain will be tax-free within the confines of the new capital gains exemption.

Real property funds like these bring commercial real estate investment within reach of the average investor, but it should be recognized that the prospects for such a fund depend on the abilities of the fund manager to pick the properties, and to spread risk among different properties and local and regional economies.

One other difficulty encountered by these funds is how to determine the value of the real estate other than upon the sale of the actual property.

Unit holders of the Royal Lepage fund found this out the hard way. When it was still in the hands of the Real Property Trust, differing opinions on the value of the property led to a reassessment of the property values followed by devaluation in the unit value of the funds. Many investors, not accustomed to real estate actually being worth less, wanted to sell. Had the investors been permitted to liquidate at that moment, it would have forced some properties to be sold at fire sale prices. Hence, a freeze was instituted and investors were not permitted to sell for a period of one year.

Real estate should be viewed as a long-term hold. If the fund is run by experienced real estate professionals, your patience should be rewarded.

United States Real Estate

As a result of the Foreign Investment in Real Property Taxation Act (FIRPTA), in which the U.S. government levies tax on the capital gains of your real estate, and the tax-free capital gains exemption introduced in Canada, the tax rules upon the sale of any U.S. real estate owned by Canadians have become complex. You will now be taxed in the United States at your marginal tax rate on 40% of the gain. This means that there will be no tax to pay in Canada. Alternatively, you have the option of paying no tax in the United States, but paying tax on 50% of the gain in Canada, in which case you will not be eligible for the Canadian capital gains exemption.

In both cases tax will be withheld; however, if you elect to pay tax in Canada, you will receive credit on your return.

For property owned prior to September 26, 1980, the gain in value will be calculated from January 1, 1985. For property purchased after that date the gain will be calculated from the purchase date.

If the gain is small, say under $50,000, it is likely it would be better to pay the tax in the U.S. If the gain is in excess of that, it may be wise to pay the tax in Canada. In any event, you should seek the advice of a professional.

All foreign owners are now required to file an information form, which includes the market value of the property held as of January 1, 1983, or the purchase date, whichever comes later. Foreign owners are also required to report the net income (total income minus expenses), and tax should be remitted at the rate of 30% on the income to the IRS. This is the responsibility of the tenant or property manager. If expenses exceed income, a rental information form can be completed which will make it unnecessary to withhold tax.

There are, of course, pitfalls. The property you own may be part of a complex that does not allow you to rent at all, or you may only be able to rent it on a restricted basis. Or your rent may not be high enough to carry the costs. Usually, rental agents are available, either through the development itself or through a real estate agent in the local community. Check their rates – they can be high (as much as 45% of the rent). A Canadian investor could also lose if the U.S. dollar weakens in relation to the Canadian dollar. While the reverse has been occurring in the past few years, this trend may not continue forever.

The best reason to invest in a sunshine property is for the fun of it.

Time Sharing

Originally an import from Europe, time sharing has enjoyed explosive growth in North America, particularly in the U.S. Instead of owning a unit for the whole year, you buy it for a specific time period every year. With time sharing you buy only what you need. The advantage is that you freeze the cost of your holiday accommodation, except for annual maintenance fees.

To combat the problem of having to go to the same place at the same time every year, time-sharing owners can also join a time-sharing network which allows them to exchange their time and space with someone else either in that particular development or in one of the associated projects located somewhere else in the world. The two largest time-sharing associations are Interval International, operating out of Miami, Florida, and Resort Condominium International, located in Indianapolis, Indiana.

Although the time-sharing industry has been plagued with high-pressure sales techniques, many people who have bought these units have seen their market value increase substantially.

MANY THINGS THAT DON'T LOOK LIKE INVESTMENTS CAN BE VERY GOOD ONES

Some people have made a great deal of money investing in hobbies like coins, stamps, and art. These investments require specialized knowledge and tend not to be liquid. We know one Toronto art investor who had to sell an impressive Emily Carr painting at a substantial loss a few years ago when money was tight. If he'd been able to hold on to it for a few more months he could have realized a substantial profit.

The problem is that the price you can get for all but the very best and most expensive items of this kind is affected by factors over which you have no control—the stock market, interest rates, the state of the economy. Essentially they're luxuries, and purely speculative investments. When there's not much money around there's even less available to buy collectibles.

There are, however, various purchases we all make that can—for a few extra dollars and a little extra work—turn out to be sound investments. If you like traditional pieces of furniture, for example, consider buying certified antiques for your house. Although they may cost more and may need greater care, you will have turned a consumption item into an investment. Once again, it won't be a very liquid investment and you won't have any guarantee that you can get back the full price you paid for it, but the furniture should hold its value, even against inflation.

Obviously, this kind of investment makes sense only if it pleases you. But by spending a few extra dollars and a little more time, you can combine investment value with personal satisfaction.

DEALING WITH YOUR INVESTMENT ADVISERS

Your stockbroker may tell you that Deep Hole Mines is a great buy, but stockbrokers earn their commission *only* if you buy something. (If yours tells you there's nothing worth buying right now, he or she is a gem.) Your insurance agent may tell you what a great investment a whole life policy is, but the agent gets a commission too. And the same is true of most mutual fund salespeople and real estate brokers. Your problem is to decide just who all these people are really working for—you or themselves.

PROFESSIONAL MONEY MANAGERS: MUTUAL FUNDS AND INVESTMENT COUNSELLORS

For the fortunate few with hundreds of thousands of dollars to invest, the services of a personal investment counsellor will be available and may well be rewarding to the ego as well as the pocketbook.

But for the common herd with only a few hundred or thousand to invest, a basic reality is that most of us don't have the time, expertise, or inclination to choose and manage investments effectively and consistently—whether the investment is in the stock market, precious metals, real estate, or agricultural commodities.

Therefore, it would seem logical—and the authors' experience as financial planners bears this out—that most of us, most of the time, for most of our money, should invest through the medium of an investment fund where our dollars are pooled with those of thousands of other people.

Frankly, we are favourably impressed with the overall track record of the leading mutual fund organizations on both sides of the border. Consistent returns of 15% to 20% compounded over many years are not uncommon. In addition, the pooling of investment allows a degree of diversification which substantially reduces risk. And perhaps most basic of all is the liquidity of investment funds — an especially important advantage where the underlying investment is illiquid, as with real estate.

Many of these funds have front-end charges, which can be as high as 9% of the money deposited with them. The charges pay in part for a sales force that in theory keeps cash flowing into the fund to allow the manager to take advantage of good opportunities. Some funds have no front-end charge.

In fact, many front-end loaded funds outperform "no load" funds and quickly wipe out the effect of any front-end charge. Before you pay a front-end charge, however, be sure you are happy that past performance has justified the charge and that the salespeople have earned their commission. Furthermore, try to negotiate a reduced commission.

While past performance is important, there is no guarantee that things will remain the same in the future. Fund managers come and go, and astute investors will check the ranks of management in a fund they are considering, in order to make sure there is depth and continuity — not just one "genius" whose death or retirement could seriously affect fund performance.

You can purchase mutual funds from salespeople who represent a specific fund or through investment dealers or mutual fund brokers. Brokers have access to many different funds with several different companies. Often these funds can be moved around as the market dictates. There are usually charges associated with such moves.

A well-managed mutual fund is, for most people, the best way to invest in the stock market. You will, however, have to earn more after tax than the interest cost of your mortgage to make it an investment that is better than paying off your mortgage. A mutual fund requires little of your time or knowledge, and you are drawing upon the expertise of a professional money manager to call the shots for you. Over the years, many of these funds have developed a bad reputation, largely because of the method of distribution. The returns on some of them, however, have been substantial and should be considered seriously by anyone interested in a stock market investment.

If you have a sizeable amount of money to invest — say $100,000–$200,000 or more — you could make use of one of the many investment counselling firms. These firms generally charge a fee based on a percentage of your total investment; their rates are relatively modest — ½% to 1% against a minimum fee is not unusual. Their fee structure gives them an economic interest in building up the total worth of your investments because that way their income rises as well.

Investment counselling fees are tax deductible. Regrettably, investment counsellors are not available to those with only small amounts of money to invest, except indirectly through "in house" mutual funds they manage for smaller customers.

CANADIAN DIVIDEND INCOME

The 1977 Federal Budget introduced some very favourable tax breaks for those receiving dividend income from a tax-paying Canadian company. At that time, changes were introduced to integrate corporate and personal tax rates to assure that there would be no relative advantage in receiving income directly or through a company. A system of a federal gross-up of income, combined with a federal tax credit, substantially reduced the amount of tax on Canadian dividends.

In subsequent Federal Budgets in 1981 and 1986, the tax advantage was reduced by reducing the rate of dividend tax credit. (In 1986, the gross-up rate was also reduced.) In addition, for those with substantial amounts of dividend income and little or no income from other sources, the Alternative Minimum Tax (AMT) effectively eliminated any tax advantage in Canadian dividend income. Table 6.2 illustrates the effect of these changes on taxpayers facing tax on regular income at a marginal rate of approximately 50%.

For taxpayers in lower tax brackets, the relative effect of the gross-up and tax credit is even more pronounced. However, the effect of the Alternative Minimum Tax has to be calculated before making any judgments on the ideal "mix" of income from dividends, interest and potential capital gains.

Table 6.2
The Effect of Changes in the Tax Treatment of Canadian Dividend Income: 1977–1986

	1977 (Budget)	*1981 (Budget)*	*1986 (Budget)*
Gross up	50%	50%	33⅓%
Dividend tax credit	25%	22⅔%	16⅔%
Cash dividend	$1,000	$1,000	$1,000
Gross up	500	500	333
Taxable dividend	1,500	1,500	1,333
Federal tax-34%	510	510	453
Dividend tax credit	375	340	222
Net Federal tax	135	170	231
Provincial tax-50%	68	85	116
Total tax	203	255	347
Effective tax rate	20.3%	25.5%	34.7%

SETTING YOUR OWN INVESTMENT OBJECTIVES

It is important for you to set your own investment objectives before seeking an adviser. This will give you more control over your financial destiny, and will help the adviser to do a better job.

The first question you have to ask yourself is, "Just how surplus is the money I am thinking of investing?" Then decide how much of your savings you might be able to expose to risk on a long-term commitment, and how much you have to keep fairly liquid.

If you really are generating extra money, money you will not need under any circumstances in the foreseeable future, you can consider less liquid, higher-risk investments. They have the greatest profit potential. On the other hand, if your excess money is the only cushion you have against a rainy day, you can't afford to take the chance of losing it, and you are probably not wise to tie it up in an illiquid form. In that case, you should look into term deposits, Canada Savings Bonds, or the newer variety of premium savings accounts that pay significantly higher interest rates on minimum balances in the $5,000-$10,000 range.

The next question you have to ask yourself is, "Do I need an income from this surplus money?" If you do, then consider Canada Savings Bonds or term deposits, mortgages, or other income-earning investments such as preferred shares or high-dividend common shares. If not, look at long-term investment situations such as land purchases, art, or growth stocks.

Don't neglect the tax implications of any investment you want to make. Try to maximize the untaxable investment earnings (the basic $1,000 worth of interest or "grossed-up" dividend income and the tax-free half of capital gains).

Only after you have made these basic decisions should you start worrying about the rate of return or profit you hope to earn. Your minimum objective should be to preserve the value of your money against inflation; that probably rules out bank accounts for anything but small amounts you may need on short notice or for short-term accumulation.

DO'S AND DON'TS

Do Buy a house if you do not already own one. This converts money you would normally spend on rent into the only tax-free investment available to anyone in Canada, other than the death benefit in your life insurance.

Do Make sure you are taking advantage of tax shelters, such as RRSPs. If your marginal tax rate is over 20%, it is hard to match the real yield you will get from investing pre-tax dollars.

Do Use CSBs and term deposits to provide liquidity and generate that first $1,000 of tax-free interest income.

Do Consider the stock market, but start with "safe" investments — blue-chip stocks that pay regular dividends.

Do Consider investing in mutual funds if you do not have the time, interest, or knowledge to invest in stocks on your own.

Do Consider investing in income-producing real-estate property or in raw land. Obviously your choice will depend on your own financial objectives, but remember that neither is a very liquid investment.

Don't Consider investing in speculative stocks unless you have money that is really surplus. Remember, there is risk of loss here, so it is no place for grocery or retirement money — and no substitute for paying off your mortgage.

Don't Tie up money which you may need in the short run in fixed, long-term investments.

Don't Let tax advantage blind you to inherent investment risk.

Don't Be impatient or greedy. Tortoises win more than jackrabbits and hogs.

Table 6.3
Summary of Investment and Tax Deferral Plans

Plan	Approximate Return	Recommended for	Tax Status	Remarks
Mutual funds available from banks, mutual funds, trust companies, and insurance companies	Variable.	Someone who wants to take some risk after having accumulated a base of guarantees.	Gain normally treated as capital gain.	A lump sum deposit. Can get "no load" funds with trust company, no guarantee. They will out-perform lowest fund. Load pays for salesperson who may be only reason you are in plan. Don't hesitate to pay it if it makes you save. Don't expect miracles – hold at least four years.
Stock purchase plans	Variable.	People willing to take some risk to obtain tax-favoured growth and dividends.	Dividends taxable but eligible for dividend tax credit; capital gains exempt up to $500,000 (or less between now and 1990); company contribution taxed as income.	Good forced savings plan. Return will depend on performance of stock. Could lose money. Usually company contributes as well. Be aware of company vesting provision.
RESPs	Variable.	People saving for children's education.	Growth in value taxable upon withdrawal in hands of child.	Child must go to a degree-granting institution and get past first year; otherwise, you receive only a return of contributions. A long-term plan.

Plan	*Approximate Return*	*Recommended for*	*Tax Status*	*Remarks*
Real Estate Funds	Variable.	Someone who is seeking tax-deferred income gain and/or stake in growth potential of commercial real estate.	No tax paid until cashed, then recaptured depreciation and capital gain taxable (in excess of exempt gains).	Some funds have front-end charge. Underlying real estate most important. Minimum deposit $2,500. Be aware of liquidity limitations.
RRSPs	Varies depending on type of investment; generally, guaranteed return investments are recommended.	People trying to accumulate money for retirement.	Contributions tax deductible; all value taxable on withdrawal.	The most popular tax shelter and an excellent way to accumulate funds for retirement. Make sure you get the right one for you. A long-term plan.

CHAPTER 7

Employee Benefits

The term "employee benefits" covers an increasing number of non-cash forms of compensation, and the array is wide enough to require some definitions.

By "employee benefits" we refer to benefits (some of which are more commonly referred to as perquisites or "perks") that fall into one of the following categories:

1. *Group insurance* including life, disability income, accidental death and dismemberment, medical and dental coverage (usually referred to as "group benefits").
2. *The provision of goods or services* including the use of money through loans on terms which are more favourable than if you provided them yourself out of your after-tax income.
3. *Deferred income plans* including Registered Pension Plans (RPPs), Deferred Profit Sharing Plans (DPSPs), group Registered Retirement Savings Plans (RRSPs), non-registered supplementary retirement income plans (SRI), and contractual deferred compensation plans.

All employee benefit plans, to be of use to you, should offer one or a combination of the following advantages:

1. *Reduced cost* compared to what you would have to pay to provide the product or service yourself. This advantage is often greatest in the area of group insurance benefits, but can also apply to items such as company leased or purchased cars, or loans (where the company can borrow at a lower rate than you can).
2. *Access to benefits* not available to you as an individual. For instance, if you are uninsurable for life or disability income insurance, group insurance may be your only source of coverage. Even if you are quite healthy, the medical and dental coverage available to you as an individual is distinctly inferior to what a good group program can provide.
3. *Tax advantage.* This will usually take the form of tax-free or only partially taxable treatment of amounts paid on your behalf by your employer (e.g., for group insurance premiums or to lease a car for your use).

In some cases, tax advantage takes the form of a deduction for contributions you may make to the plan. For example, contributions you make to RPPs or RRSPs are deductible within certain limits. In addition, premiums you pay for government and private health and dental plans may be deductible under certain circumstances.

WHY BOTHER LEARNING ABOUT EMPLOYEE BENEFITS?

Whether you are single or married, or have dependent children, you should take an interest in non-cash employee benefits for a number of reasons.

First, you may have access to attractive optional benefits (e.g., voluntary group life insurance), but only if you learn about the plans and make a decision to participate.

Second, there may be deadlines for participation, beyond which you will not be eligible, or only on less favourable terms. For example, in many plans, if you don't sign up for life and disability insurance within ninety days of being employed, you'll have to pass a medical exam.

Third, if you're part of a two-income couple, you and your partner should review your benefit plans carefully to avoid duplication of cost on contributory plans, and to make sure you're choosing the particular benefit plan with the best combination of cost and benefits.

Finally, if you're in a position to negotiate your total compensation package, you should be aware of what the best trade-offs may be between taxable cash compensation and lower cost, tax favoured non-cash benefits. When you make those comparisons, make sure you measure the total impact of foregoing cash income. For example, if you agree to reduce a bonus or pass up a salary increase in order to obtain non-cash benefits, measure the possible effect on your pension and group life and disability insurance benefits, all of which can be adversely affected. For this reason, you are better generally to trade cash bonuses rather than salary.

GETTING THE MOST FROM GROUP BENEFITS

Here's a practical checklist on how to gain maximum advantage from participation in group insurance programs at your work.

1. Comparison shop where it's appropriate. Especially if you're under age 40, don't take for granted that the group insurance rate is better than what you would face as an individual on personal insurance. Individual life insurance rates, in particular, have reduced steadily over the last decade — especially if you qualify as a non-smoker.

   But keep your perspective straight; that is, take all the "free" group coverage you can get from non-contributory employer pay-all plans. Compare rates only where *you* are required to pay all or part of the premium.

2. Take full advantage of coverage you can't get as an individual. If you are uninsurable for life and/or disability income insurance, take as much as you can get, even if you have to contribute to the cost. Apply the rule to medical and dental coverage as well—even if you're in excellent health. The fact is, there is virtually no first-class medical and dental coverage available to individuals at any price. If you don't believe this, check with some insurance companies that advertise individual medical coverage, or an organization like Blue Cross.
3. Try to get the best tax treatment possible. If you are required to contribute to the cost of the program, ask to have your contributions directed toward provincial hospital and medical premiums, if any; life insurance premiums for any amounts in excess of $25,000; and disability income insurance premiums.

On the first two items, payment of the premium by your employer creates a taxable benefit for you. If your employer pays the premium for disability income insurance, the premium is not considered to be a taxable benefit; but, if and when you ever receive income benefits, the benefit payments will be taxable, less any payments you have made. If, on the other hand, you pay all the premiums, none of the benefits will be taxable.

Payments by your employer do not create taxable benefits on the following insurance benefits: Dependent Life; Accidental Death and Dismemberment; Medical and Dental. Of these, the most significant is the last. For this reason, if you're in a position to negotiate your total compensation, you may be motivated to ask for extensions of medical and dental coverage in return for giving up cash compensation. By doing so, you effectively convert taxable compensation to non-taxable.

THE REAL MEASURE OF TAX ADVANTAGE

If you're familiar with the concept of progressive tax rates, you'll know that you pay tax at higher rates on the "last" income you earn, and that it's at your marginal or highest rate that you gain tax advantage.

What you may not know is that the degree of real advantage is a lot greater than the marginal tax rate numbers suggest.

Example

In 1986, on taxable income from $13,054 to $18,275, you'll pay federal tax at a rate of 20%, and a combined federal and provincial rate of 30% (Ontario; not including temporary surtaxes; rates will be higher or lower in other provinces).

If you are able to trade $500 of cash for a non-taxable benefit such as medical or dental coverage, the full $500 will be available to pay for benefits, whereas you would have only $350 cash left over after tax. The $150 difference represents an increase of almost 43% in the amount available to buy benefits.

At the end of this chapter, we have provided a summary of the tax treatment of contributions to, and income from, a wide range of non-cash benefit plans.

NON-CASH PERKS CAN PERK UP YOUR PAY PACKAGE

In the parlance of employee compensation, group insurance plans are known as benefits. Non-cash benefits such as company cars, loans, and personal financial planning are known as perquisites or "perks" – probably because they are usually made available only to high-ranking executives. Let's examine how they work.

Car Benefits

Let's say your employer authorizes you to buy a $10,200 car, and agrees to pay you a big enough bonus to take care of it. If you are in the 34% marginal tax bracket, this will require a bonus of $15,454 to leave you enough after-tax money to pay for the car.

On the other hand, if your employer decides to buy or lease a car for your use, it costs him or her less. The company's direct cost is fully deductible as a business expense, just as your bonus would have been. You will have to declare a certain portion of the total value of the car as a taxable benefit to you (⅔ of the car lease or 2% of the original cost as a standby fee per month), but the cost of grossing up your extra tax will be only $3,503 for a total cost of $13,703, an 11% saving compared to grossing up a bonus.

If your employer will not buy or lease a car for you, consider a car allowance which may come to you tax-free, provided it is reasonable in terms of your actual expenses on company business.

Employee Loans

The November 1981 Budget signalled the end of the major advantage of interest-free loans. The general $500 deduction in calculating the amount of taxable benefit was eliminated and the $50,000 exemption on housing relocation loans was phased out over 1982 and 1983 ($40,000 in 1982, $20,000 in 1983, nil beginning in 1984). In the May 1985 Federal Budget, the trend was reversed somewhat. A change was introduced to allow an interest-free loan up to $25,000 with no taxable benefit imputed, provided the loan proceeds were used to purchase a home as a result of a job transfer involving a move at least 40 kilometres to the new place of employment.

There remains, as well, some interesting advantage in low-interest or interest-free employee loans simply because the "prescribed rate" used by Revenue Canada to measure the amount of taxable benefit is less than the market rate the employee would have to pay. The advantage holds even if the employee has to forego salary equal to the employer's interest cost on the money.

The prescribed rate is that applied to arrears and overpayments of tax, and is calculated quarterly based on the treasury-bill auction rate the last Thursday in each calendar quarter.

Example

1. Amount of loan: $10,000
2. Market interest rate
   Employee: 12%
   Employer: 10%
3. Prescribed interest rate: 10%
4. Employer interest cost: $1,000
5. Foregone salary: $1,000
6. After-tax value of foregone salary: $560 (44% tax bracket)
7. Deemed taxable benefit to employee ($10,000 × 10%): $1,000
8. Additional tax payable from benefit: $440
9. Total cost to employee: $1,000
10. Market cost to employee: $1,200
11. Saving: $200 or 16.6%

The saving would allow faster repayment of the loan and further savings in total financing costs.

Note that the example above applies to situations where the loan was *not* for investment and therefore interest on the loan is *not* tax deductible. If the loan proceeds are used to make an investment, whether in company stock or for some other investment, the figures in our previous example would be altered somewhat, but the relative advantage would remain the same.

Example

1. Amount of loan: $10,000
2. Market interest rates
   Employee: 12%
   Employer: 10%
3. Prescribed interest rate: 10%
4. Employer interest cost: $1,000
5. Foregone salary: $1,000
6. After-tax value of foregone salary: $560 (44% tax bracket)
7. Deemed taxable benefit to employee: NIL
8. Additional tax payable: NIL
9. Market cost to employee: $1,200 less 44% deduction = $672
10. Saving: $112 or 16.6%

Club Memberships

For many years payment by the employer of fees for luncheon and country clubs has been one of the most common and popular perks. In recent years, fitness clubs have overtaken most other clubs in popularity.

Ostensibly, employers' motivation in paying such fees is to help their executives promote the business through their social activities, and to help them stay fit and healthy to survive the stress created by business pressures.

It seems Revenue Canada accepts the latter argument wholeheartedly because they do not consider the payment of pure fitness club fees a taxable benefit. Regarding social clubs, they accept the argument only partially. In effect, they consider the payment of fees for such clubs as a taxable benefit unless the employer agrees not to deduct the payment as a business expense. Obviously, this treatment is most attractive where the corporate tax rate is considerably less than the executive's personal marginal tax rate. That situation is restricted to the owners of small Canadian-controlled companies who qualify for the "small business deduction," and to a lesser extent, to executives in Quebec.

Personal Financial Planning

Personal financial planning has been growing in popularity as an employee benefit in recent years. Fees paid to the consultant by the employer are a taxable benefit to the employee. However, the extra tax cost is slight compared to the typical advantages generated; thus this benefit is an excellent way for employers to help employees stretch their compensation dollar and increase understanding and appreciation of the rest of the employee benefits program. Financial planning is now being provided to senior executives on a regular basis, upon retirement and upon termination of employment, and in the form of seminars to others in the company. This latter approach is non-taxable to the employee; however, it is most effective if followed up on a one-to-one basis.

Flexible or Optional Compensation

This approach, which has gained favour with many employers in recent years, allows you a "budget" — a stated dollar amount or percentage of salary — which you can direct the company to use on your behalf in a number of different ways. Some examples:

- Payment of deductibles and co-insurance amounts under group medical and dental coverage or amounts in excess of a limit in the basic contract, such as for orthodontic or major restorative procedures (non-taxable).
- To fund a company contribution to a Deferred Profit Sharing Plan (non-taxable).
- To fund extra vacation (taxable).
- To cover deemed interest cost on an interest-free employee loan (tax treatment depends on the purpose of the loan).
- To repay principal on an employee loan (taxable).
- To cover all or part of a fee for financial counselling (partially taxable depending on how advice is delivered).

- To cover fees for fitness club membership (non-taxable) or to a country club (non-taxable to employee if not deducted by the company).

DEFERRED INCOME PLANS

In recent years a number of factors have combined to make more Canadians interested in deferred income plans than ever before. These factors include a steadily increasing tax burden since the early 1980s, widespread publicity on RRSPs, greater awareness of the need for adequate retirement income, and to some extent, disillusionment with major tax shelter investments.

The term "deferred income plan" covers everything from an RRSP through a company pension plan (RPP) or Deferred Profit Sharing Plan (DPSP) to a sophisticated executive deferred compensation plan — in effect any mechanism whereby tax payable on current income may be deflected by delaying receipt of the income and/or making tax deductible contributions to a qualified "statutory" plan.

Of the three major statutory plans, RRSPs are dealt with at length in Chapter 9 on Tax Shelters and company pension plans (RPPs) and Deferred Profit Sharing Plans (DPSPs) in Chapter 11 on Retirement. In the context of a discussion on employee benefits, it's worth noting that both RPPs and DPSPs are highly tax effective because they provide total tax deferral; i.e., on the initial contribution by the employer *and* on the income or growth earned on it subsequently.

An RRSP, since it is a personal tax deferral vehicle, does not technically qualify as an employee benefit plan. But it is equally tax effective in that the cash compensation from which an RRSP contribution could be made is tax deductible to the employer while the deductible RRSP contribution "washes" any tax liability from the employee's personal tax return.

Let's look at some other deferred income plans and how they work.

Deferred Compensation

The term "deferred compensation" refers to a variety of arrangements which act as substitutes for, or extensions to, RPPs or DPSPs.

Deferred compensation plans fall into two broad categories: funded and unfunded. Let's deal first with the latter.

Unfunded plans, as the name suggests, are merely contractual agreements whereby the employer commits to paying the employee a lump sum or a stream of income payment at some time in the future. No money is actually set aside to fund the commitments, although the amounts owing would be noted as a contingent liability on the books of the company. In most cases, the date or dates for delivery of deferred compensation are specified in the agreement, although these can usually be altered with the approval of the employer.

If you are able to negotiate an unfunded deferred compensation plan, you should consider requesting that benefits be payable in one or more of the following forms.

1. In the event of your death, as a "death benefit." This will make the first $10,000 tax free and the remainder taxable at your beneficiary's rates.
2. At retirement in the form of a lump sum "retiring allowance" equal to $2,000 multiplied by the number of years of service you have with the employer. For example, if you have 30 years of service by your retirement date, arrange to receive a retiring allowance of $60,000.

   The key point here is that you could defer tax on all of the $60,000 by "rolling" it to an RRSP and keeping it tax protected as late as the end of the year you reach age 71.
3. As an alternative or supplement to a lump sum retiring allowance, have funds paid to you as an income. This type of plan is often referred to as Supplemental Retirement Income (SRI), or a "Top Hat Pension," because it is used to offset the effect of limits on the maximum benefits from basic pension plans (RPPs).

Funded Deferred Compensation: The Employee Benefit Plan Trust (EBPT)

Another method of delivering deferred income has been through an Employee Benefit Plan Trust. Under this arrangement, the employer allocated funds to a trust for payment to the employee at some time in the future, subject to the following tax treatment.

1. The employer *could not* deduct contributions at the time they were made, but the employee was not taxed on them.
2. The employee was taxed on payments when received, at which time the employer could deduct the payments.

The Employee Benefit Plan Trust approach has offered more flexibility than a retiring allowance or supplemental retirement income plans because payment of benefits was not tied to retirement from the company.

At the practical level, however, the EBPT was often rejected by employers because it called for specific allocation of funds to the plan trust, but provided no current tax deduction for such contributions.

Currently the tax treatment of Employee Benefit Plan Trusts is uncertain as a result of the February 1986 Federal Budget. You and your employer should consult with the company's tax advisers before making any moves in this area.

GOVERNMENT BENEFITS

The government also provides benefits which can play an important part in total personal financial planning.

Canada and Quebec Pension Plans

Canada and Quebec Pension Plans came into effect on January 1, 1966, and were fully effective by 1976 after a ten-year transitional period. They were indexed in January 1974 to the Consumer Price Index.

Table 7.1
CPP/QPP Projections (Maximum)

Year	*Contribution* *Employee*	*Employer*	*Monthly Pension Benefit*
1986	$419.40	$419.40	$486.11
1987	436.18	436.18	505.59
1988	453.63	453.63	525.81
1989	471.78	471.68	546.84

Both plans are earnings-related contributory plans. All employees between the ages of eighteen and sixty-five must participate. In 1986, your first $2,500 of annual earnings is exempt from contribution, and on earnings above that amount you have to contribute 1.8% of your salary to a maximum of $23,300 ($419.40 per year). Your employer also contributes 1.8%, making the total contribution 3.6% of qualifying income.

Maximum monthly benefits payable through CPP and QPP include:

CPP Disability Benefits of $456.64 in 1986; QPP, $597.96.

CPP Survivor Benefits of $273.35 under sixty-five, $291.67 over sixty-five in 1986; QPP, $415.67 and $291.67 respectively.

CPP Orphan Benefits of $91.06 per child in 1986; QPP, $29.

CPP Lump Sum Death Benefits of $2,580 in 1986; QPP, $2,580.

The amounts payable will be adjusted by indexing in future years.

Government Health Services Plans

In Canada health care falls under the jurisdiction of the provinces rather than the federal government. Since 1958, all the provinces have had their own hospital plans, and in 1966 the federal government introduced the Medical Care Act, which came into force in July 1968. Now benefits are defined as services which are medically required and are rendered by physicians, surgeons, or qualified health professionals. Services not deemed to be medically required are not covered.

Your basic provincial plans can be integrated with insured *Extended Health Care Benefits* (drugs, etc.) for maximum coverage.

Unemployment Insurance Benefits

In 1986 the employee contributes 2.35% of insurable earnings up to a maximum of $495/week, or $11.63 per week. The employer pays 1.4 times the employee's contribution, or $16.28 per week. Maximum benefits are $297 per week, payable for 15 weeks in the event of disability or up to 51 weeks because of other unemployment causes. All premium contributions are deductible and benefits are taxable as income.

WHEN TO EVALUATE EMPLOYEE BENEFITS

Since you will be locked into the employee-benefit program once you start working, the best time to evaluate employee benefits is before you take a job. Make sure you are not missing the savings that can come from group coverage or from the structure of our taxation system.

NEGOTIATING YOUR COMPENSATION PACKAGE

Start by Calculating the Cash You Need

There must be a hundred old jokes about people who "save" so much by buying so many "bargains" that they don't have enough left over to pay the rent. The moral of all these jokes is the same: we can't start financial planning until we know how much money we will need to live on.

The same goes for negotiating a compensation package. We all need a certain number of after-tax dollars every year to pay for things such as rent, mortgages, food, and new shoes for the baby. Employee benefits would be pretty small comfort if we traded them for dollars we actually needed to live on.

Deciding how much cash you really need isn't simply a negative exercise that will tell you what employee benefits you can't afford. It will help you identify surplus income — the income you may be making over and above your minimum living requirements. Once you have identified this surplus income, you know how much money you can realistically consider trading for non-cash benefits.

Whether you are young or old, don't hesitate to discuss your benefit package with your employer. Many employers in Canada today are not getting maximum value for what they spend on salary and benefits. A harder look at our tax laws can save them — and their employees — money. So if you are satisfied that there are some spots where your benefit package is "soft," point them out to your company. Or if you read about an innovative approach to compensation, bring it to their attention. They may even be grateful.

And a special word to young employees. There is a tendency for younger people, particularly younger women, to under-use the benefits available to them. In many cases you don't really have a choice of taking the benefit or the money. The company offers you the benefit and you should take it. Simple prudence makes most of them good investments for you.

DO'S AND DON'TS

Your employee benefit package can be better than money. The rules are pretty simple.

Do Make sure you are taking advantage of all benefits that offer you savings on group rates, particularly if you have special needs or special problems getting these benefits on your own.

Do Make sure your benefits are arranged to maximize non-taxable payments by your employer. That could mean re-examining the practice of having every benefit paid for on a fifty-fifty basis between the employee and the employer.

Do Look for special benefit arrangements that might make sense in your situation — 100% medical or dental plans, deferred profit-sharing plans instead of pension plans, company-owned or leased cars, expense accounts, club memberships, fitness clubs, employee loans, or personal financial planning.

Do Avoid duplication of employee contribution costs if you and your spouse are both covered by group benefit plans at work.

Don't Assume that because you have no dependants you don't need to bother with group benefits. Disability income, medical and dental insurance are still of crucial importance.

Table 7.1
Canadian Income Tax Treatment of Certain Payments by Employer and Employee

	If Paid by Employer		*If Paid by Employee*	
Type of Payment	*Deductible by employer*	*Income to employee*	*Deductible by employee*	*Comments*
Retirement plans				
1. Registered Pension Plans	Yes	No	Yes	*Current service contributions* Employer and employee can each deduct amounts paid up to $3,500 per year. *Past service contributions* Employee is limited to $3,500 per year. Employer's contributions must be approved by Minister. (Due to be changed in 1987.) All benefits received out of plan are taxable.
2. Deferred Profit Sharing Plans	Yes	No	No	Employer contributions limited to the lesser of $3,500 (or 20% of employee's salary) *minus* employer current service pension plan contribution. All benefits are income to employee.
3. Retiring allowance for long service or in respect of loss of office	Yes	Yes See comment	N/A	Employee may deduct up to $2,000/year of service from income if paid into a Registered Retirement Savings Plan, Registered Pension Plan or a Deferred Profit Sharing Plan ($3,500 in some cases).

	If Paid by Employer		*If Paid by Employee*	
Type of Payment	*Deductible by employer*	*Income to employee*	*Deductible by employee*	*Comments*
4. Administration costs of group Registered Retirement Savings Plan	Yes	See comment	Yes	Administration costs paid by employer are included in income of employee but are deductible to employee as part of his or her contribution to the plan within prescribed limits. Administrative costs paid by employee are also deductible to employee as part of his or her contribution to the plan within prescribed limits.
Other Deferred Compensation Arrangements				
1. Stock option plans	No	Yes	N/A	Excess of market value of shares at time option is exercised over option price is income to employee in year option exercised, if public or non-Canadian company. If a private Canadian company, or a qualifying plan for Canadian public company shares, one-half the gain on exercise is taxable as income.
2. Deferred compensation contract	No	See comment	N/A	Amount contributed by the employer is generally not deductible by employer or taxable to employee until actually paid to employee.

	If Paid by Employer		*If Paid by Employee*	
Type of Payment	*Deductible by employer*	*Income to employee*	*Deductible by employee*	*Comments*
Life and Health Plans				
1. Group term life insurance	Yes	Yes/No See comment	No	Employer premiums paid for coverage in excess of $25,000 for any one individual are income to employee.
2. Private health service plans	Yes	No	Yes/No See comment	Premiums paid by employee form part of medical expenses and as such are deductible to the extent medical expenses exceed 3% of net income.
3. Provincial hospitalization and medical plans	Yes	Yes	No	
4. (a) Group sickness or accident insurance, group disability insurance, and group income maintenance insurance	Yes	Yes/No See comment	No	Employee may exclude benefits from income when received to exent of his or her contribution. If all benefits are funded by employee (with no employer contributions) all benefits are tax free.
(b) Supplementary unemployment benefit plan premiums	Yes	No	N/A	Benefits out of plan are income when received.

	If Paid by Employer		*If Paid by Employee*	
Type of Payment	*Deductible by employer*	*Income to employee*	*Deductible by employee*	*Comments*
5. Group dental plans	Yes	No	No	
Other				
1. Interest-free loan to employee	N/A	Yes See comment	N/A	If interest-free loan is used to purchase stock, a benefit is deemed but the employee may claim an offsetting deduction under carrying costs. Otherwise there is a deemed taxable benefit equal to prescribed rate minus rate charged, if any, unless loan is $25,000 or less and is used to purchase a home 40 kilometres closer to place of employment.
2. Counselling Services				
a. Personal financial counselling	Yes	Yes	No	Financial or retirement planning seminars are non-taxable to the employee.
b. Retirement counselling	Yes	No	No	
c. Investment counselling	Yes	Yes	Yes	
d. Executive compensation	Yes	No	N/A	
3. Personal use of company automobile				
a. Standby charge	Yes	Yes	No	Subject to statutory minimum standby charge of 2% per month of original capital cost if company-owned, or ⅔ of lease cost if leased.

	If Paid by Employer		*If Paid by Employee*	
Type of Payment	*Deductible by employer*	*Income to employee*	*Deductible by employee*	*Comments*
b. Expenses	Yes	Yes	No	Subject to pro rata reduction for personal use less than 12,000 kms. Operating expenses create a taxable benefit for pro rata personal use to total use.
4. Personal use of aircraft	Yes	Yes	No	Personal use is measured as taxable benefit to employee on basis of flying time.
5. Dues to recreation and social clubs	No	Yes/No See comment	No	Initiation fees paid by employer are not deductible. Regular membership dues are deductible to the employer. If club is used for business purposes, dues are not included in employee's income, provided employer does not deduct cost from its income.
6. Professional membership dues	Yes	Yes	Yes	
7. Employee's moving expenses	Yes	No	Yes	Deduction to employee is based on certain income and geographical restrictions.

CHAPTER 8

Minimizing Your Income Tax

In 1915 the government of Canada imposed a "temporary" 3% tax on incomes to last only until the end of the war. It didn't quite work that way. Progressive income tax has become a permanent and increasingly significant fact of Canadian economic life.

It is hard to argue with the idea behind progressive income tax. The theory is that the more you make, the more you can afford to pay the government to help finance all the services available to you. So the more you make, the more income tax you will pay, and the higher your marginal rate of income tax becomes. The marginal rate is simply the tax you pay on the last dollars you earn.

In 1986, some Canadians will pay a marginal tax rate as high as 63%. That means that if they earn an extra dollar on the last day of the year, they keep only 37¢. Even if you had a taxable income of only $18,275 in 1986 your marginal rate would vary from 34% to 44%; depending on the province in which you live, the government takes 34¢ to 44¢ of that last dollar. The table in the appendix indicates the 1986 marginal tax rates in the various provinces. Tax rates like these take a lot of the fun and purchasing power out of your next raise. That's the bad news. The good news is that it is quite *legal* as well as profitable to arrange your affairs to attract as little taxation as possible.

WHERE DOES YOUR INCOME COME FROM?

How you'll do that depends upon the kind of income you earn. Tax treatment differs for different income sources. The first step in sensible tax planning is to identify your particular type or types of income from four basic categories:

1. Income from employment
2. Income from self-employment; professional or business income
3. Pension income
4. Income from other sources, primarily investments.

Income from Employment

If you earn a salary, commissions, or an hourly wage from somebody else, you're an employee.

Income taxes are one of your largest expenditures. The following table shows how much you pay on various amounts of employment income and the marginal tax rate at each level. This table is applicable to residents of Ontario, but rates for the other provinces are included in the appendix, although they do not include special provincial tax credits.

Table 8.1
Illustration of Total Tax Payable for 1986*

Employment Income	*CPP*	*UIC*	*Approximate Tax Payable*	*Average Tax Rate*	*Marginal Tax Rate***
$ 15,000	$225.00	$352.50	$ 953	20.4%	25.7 %
20,000	315.00	470.00	2,263	23.9	28.8
25,000	405.00	587.50	3,648	25.6	30.3
30,000	419.40	604.90	5,184	27.0	34.8
40,000	419.40	604.90	8,806	30.1	37.9
50,000	419.40	604.90	12,674	32.3	47.0
75,000	419.40	604.90	24,749	38.5	55.4
100,000	419.40	604.90	38,474	43.1	55.4

*Assuming a married couple with two children under 18, no RRSP or pension plan, one spouse does not work, and they live in Ontario.

**Includes surtax of 1½% of basic federal tax for 1986.

On your tax return you will have to show as income your total earnings plus whatever taxable benefits you receive from your employer. To check your opportunities and reduce your tax, ask yourself a few simple questions.

What can my company provide as a tax-free benefit?

Some employee benefits are taxed in your hands, and you have to add their value to your income for tax purposes. Others are not, although your employer can still deduct them as an expense of doing business. In effect this permits him or her to buy certain things for you which, if you had to pay for them yourself, would cost you much more simply because you would be paying with after-tax dollars.

Tax-free or tax-deferred benefits include:

- Group Registered Retirement Savings Plan
- Registered Pension Plan
- Deferred Profit-Sharing Plan
- Group term life insurance up to $25,000
- Private health service plan
- Group dental plan
- Club dues (if used for business purpose, and your employer does not deduct the expense)
- Products or services purchased from employer at the cost to the employer.

Do I really need cash from my next raise or bonus this year?

If you take the money this year, you will be taxed on it this year. If you are going to save it anyway, it might make sense to defer receiving the extra money you could have earned. That way you can earn interest on dollars that would have been paid out in taxes and possibly take the raise in a later year when your total income may be smaller and your marginal tax rate lower. Three options are available if you decide to defer income.

1. Maximize your pension or RRSP contribution and/or direct your employer to divert cash bonuses to buying past service pension benefits for you.
2. Have your employer contribute to a Deferred Profit-Sharing Plan.
3. Opt for a deferred compensation agreement.

For further details about these plans refer to Chapter 7.

Am I taking all the deductions I am entitled to?

The following is a list of expenses and contributions you can deduct from employment income, with the 1986 maximum where applicable.

Table 8.2
Deductions to Arrive at Net Income

	Maximum Deduction Where Applicable
Employment expense (20% of income)	$ 500.00
Canada or Quebec Pension Plan Contributions (1.8% of income)	$ 419.40
Unemployment Insurance Premiums	604.92
Registered Retirement Savings Plan (RRSP) if not in a RPP or DPSP	7,500.00*
If in Registered Pension Plan (RPP), combined RRSP and employee RPP contributions	3,500.00
Professional and Union Dues	Amount Paid
Tuition Fees	Amount Paid (if over $100)
Child Care Expenses	8,000.00
Carrying Charges on Investments:	
—interest expense	
—safety deposit box	Amount Paid
—accounting, management, and investment counselling fees	

*proposed.

Table 8.3
Deductions to Arrive at Taxable Income, 1986

Medical Expenses	Actual less 3% of net income
Charitable donations	Up to 20% of net income

Personal Exemptions	*Canada*	*Quebec*
Basic	$4,180	$5,280
Spouse	3,660	4,560
Child under 18 (or 21 in Quebec)	710	1,870 (first child)
Child 18 or over (or 21 in Quebec)	1,420	1,370 (other child)
Age (65 or over)	2,610	2,200
Spouse's age (balance not used by spouse can be transferred)	2,610	2,200

If you are entitled to a deduction, claim it. If you're an employed person you can reduce the amount of tax you pay by arranging your benefits to maximize the number of non-taxable benefits paid for with pre-tax dollars, and by deferring any surplus income you may be entitled to. Once you have taken those steps, be careful to maximize the deductions available to you, especially those for RRSPs. Beyond that, to reduce taxable income further, you'll have to get into major tax shelters which typically involve high-risk investment.

Make sure you do not lose spousal and child exemptions needlessly.

In 1986 maximum personal exemptions are:

1. Basic: $4,180.
2. Spouse (or equivalent to married for single parent): $3,660 less 100% of *net* income over $520.
3. Other dependent relative: ($1,420 less 50% of net income over $1,340).
4. Children under eighteen: $710 less 50% of net income in excess of $2,760.
5. Children age 18 and over: $1,420 less 50% of net income in excess of $1,340.
6. Children over 21 may be claimed if they are in full-time attendance at a school or university or if they are infirm.
7. When claiming the equivalent to married exemption for a child, claim the child who would otherwise provide the smallest deduction.

Keep in mind that it is *net income* that determines the personal exemption deductions. If the income of your spouse or child exceeds the allowable limit, you may be able to reduce it by claiming the following deductions in calculating their net income:

- employment expenses
- CCP/QPP contributions
- UIC premiums
- union, professional, or like dues
- child-care expenses
- tuition fees (only the student can claim)
- education deduction (student can claim, or supporting parent if student's *taxable* income is nil)
- contribution to an RRSP (up to 20% of earned income)

Here's how it could work. Let's assume your son is 19 years of age, is a full-time student at a university, and earned $6,000 with part-time and summer employment. His tuition fees are $1,500, and he has attended university during 8 months.

Gross income		$6,000.00
Less employment expense (20% to a maximum of $500)	$ 500.00	
CPP/QPP	63.00	
UIC	141.00	
Tuition fees	1,500.00	
		$2,204.00
Net income		3,796.00
Personal exemption		4,180.00
Education deduction (8 mos. at $50)		400.00
Taxable income		NIL
Tax payable (Ontario resident)		NIL
Allowable net income (without loss of exemption)		$1,340.00
Loss of exemption		$1,228.00 (max.)
Parent provides funds for		
RRSP contribution 20% of $6,000 (500 + 141)		$1,072.00
Results		
Net income		$3,796.00
Taxable income		NIL
Exemption regained (50% x 1,072)		$ 536.00
Tax savings to you (at 50%)		$ 268.00

If your child is 18 or over and earns little or no employment income, you should consider "income splitting" with him or her (or them) by lending cash to them and having income from investment of the cash taxed at their rates, not at yours. Note that this will make sense only on cash that is generating *taxable* investment income; i.e., the amount over $1,000.

Income from Self-Employment

If you carry on an unincorporated business or profession, you are self-employed and therefore enjoy more tax flexibility. On self-employed income, unlike regular employment income, you lose the standard $500 employment expense deduction, but you can claim all expenses incurred for the purpose of earning self-employed income, including car expenses, an office in your home, promotion, and entertainment. Following is an alphabetical list of the most common allowable expenses. Be sure you make full use of all deductions permitted in each category.

Table 8.4
Allowable Business Expenses for Self-Employed Individuals
(where applicable and reasonable)

Accounting fees	Lease payments
Advertising and promotion	Legal fees
Automobile	Materials
Bad debts	Moving expenses
Business taxes	Patronage dividends paid out
Canada (and/or Quebec) Pension Plan	Postage
	Professional fees
Cancellation of lease	Property tax
Capital cost allowance	Property maintenance and repairs
Convention	Rent
Cost of goods sold	Supplies and stationery
Depreciation	Salaries
Discounts allowed	Telephone
Entertainment	Travel
Insurance	Unemployment Insurance premiums
Interest on business loans	
Landscaping	Utility expenses

There's a catch to your right to deduct all these expenses—you must be able to prove them.

The most common problems of self-employed people are, on the one hand, forgetting to deduct legitimate expenses and, on the other hand, showing excessive zeal in how much they deduct on others. If you earn gross income of $18,000 and try to deduct $10,000 for promotion and entertainment, you will likely get a visit from the tax auditor. And when the auditor comes to see you, he or she will be armed with a rule that can make your life miserable: the burden of proof for every deduction is on you.

Keep detailed records of your income and your expenses. Don't discard these financial records — not even that old shoe box full of receipts — without written permission from your District Taxation Office. Keep receipts for each expenditure, a separate bank account for business transactions, deposit receipts intact, and pay by cheque whenever possible.

But don't try to do it all yourself. Get professional accounting help when you are doing your taxes, maintaining your records and, most important, dealing with the tax people should they come to talk about a return. When that happens, the biggest mistake you can make is to answer a whole lot of questions when you're really not sure of the details. The best procedure is to answer frankly. Where you are not sure, say so and arrange a meeting between the tax people and your accountant in your accountant's office.

Although it is legal for you to arrange your affairs to attract as little tax as possible, you face heavy fines and possibly even imprisonment if you attempt to evade taxes you are legally responsible for paying. If you keep records scrupulously and calculate your deductions honestly, you'll still pay your fair share of taxes; but you won't pay any more than you should.

When does it make sense to incorporate?

If you are self-employed, it may be worthwhile to incorporate. The type of business operated and the amount of taxable income earned are key considerations.

Canadian-controlled private corporations qualify for a special low rate of tax on the first $250,000 of taxable income each fiscal year.

This low rate of tax is about 26% but varies by province. The small business deduction allows the owner of an incorporated business to enjoy a worthwhile tax deferral advantage.

If profits of the business exceed the income required by the owner, he or she may leave the excess in the business after paying tax of about 26%. If this profit was paid out as salary, the owner might well pay a substantially higher rate. No further tax is payable until such time as the remaining 74¢ of "after-tax" profits are paid out as dividends. At that time, a corporate distribution tax is payable equal to 12½% of the dividend paid, and the owner will pay tax on the dividend.

This sounds like a lot of tax to pay when the dividend payment is made. In fact, the 12½% dividend tax was introduced to equalize the after-tax cash to an owner/manager whether he or she pays himself or herself a salary or a dividend. The only difference now is that by keeping excess earnings in the company you pay the tax later and can use the current tax saving to earn income. In 1987, however, the 12½% of distribution tax will disappear; however, the gross up and tax credit allowed on dividends decreases. The net effect will be slight.

Current tax savings can still be achieved by paying dividends as part of compensation rather than taking all salary. If both spouses own shares, significant savings can be realized by splitting dividend income.

Effective January 1, 1980, the ground rules for payment of reasonable salaries to a spouse or other family members became the same for all businesses, whether incorporated or not, so that splitting *salaries* to reduce taxes is not a consideration in deciding to incorporate.

When paying dividends, it is important that you utilize the dividend tax credit fully. This will often require payment of some salary, especially where dividend payments are less than $3,800.

In most cases it is advisable to take out a sufficient salary to make the maximum contribution to CPP or QPP. In 1986, the requirement is $25,800 per annum. If you wish to make the maximum contribution to an RRSP, salary of slightly more than five times the annual maximum is required (e.g., in 1986, to qualify for the maximum contribution of $7,500 requires qualifying income of a little more than $37,500). Dividends do not qualify as earned income in determining allowable contributions to an RRSP and do not qualify for the $500 employment expense deduction.

In short, current personal cash requirements should be paid as salary unless a tax saving is possible by payment of dividends to a spouse.

It is important to realize that the amount and type of income you receive each year from the business is fully under your control.

When properly documented, a management bonus can be set up at the end of the fiscal year as an expense to the company and can be paid out at any time over the next 180 days.

If you are self-employed and profitable, consider incorporating, but do so only after discussion with a chartered accountant who specializes in working with small owner-managed businesses.

Pension Income

If you receive annuity income from a private pension, an RRSP or a Deferred Profit Sharing Plan and are 65 years of age or over, you qualify for a pension deduction of up to $1,000 deduction against that income. Those who receive income from a Registered Pension or Superannuation Plan (RPP) qualify for this deduction at *any* age.

The best way to maximize the benefit of this deduction is to arrange your retirement income so that both you and your spouse have qualifying income to "use up" the available exemptions and deductions. That not only reduces the marginal tax rate by having the same gross income treated as two different incomes for tax purposes, but it also permits you to claim the $1,000 deduction twice.

Let's compare two couples aged 66, both retired and living on retirement income equal in total to $2,000 per month. Both couples live in Ontario. One has arranged to have income split (paid to both spouses).

The other draws a pension that is paid only to the spouse who was employed. Table 8.5 shows the tax result.

Table 8.5
Tax Result of Split Pension vs. Single Pension*

	Split Pension		*Single Pension*	
Income	*Husband*	*Wife*	*Husband*	*Wife*
Private pension, annuity	$12,000	$12,000	$24,000	NIL
Old Age Security	$ 3,460	$ 3,460	$ 3,460	$3,460
Canada Pension Plan	$ 5,833	NIL	$ 5,833	NIL
1. Total Income	$21,293	$15,460	$33,293	$3,460
Deductions				
Personal Exemption	$ 4,180	$ 4,180	$ 4,180	$4,180
Age Exemption	$ 2,610	$ 2,610	$ 2,610	NIL
Age Exemption transferred from spouse	NIL	NIL	$ 2,610	NIL
Married Exemption	NIL	NIL	$ 720	NIL
Pension income deduction	$ 1,000	$1,000	$ 1,000	NIL
2. Total Deductions	$ 7,790	$ 7,790	$11,120	$4,180
3. Taxable Income (1-2)	$13,503	$ 7,670	$22,173	NIL
4. Income Tax Payable	$ 3,425	$ 1,794	$ 6,200	NIL
5. After-tax income (1-4)	$17,868	$13,666	$27,093	$3,460
6. Combined income for couple	$31,534		$30,553	
7. Advantage in splitting income	$ 981**			

*Figures are for 1986 in Ontario.

**The relative advantage of income splitting increases significantly as the amount of total income increases.

Even though you may be years away from drawing a pension it makes sense to plan now to have the income paid on a split basis. You can do this in a variety of ways. If your spouse doesn't work, you can contribute to a spousal RRSP in his or her name and deduct the contribution from your income. The tax saving now is the same to you, but the tax saving later—when the income is being drawn—is worth planning for. The higher the retirement income, the greater the potential tax saving. In addition, you may be able to split investment income, a subject dealt with in more detail later in this chapter under the heading "Split investment income with family members."

Income from Other Sources

It's worthwhile knowing how our tax laws treat income from other sources so that you can enjoy further tax savings.

Try to earn $1,000 in investment income.

Your first $1,000 of investment income, if it comes from eligible Canadian sources, is tax free. If you are in the 50% marginal tax bracket you would have to earn $2,000 of salary to have the same after-tax cash in hand. Any other investment that yields taxable benefits to you also will have to perform twice as well to be of equal value.

The rule is simple: every taxpayer should try to earn $1,000 of interest or dividend income from Canadian sources. Ideally, all investment income above $1,000 should be earned and taxed in the hands of the spouse with the lower income, or dependent children 18 years of age or over.

Dividend income from eligible Canadian shares also qualifies for the $1,000 deduction.

You can use your $1,000 investment deduction for income from interest or dividends from eligible Canadian securities, but you can't use it twice.

The tax effect of dividend income is a little more complicated. The actual income you get is "grossed up" by one-half and then qualifies for a 22⅔% federal dividend tax credit. Effective January 1, 1987, the gross up reduces to 33⅓% and the federal dividend tax credit to 16⅔%. The effect is to increase the effective tax rate considerably; e.g., for a person in a 50% marginal tax rate on ordinary income, the effective tax rate on dividends increases from 25% to 34%. Table 8.6 shows how it works.

Table 8.6
Tax Effect of Dividend Income

Dividend income (e.g., from 8% on $8,338)		$ 667
Gross-up (50%)		333
Taxable dividend		$1,000
Less:		
Investment income deduction		1,000
Change in taxable income		$ 0
Income Tax Payable	NIL	

The dividend tax credit is still available as a deduction against other income. Table 8.7 shows how it works.

Table 8.7
Tax Effect of Dividend Tax Credit, 1986

	With a Dividend Tax Credit	*Without a Dividend Tax Credit*
Federal Tax (assumed)	$6,000	$6,000
Less:		
Federal dividend tax credit (22.667% of grossed-up dividend)	227	—
Basic federal tax	5,773	6,000
Plus:		
Provincial tax of 50%*	2,886	3,000
Total Tax	$8,459	$8,800
Summary:		
Tax reduction		341
Tax-free income		667
Total		$1,008
After-tax rate of return on $8,338	12.08%	

*Ontario.

Split investment income with family members.

When you are earning more than $1,000 of taxable investment income, you should consider transferring cash to your children age 18 or over to avoid having income over $1,000 taxed at your marginal rate. In their hands, investment income may be free of tax or taxed at low rates compared to yours.

Before May 22, 1985, income splitting with spouse or children was relatively straightforward. Once you had determined the amount of income you wanted to transfer, you simply wrote a cheque to your spouse, your children or, if the child was a minor, to a trust on her or his behalf. The amount of the cheque would be approximately equal to the amount of income you wanted to transfer divided by the rate of return you expected to get and the portion of the tax year remaining at the time the loan was made.

Example
You decide to transfer $2,000 of 1986 income to your 20-year-old daughter on August 31, 1986. You expect she can earn 10% on the money:

$$\text{Amount of capital required} = \frac{\$\,2{,}000}{.10 \times 4/12} = \$60{,}000$$

i.e., $60,000 @ 10% for a full year would yield $6,000; for 4/12 or 1/3 of a year, $2,000.

If you made the loan on June 30, the amount required would be $40,000; on March 31, $30,000; on January 1, $20,000.

The May 23, 1985 federal budget and what it did to income splitting.
On May 23, 1985, Finance Minister Michael Wilson introduced Budget papers which effectively eliminated income splitting opportunities between spouses, at least using the traditional method of the high-tax-rate spouse lending cash to the low-tax-rate spouse.

The Budget also put some restrictions on income splitting with children age 15-17, and serious restrictions on income splitting with children under the age of 15.

Here is a summary of the changes announced and their practical effect on income splitting techniques and timing.

1. The definition of "transfer" under the so-called attribution rules in the Income Tax Act was extended immediately to cover cash loans after May 22, 1985, between spouses and to persons under age 18.

   The attribution rules state that income on such a transfer is attributed for tax purposes back to the transferor of the property or cash, and taxed at his or her rates, not those of the recipient or transferee. Previously, loans had been exempted from the effect of these rules.
2. On loans made before May 23, 1985, the new rules will not apply until January 1, 1988, on demand loans, and term loans maturing before that date. On term loans maturing after that date, the new rules will apply only after the maturity date of the loan.
3. The practical effect of these changes is most severe on income splitting with *spouses* because there is no age limit on the application of the attribution rules (as there is with children), and they apply to capital gains as well as income. (They don't apply to capital gains on transfers to children of any age.)
4. If you are a two-income family where one spouse's marginal tax rate is substantially lower than the others, to the extent it's practical, have all expenses paid by the high-tax-rate spouse, and all savings done out of the income of the low-tax-rate spouse.

Before you adopt this approach, make sure both you and your spouse are comfortable with the idea, especially the high-tax-rate spouse, who may feel vulnerable in the event of marriage breakdown.

5. If you want to split income with children remember *the attribution rules have never applied, and still don't apply, on transfers to children age 18 or over*. Thus, the Budget announcements had no effect on such transfers.
6. For income splitting with children under age 18, however, the changes create serious restrictions; but these problems can be circumvented legally and practically by one or more of the following techniques:
   (a) Have the child (or the trustee of a trust for the child) invest for *capital gains*. They are not subject to the attribution rules. In this way, the high-tax-rate parent can keep his or her lifetime capital gains exemption intact.
   (b) For children age 15–17, purchase compound interest instruments of three- to one-year maturities to assure that no income will actually be paid, and therefore taxable, until the child reaches age 18 when the attribution rules no longer apply.

   Note that the three-year tax rules on accrual or compounding income restrict the use of this approach to three-year compound interest periods or less. In other words, if the trustee bought a five-year GIC for a 13-year-old child, no income would get paid until the child reached age 18, but the trust would be required to report the income at the third anniversary as income to the parent making the loan because at that point, the child would be only 16 and the attribution rules would apply.
   (c) For children age 0–14 inclusive, purchase a high cash value "tax exempt" life insurance policy (with or without participating "dividends") as a means to create totally tax deferred income; i.e., the three-year tax rule would not apply on accruing income. Tax would be paid only when the policy was cashed in.

   If you consider this approach, make sure the net return, including the tax deferral advantage, is competitive; and remember that unless you and your spouse are very well insured, it will make more sense to pay something extra to have the policy on your life or your spouse's rather than the child's. A child's death is traumatic emotionally but not significant financially.

   An alternative, if you're willing to take on some investment risk, is to invest in growth property (e.g., mutual funds) because capital gains are not attributable at any age.
   (d) For children 0–14, if you're willing to bet they'll qualify for post-secondary education, invest in a Registered Education Savings Plan (RESP). It will avoid the three-year accrual tax rules; but you should be aware that, if the funds are not used to fund some-

one's higher education, you will get back only your *original* deposit or deposits; and lose all interest, dividends or capital gains.

(e) Open a separate bank account in each child's name and deposit the Family Allowance cheque. This amount of "income splitting" is permitted without the formality of loans and trusts.

How much is "enough" income splitting?

If you have children age 18 or over, you can generate interest on a current basis without running afoul of the attribution rules. To maximize advantage, remember the following points:

- Tuition fees are deductible to the student, not to the parent.
- If your child's taxable income is nil, you can take the Education Deduction of $50/month for every month the child is away at school.
- If your child's net income falls below the "threshold" amount, you won't lose the dependant exemption.
- Even if your child's net income is large enough to cost you all or part of the dependant exemption, you can still gain advantage from further income splitting because, once you have lost the exemption, you'll gain from the difference between the child's low or nil rate of tax and your much higher rate.

Let's look at an example. Suppose you have a daughter aged twenty, attending university, who earns $2,500 working summers and pays $1,500 tuition fees.

Gross income		$ 2,500
Deductions		
Employment expense	$ 500	
CPP/QPP, UIC	90	
Tuition	1,500	
		$ 2,090
Net income		410
Maximum net income allowable (without loss of dependant exemption of $1,420)		1,340
Additional income transferable		930
Capital to be transferred (say, at 10% interest)		$ 9,300
Net tax saving (at your 50% tax rate)		$ 465

This example illustrates a "perfect" solution in that your daughter pays no tax and you suffer no loss of dependant exemption for her.

Now let's look at an example that is not perfect, but is more productive than the one we've just seen. The facts are the same as before, but let's assume you are lucky enough to have $37,700 generating taxable interest income. You are motivated to shift the income to your daughter to help pay for her books and room and board.

Daughter's net income (before investment income)	410
Plus investment income ($37,700 @ 10%)	3,770
Total net income	4,180
Maximum net income allowable before loss of dependant exemption	1,340
Loss of exemption to you	1,420
Extra tax cost from loss of exemption	710
Tax saving on transfer of $3,770 income	1,885
Net advantage in income splitting	1,175

In this example, your advantage is $710 greater than in the previous "perfect" solution.

Now let's suppose you are really cash rich and have $100,000 generating taxable interest, and are motivated to split income with your daughter to help her save for expensive post-graduate work in a few years.

Daughter's net income (before investment income)	410
Plus investment income ($100,000 @ 10%)	10,000
	$10,410
Less personal exemption: $4,180 investment income deduction: $1,000	
	($5,180)
Taxable income	$5,230
Total tax payable by daughter	$1,110
Tax cost to you of loss of exemption	710
Total tax cost in transfer	$1,820
Total tax saving in transfer	5,000
Net advantage	$3,180

Advantage would continue to increase until your daughter's marginal tax rate equalled yours.

Fine tuning on income splitting.

More income-splitting advantage could be gained by creating a deduction for RRSP. These deductions, to the extent they wipe out the child's taxable income, can free up the $50 per month education deduction to be used in your return rather than being relatively wasted in your child's hands.

CAPITAL COST ALLOWANCE

If you earn income from rental property, capital cost allowance can protect much of that income from taxation.

You are allowed to claim capital cost allowance on buildings, equipment, and many other classes of depreciable property. This means you are able to assume for tax purposes that your property is actually decreasing in value. You can then treat the reduction in value just as if you had actually spent the money.

Generally, you can claim capital cost allowance up to the prescribed rate (e.g., 5% on most buildings) only to the extent it offsets income from the investment itself. You cannot use it to create losses against other income. When this has been allowed, an interesting tax shelter resulted, the best known being the now defunct MURB program on rental property.

Note that for the tax year in which you acquire depreciable property you can deduct only half the prescribed amount.

INTEREST EXPENSE

Proper planning of your debt can have a major impact on your after-tax income. The reason is that some interest is tax deductible, while other interest is not.

Interest on loans made for the following purposes is generally tax deductible:

- RRSP (but not spousal RRSP) where loans were made prior to November 12, 1981.
- To start or operate a business.
- To purchase business interests.
- To purchase stocks, bonds, debentures, or mortgages where there is a reasonable expectation of income.
- To purchase a car for business use.
- To purchase tax-sheltered investments.

The financial corollary of tax deductible interest is that you should be aggressive in paying off loans on which interest is non-tax deductible. Your net "return" is equal to the full rate of interest — a result that is difficult to match, especially if you face tax at high marginal rates.

CAPITAL GAINS AND LOSSES AND THE CAPITAL GAINS EXEMPTION

A *capital gain* results when you sell or are deemed to have sold an investment for a higher price than what you paid for it. A *capital loss* is the opposite: it is the negative difference between the price at which you bought an investment and the lower price at which you sold it. It's worth noting that, if you buy and sell assets or property for a living — or very frequently as an investor — you may find that the tax authorities will consider your gains and losses as income and expenses. And that will have a profound effect on the tax treatment you receive.

The Era of Tax on Capital Gains: 1972–1984

Before 1972, capital gains and losses were neither taxable nor deductible in calculating income for tax purposes. From January 1, 1972, to December 31, 1984, one-half of capital gains were to be included, and one-half of capital losses could be deducted from income for tax purposes. No capital gains tax schedule was introduced and no distinction was drawn between short- and long-term gains. Regular tax rates would apply to the taxable half of gains and the deductible half of losses.

More complex rules were established for property acquired before January 1, 1972, and some latitude was provided for "using up" capital losses incurred in years when they could not be offset completely against capital gains. Losses could be carried back one year (and later up to three years) and forward indefinitely, in the search for a capital gain to offset. In the meantime, for each year that capital losses remained outstanding, up to $2,000 could be written off against other income.

The May 23, 1985 Federal Budget: A Lot of Good News, A Little Bad

As most Canadians are aware by now, Finance Minister Michael Wilson startled much of the financial world when he announced a lifetime capital gains exemption of up to $500,000. The exemption applies only to individuals — not trusts or corporations — and is being phased in as follows:

1985-$20,000
1986-$50,000
1987-$100,000
1988-$200,000
1989-$300,000
1990-$500,000

Even more surprising than the exemption itself is the fact that it applies against gains on all forms of capital property located anywhere in the world. For example, if you bought and later sold a condominium in Florida or Arizona for a gain, the exemption would apply exactly as it would if you had made the gain on a Canadian common stock.

For this reason, the exemption has been widely criticized, and many pundits have predicted that it will be withdrawn or restricted.

Clouds in the Silver Lining

With the introduction of the capital gains exemption, a number of measures were introduced to reduce or offset its practical effect. Here's a list of the more significant measures.

- You can still write off capital losses, but only against capital gains, not against other income.

- Gains on certain stock options will no longer be considered capital gains. One-half the gain will be taxed as regular income.
- The exemption will not apply in determining net income or taxable income for purposes of calculating allowable deductions for dependants such as spouse and children, and for medical expenses.
- The exemption will not apply in determining taxable income for purposes of determining the application of the Alternative Minimum Tax. (See the discussion later in this chapter.)
- Measures were introduced to prevent dividend income being converted to capital gains for tax purposes; e.g., through stock dividends.

The capital gains exemption already has been, and will continue to be, an incentive for Canadians to invest in the equity area with the attendant opportunities for growth and risks of loss. To get maximum use from it, employ the following techniques:

- Try to arrange your affairs so gains are distributed as widely as possible among family members (call it "growth splitting").
- Avoid triggering gains in excess of the cumulative exemption for any given year until 1990.
- Don't leave lifetime exemptions unused; e.g., in your will, provide your executors with the choice of "rolling" capital property to your spouse on a tax-deferred basis, in case you have used up all of your $500,000 exemption in your lifetime; or electing to have gains taxed in your final tax return, at least to the extent your exemption remains unused—or a combination of the two.

  Example
  You die with an unrealized accrued gain of $300,000 on your common stock portfolio. Before your death, you had used up $400,000 of the lifetime exemption of $500,000.

  Solution
  Elect to trigger gains at death on enough stock to produce $100,000. Roll the rest to your spouse on a tax-deferred basis. This will maximize use of your exemption and minimize encroachment on your spouse's.
- Be more conservative than you otherwise might have been, because gains subject to the exemption can be up to 25% to 30% less than those on taxable gains, and still leave you as well off after tax.

THE ALTERNATIVE MINIMUM TAX

In the summer 1984 federal election campaign, NDP leader Ed Broadbent succeeded in "shaming" his two opponents, then Prime Minister John Turner of the Liberals and soon-to-be PM Brian Mulroney of the Conservatives, into adopting a tax policy he had been demanding for some time. In the campaign it was referred to as a "minimum tax on the rich." In the May 1985 Federal Budget, it appeared in the form of a discussion paper reviewing the comparative pro's and con's of three different approaches to the idea of a minimum tax on high-income earners. When Finance Minister Michael Wilson put his proposal before the House of Commons in early December 1985, it was in the form of an "Alternative Minimum Tax" (AMT), one of the three approaches examined in the Budget discussion paper.

How Does AMT Work?

The formula for calculating AMT is complex and tax planning for those affected will be equally complex. Here we can provide only an outline of the mechanics of the calculation, its impact on tax payers with different sources of income and tax deductions, and planning moves which can reduce its impact.

The AMT is a second tax calculation that adds back the following "tax preference" items to the calculation of regular taxable income:

- contributions to RRSPs and Registered Pension Plans;
- tax exempt capital gains;
- taxable capital gains;
- capital cost allowance deductions arising from tax shelter investments in MURBs, and exploration, development, and oil and gas property expense deductions for resource exploration and development projects;
- Canadian source dividends.

From this adjusted taxable income a deduction of $40,000 is made. Then a flat federal tax rate of 17% is applied to the remainder. Provincial rates are then applied on the federal rate. The total varies from province to province; however, the combined rate will equal about 26%. Where AMT exceeds regular tax, only foreign tax credits, child tax credits and refundable investment tax credits are allowed (i.e., excluding the non-refundable but deductible Canadian dividend tax credit).

Impact of AMT

Finance Minister Michael Wilson estimated that the AMT would affect fewer than 100,000 of the more than 15,000,000 returns filed in Canada each year. Of these, most will be in one or more of the following categories:

- Those with large tax-shelter deductions from MURBs, oil and gas and mining exploration schemes, relative to non-preference income such as salary, self-employed income or interest.
- Those with large amounts of Canadian dividend income relative to non-preference income. These could include, for instance, relatively high-income retired persons with little or no pension income, and a preponderance of Canadian dividend income.
- As a sub-division of the high Canadian dividend income category, owner/managers whose corporations qualify for the preferred corporate tax rate through the "small business deduction" and take their compensation by way of dividends.

- Retirees transferring all of their pension income into RRSPs.

Examples
Investors 1986 (single taxpayer, personal exemption $4,180)

1. Taxable Canadian dividend income	$ 60,000	
Regular tax	0	
AMT (approximately)	4,000	
Increase		$4,000
2. Capital gain	$250,000	
Lifetime exemption claimed	50,000	
Non-exempt capital gain	200,000	
Taxable capital gain	100,000	
Regular tax - approximately	42,700	
AMT - approximately	46,100	
Increase		$ 3,400
3. Capital gain	$250,000	
Lifetime exemption claimed	Nil	
Non-exempt capital gain	250,000	
Taxable capital gain	125,000	
Regular tax - approximately	56,600	
AMT - approximately	52,500	
Increase		Nil

Owner Managers (at regular small business corporate tax and dividend distribution tax)

4. Salary only	$100,000	
Corporate tax	Nil	
Personal tax	$ 39,500	
AMT	N/A	
Increase		Nil
5. All dividends		
Corporate tax	$ 33,300	
Regular personal tax	6,222	
AMT	14,422	
Increase		$8,200

As with all but the most routine tax matters, the AMT deserves not only your careful attention, but that of expert advisers before you make any decision regarding your own situation.

TAXES ARE A FACT OF LIFE

Arranging your affairs to minimize your taxes is legal and prudent, given the high rates of personal tax in Canada today. But any effort to evade taxation, by failing to report income or by trying to get away with inflated deductions, can cause you far more grief than it's worth. The penalties are severe.

Perhaps the most important element of financial planning in connection with taxation is to learn to think in terms of your disposable income — that is, your income after taxes — when you are making your financial plans. If your gross income is $24,000, and you plan to spend $24,000 in that year, you'll end up in financial trouble. Taxes are an inescapable fact of life. Plan to minimize their impact, but learn to live with them sensibly.

DO'S AND DON'TS

Do Review all deductions available to you and make certain you are claiming all those you are entitled to.

Do Investigate deductions you don't qualify for now but might if you made a few changes (e.g., investment income deductions of $1,000).

Do Talk to your lawyer and accountant before taking title to your new home and then decide whether it should be in your name, your spouse's, or held jointly. If you're married and have two residences, arrange that your non-principal residence is owned by the spouse with the lower tax rate.

Do Look for opportunities to split investment income with other family members in lower tax brackets.

Do Look for tax-sheltered or tax-deferred types of investments after you have earned $1,000 of interest or dividend income and exploited opportunities for income splitting.

Do Take maximum advantage of the RRSP and pension deductions available to you.

Do Discuss a complicated tax return with a professional, preferably a chartered accountant who specializes in income tax.

Do Make any big donation to charity in December, not January, because it qualifies in the year in which you make the deduction.

Don't Forget to use an RRSP to reduce a child's net income to the maximum allowable without loss of the full exemption; and/or to reduce their taxable income to nil in order to allow you to claim the $50/month Education Deduction in your name.

Don't Forget to test for the impact of the Alternative Minimum Tax in determining the mix of salary and dividends you should take as an incorporated owner/manager, and the mix of interest and dividends you should create if you are living substantially on investment income.

CHAPTER 9

Tax Shelters: A Modern Necessity

Fifty years ago, no one thought much about tax shelters because there was little or no tax to be sheltered from. Governments weren't expected to provide as many services as they are today, and they didn't require the massive revenues our modern tax system generates.

Today the Canadian wage-earner has to cope with many different kinds of taxes—property tax, sales tax, capital gains tax and, most significant for most people, income tax. We will deal only with the last two, although in Canada the so-called "capital gains tax" is really just regular income tax rates applied to one-half the gain, over what's left of the taxpayer's lifetime exemption of up to $500,000.

Even at modest earnings levels, income tax can be a real burden. If you make $24,000 and support a spouse and two dependent children, Revenue Canada is going to take about 30¢ out of the next dollar you make (1986 rates). In recent years effective tax rates have been increasing, and the odds are that tax rates will get even higher. People tend to demand more services from government, and government insists on providing more services and building bigger and more inefficient bureaucracies to provide them, "forcing" the government to take a greater share of our incomes to pay for them. This is especially true when governments are committed to reducing huge deficits, and therefore are reluctant to finance increased government expenditure through increased borrowing.

The combined effect of income tax and inflation on people's ability to save money can be devastating. As a result, it is absolutely vital that we take maximum advantage of any legitimate tax concessions offered by government.

TAKING ADVANTAGE OF TAX SHELTERS

Tax shelters are usually created as incentives for people to invest in ways judged to be socially useful. For example, the government has said, "Since we don't want you to be dependent on the state when you reach old age, we'll make it attractive to save for retirement by allowing you to defer tax on the money you contribute to an RRSP. And to stimulate investment in the multiple unit residential market, the Canadian feature film industry, the search for oil and gas, and the development of new technology, we will offer special tax incentives to invest in multiple unit residential buildings (MURBs), Canadian films, oil and gas exploration funds, and research and development."

If you take intelligent advantage of the tax shelters available to you, you should be further ahead in the financial ball game than you otherwise might be. By "intelligent" we mean that, in engaging in tax shelters, you do not let the tax shelter compromise your judgment of the investment qualities of the tax shelter.

Remember, it is perfectly moral, ethical, and legal for you to arrange your affairs to attract as little tax as possible. But the transactions you enter into have to be real transactions. They have to have some purpose beyond simply avoiding taxation. The best common-sense test you can run on any tax avoidance suggestion is simply to ask yourself, "If the tax people come to talk to me about this, am I prepared to answer all their questions honestly, provide them with all information about this transaction, and fight any disagreements they might raise?"

In this chapter, we deal with tax shelters of interest to most people and with a few exotic ones of real interest only to those who earn $75,000 or more a year.

REGISTERED RETIREMENT SAVINGS PLANS (RRSPs)

RRSPs were introduced in 1957 by the federal government as a response to strong lobbying from groups of professional practitioners who could not participate in company-subsidized pension plans and were demanding a personal alternative.

Initial contribution limits were small by today's standards—only the lesser of $1,500 or 10% of qualifying income. Obviously, the idea was sound, because more and more Canadians have taken advantage of the RRSP tax advantage in steadily increasing amounts ever since. If there was ever any doubt that RRSPs had become the tax shelter of the ordinary Canadian, it was banished when a leading trust company employed as a spokesperson in its RRSP radio advertising campaign no less a financial commentator than Eddy Shack.

RRSP Contribution Limits

Between 1957 and the late 1970s, contribution limits were increased periodically until they had reached the limits most of us are familiar with:

- the lesser of 20% of earned income and $3,500 if you were in a Registered Pension Plan (RPP) or Deferred Profit Sharing Plan (DPSP) minus any contribution you made to the RPP;

or

- the lesser of 20% of earned income and $5,500 if you were not in an RPP or DPSP.

These limits remained static until 1985 when the May Federal Budget proposed sweeping changes in the whole system of RRSP, RPP, and DPSP contributions. These proposals were originally to take effect in 1986, but, with one exception, were eventually postponed until 1987. Refer to Table 11.3 on page 156 in Chapter 11, "Retirement," for a summary of the proposed new contribution rules.

Let's look at an example. Elmer and Emma Elderly are in their early 60s and have created a few nest eggs along the way. Elmer works at a large oil company, where his salary is $50,000, and he is a member of a company pension plan to which he contributes 4% of his salary. Emma doesn't work outside of the home and therefore does not belong to a pension plan — but she has built up a real-estate portfolio which yields $20,000 net rental income. Let's see what they can contribute to RRSPs.

In 1986, Elmer can contribute $1,500 ($3,500 minus 4% of $50,000, or $2,000). Emma can contribute $4,000 (20% of $20,000). In 1987, Elmer will be limited to a $2,000 RRSP contribution because he is in a "defined benefit" RPP.*

If we changed the example slightly and portrayed Emma with $30,000 of rental income, she could contribute $6,000 under the new formula (20% of 30,000), or $5,500, the flat maximum under the old formula. She would have this choice in 1986 and 1987, although in 1987 the new formula would be the lesser of $9,500 or 18% of qualifying income. Thereafter, she would have to follow the new formula.

If you are in a defined benefit RPP, be sure to check with your payroll or compensation and benefits to get confirmation of your RRSP limit in 1987 and thereafter.

Spousal RRSPs

Since 1974, taxpayers have been able to designate their spouse as beneficiary of a "spousal RRSP," with the tax deduction going to the *contributor* and title to the money to the designated spouse. In the example above, for instance, if Elmer's pension in retirement was going to exceed Emma's rental income, it would make sense for them to have Elmer contribute $1,500 to a spousal RRSP for Emma to try to get her income up as close to equality with Elmer's as possible. Equalizing incomes in retirement is ideal because it minimizes marginal tax rates and maximizes use of available exemptions such as personal, old age, $1,000 interest income and

*These figures assume proposals put forward in the May 1985 Budget are legislated. At the date of going to press, the legislation had not been introduced. It also assumes rental income will still be considered as earned income for calculating income for RRSP purposes.

the special $1,000 "pension" deduction available to everyone beginning no later than the year they reach age 65.

RRSP Accumulation Power

To appreciate the tremendous advantage an RRSP offers over investment with after-tax dollars, you have to recognize three key points:

- Your RRSP contribution is in pre-tax dollars. This means you *start off* with a lot more *capital* actually invested.
- Income or growth on your investment is not taxed as it accrues year by year. This means total pre-tax income can be reinvested and *compounded* year in, year out. It's only when you take money out of the plan that you have to pay tax.
- The degree of advantage you gain by tax sheltering is a lot greater than most people realize. Tax rates are quoted as a percentage of pre-tax income. For most of us, pre-tax income is a myth. We never see our pre-tax income – we can only brag about it. What we live on is our take-home pay. If, by tax sheltering, however, we can "get some of our tax money back," the rate of advantage is relative to how much we would have had to work with otherwise. Let's look at some examples using a pre-tax amount of $5,500.

1. Marginal tax rate (highest rate on last dollars earned)	51%	45%	38%
2. Tax at marginal rate	$2,805	$2,475	$2,090
3. Available for investment after tax	$2,695	$3,025	$3,410
4. Available for RRSP pre-tax	$5,500	$5,500	$5,500
5. Percentage *increase* in amount invested in RRSP versus non-RRSP investment	104%	82%	61%

While we have used RRSP as an example here, the arithmetic of tax deferral advantage applies to all forms of tax shelters: not only RRSPs, but also to pension and Deferred Profit Sharing Plan (DPSP) contributions, deductible investment loan interest, and major tax shelter investments. The only difference is the amount you may invest and the range of investment options open to you – a subject we turn to now.

RRSP Investment Choices

The range of investments which qualify for RRSPs is very wide, including everything from very safe deposit accounts or Guaranteed Investment Certificates through mutual funds of different kinds, all the way to your own "self-directed" investment portfolio. Generally, the criteria for choosing an RRSP investment are similar to those for general investment: liquidity, safety, income, growth potential, volatility, market value and risk of loss, and degree of personal management required – all contributing to the definition of your investment "comfort zones." You should be aware, however, of some realities which may cause you to lean more in one direction than another.

- *High income* earners in high marginal tax brackets often shy away from investments yielding high but taxable income. This is *not* a problem with RRSPs, of course, because tax is deferred.
- *Capital gains* outside an RRSP enjoy three potential tax advantages: first, no tax is payable while the gain is accruing, only when it is realized on sale of the investment and, in some circumstances, at death; second, all or part of the gain may be tax exempt under the lifetime exemption of $500,000; and third, only half the non-exempt portion of the gain is taxed.

  In an RRSP, tax is deferred, but when money comes out of the plan 100% of the gain is taxed, not 50%.
- *Dividends* from tax-paying Canadian companies also enjoy substantial tax advantage outside an RRSP because of the dividend tax credit.

In an RRSP, tax on dividends is deferred but when tax becomes payable the dividend tax credit is not available. All dividends are taxed as regular income.

All this suggests that you should start with an overall philosophy which says: keep high-interest, guaranteed-return investments *inside* your RRSP and growth and dividend-paying stocks or mutual funds outside.

That's if there's room in your total portfolio for both guaranteed income investments and stocks or mutual funds—and enough money available for guaranteed income investments to "use up" your RRSP contribution limits.

Other factors which should govern your choice of RRSP investments are:

- *Age*. Generally, you should play it safer as you get older.
- *Control over retirement date*. The less control you have over your retirement date, the more conservative your investment portfolio should be. In other words, if a mandatory retirement policy could force you out when the stock market was in a cyclical trough, you might suffer serious losses if you were forced to cash in your RRSP investments.
- *Time and expertise*. Be realistic about the time and skill you can devote to investment management. In retirement, you'll have all the time you used to devote to work, but there may be other activities you're much more interested in pursuing than reading the stock-market quotations. If you'd rather golf or travel, let a pro take care of investing your RRSP funds.

Getting Money Out of Your RRSP

With few exceptions, you're best to wait until retirement to start drawing on RRSP funds. However, you don't have to wait that long. Let's look at how and when you can get money out of your RRSPs.

Before Age 71 (i.e., the end of the year you become age 71)

You can withdraw RRSP funds in a lump sum subject to withholding tax of 10% to 30% and, ultimately, to whatever your top tax rates are for the year of withdrawal, *including RRSP proceeds and all other sources of income.*

The best reasons to withdraw RRSP funds in a lump sum would be to help finance a year or more away from work, to return to school, or to take a sabbatical. In this way, you'll attract tax at only average rates, not your highest marginal rate, as would be the case if you cashed your RRSP on top of a full year's other income.

RRSP Maturity Options

In addition to cashing your RRSP in a lump sum, you can also choose from three maturity options. These options allow you to spread payments and tax liability in a systematic way and to structure an income package suited to your current needs and concerns about future inflation. The three options are:

- *Life annuity,* with or without contingent or "backup" guarantees in the event you were to die shortly after payments started.
- *Term certain annuity to age 90*; i.e., payment to your age 90, either to you if you live or, if you don't live to age 90, to a beneficiary of your choice.
- *Registered Retirement Income Fund* (RRIF), which allows continued investment of RRSP funds, subject to a minimum withdrawal formula which will eventually pay out all funds by age 90.

Let's look at each of them more closely.

Life annuity. This is the original and oldest of the RRSP options. A life annuity can be just that—the guarantee of a regular level amount of income, usually monthly, for the rest of *your* life, no matter how short or long a time you live. Because most people fear "losing their money" if they die prematurely, few choose annuities without guarantees beyond the death of the annuitant.

Joint-survivor annuity. This option is favoured by most married couples for at least part of their RRSP proceeds. It assures income as long as *either* spouse lives—either level income until the second death or structured to yield ⅓ to ½ less income when only one spouse is still living.

Term-certain guarantee. This is a popular adjunct to a joint-survivor annuity, or it may be the only underlying guarantee beyond the life of the annuitant. Under this arrangement, payment is guaranteed for a minimum number of payments whether or not the annuitant (or annuitants, under a joint-survivor annuity) live that long. Popular term-certain guarantee periods are five, ten, and fifteen years; however, you can only elect a term certain annuity to age 90 with your RRSP money.

Discount tables are applied to determine how much less income is available per $1,000 of cash proceeds when a joint-survivor and/or term-certain guarantee is built into an annuity. Most people are pleasantly surprised at how little it costs to provide such guarantees, but they should recognize that, as a planning tool, annuity guarantees are irrevocable decisions which cannot be changed to fit circumstances as they unfold. For instance, if you opt for a discounted joint-survivor annuity to protect your spouse if he or she survives you, but he or she predeceases you instead, you can't go back to the insurance company and demand a life-only annuity for a higher amount.

Term certain to age 90. This option is cut and dried — a level income to your ninetieth birthday whether you survive that long or not. You get to name a contingent beneficiary — usually a spouse or children — in case you don't make it to age 90. If you do die before age 90, your spouse can receive taxable income payments for the rest of the guaranteed period but anyone else, including your children, would have to take remaining payments in a taxable lump sum.

Registered Retirement Income Fund (RRIF). Under a RRIF, you don't have to commit all your capital to buying an annuity. You can invest it yourself under a self-directed plan or have it invested in a mutual fund or a GIC through a trust company or credit union or insurance company. Every year, however, you must withdraw a fraction of the total fund equal to at least 1 divided by the difference between age 90 and your current age. At age 60, the fraction would be 1/(90–60), i.e. 1/30, or 3.33%. At age 71, the fraction would be 1/(90–71), i.e., 1/19, or 5.26%.

Under new rules announced in the February 1986 Budget, you can now have as many RRIFs as you want and withdraw any amount over the minimum required.

As the denominator decreases each year, the fraction will increase. Given that the capital fund is generating income or growth greater than the percentage withdrawal requirement, income will increase steadily until the last years before age 90. This should not be a difficult task, one would think, until over age 80, where the withdrawal fraction would be increasing beyond 10%; i.e. 1/(90–80), 1/10, 10%.

Age 71 Year End: Maturity Options Must Be Triggered

You can delay choosing RRSP options until the last day of the year you reach age 71. After that, any balance on which you have not elected one of the three options will be subjected to tax as a lump sum — not usually a very palatable prospect.

Before age 71, you enjoy a period of tremendous planning flexibility. During these years you can

- Elect one or more of the three RRSP maturity options.
- Cash in a lump sum.
- Continue to accumulate value in your present RRSPs.
- Make new annual contributions of up to $3,500 or $5,500, depending on whether or not you are in a pension plan (more when the new rules are finalized).
- Designate such contributions as spousal contributions.
- Use both private and government pension income, as well as employment and rental income, as a base in applying the 20% annual contribution formula (through 1986 only).
- "Roll" *all or any part* of your private and government pension income into *your* RRSP — but not to a spousal plan (it is proposed this will only be to December 31, 1989).
- "Roll" at will directly from one RRSP to another, depending on your assessment of the most competitive debt instruments, the best investment opportunities and investment fund management.

Get Time and Momentum on Your Side: Start Now

To get a tax deduction for an RRSP contribution, you can contribute at any time during the calendar year or up to 60 days after the end of the year. If you've decided to make the investment and if you have already earned $1,000 of interest or taxable dividend or capital gains, get the plan started immediately. Otherwise, you'll be earning taxable interest outside the RRSP instead of tax-sheltered interest inside.

It's especially important that you save regularly for RRSP contributions because, since the November 1981 Budget, interest on loans for new RRSP contributions is not tax-deductible. Many RRSP plans allow regular contributions with no minimum payment required after the first payment. Writing a series of post-dated cheques could be the most practical way to get money into your RRSP systematically — and to avoid late February panic loans to beat the deadline.

The RRSP is the government's way of encouraging you to save for your retirement. It's one tax shelter every Canadian should consider seriously.

RRSPs at Death

Here is a summary of tax treatment of RRSP proceeds at death of the planholder or income recipient:

- Income payments other than to a surviving spouse must be commuted to a lump sum and taxed in the hands of the recipient, subject to certain exceptions.

- Lump sums are fully taxable at the deceased RRSP holder's rates except when received by a spouse, a dependent child under the age of twenty-six, or an infirm child under the age of seventy-one. In the case of a child under the age of twenty-six an amount equal to $5,000 × the number of years the child is under age twenty-six can be taxed at the child's rate (age 71 if the child is infirm).

 A spouse can defer tax up to the end of the year he or she reaches age seventy-one by "rolling" funds to his or her own RRSP.

CANADIAN FILMS

Before 1966 Canada had no feature film industry. That year the Canadian government decided a domestic film industry would be beneficial to the country, both culturally and financially. It created the Canadian Film Development Corporation. Since then, various laws have been enacted resulting in the present allowance of a 100% rate of Capital Cost Allowance (depreciation) for films that meet specific criteria set down by the government, and certified by the Secretary of State.

In the early years many pitfalls existed for investors. Hucksters and swindlers left behind them a trail of bilked investors, creating a black cloud over film investment as a tax shelter. Also, many of the films were financed by a combination of cash-ins and promissory notes that were nothing but a sham. The notes were non-recourse (that is, the investor received a tax reduction at the time for having signed them, but was told that at no time would he or she actually have to pay off the notes; they were to be repaid out of the profits of the film, which the producers knew would be non-existent). Eventually, the Department of National Revenue caught up with this type of sham and reassessed the people involved.

Currently, the only note acceptable for tax purposes is a full recourse note, which may or may not bear interest. However, the lure of a 100% writeoff did create a deluge of new films, all neatly packaged by the investment community. There was even talk of Montreal or Toronto becoming the new Hollywood, and stars such as Michael Douglas, Bruce Dern, and Suzanne Somers could be found frequenting Canadian watering holes. Most of these movies, however, had more glitter than gold, since few investors made a worthwhile return on their money. As a result, there was an industry shakeout and the number of new films being produced now has slowed to a trickle. Instead, movies for home consumption through network TV and private video are being made. They are less expensive to produce, less risky, and with the coming of pay TV they could offer a reasonable return on an investment. Therefore, such investments cannot be looked upon merely as tax shelters, but must be measured by the normal standards of a good investment.

When considering a film investment, take a hard look at:

- The story line, script, or screenplay. Quality can be judged only by qualified experts. It is fair to state that a good film can never be produced from a bad script or screenplay, no matter what the subject matter.

- The choice of the director and the principal cast. The director or one or more of the stars may not be suitable for the particular film. Once again, a professional evaluation is necessary.
- Marketing conditions. Is the feature film or proposed television special or television series likely to receive favourable response from the marketplace? This is perhaps the hardest question of all. One must be able to evaluate whether or not a producer has attempted to test the market, or whether the proposed undertaking is based upon totally subjective decisions on his or her part. If the producer has an excellent track record of profitable films, perhaps one would be inclined to follow his instincts.

Tax considerations should be the least important. A tax loss is a loss like any other — except that instead of losing 100 cents on the dollar, you may perhaps lose only 50 cents on the dollar. But to invest for the purpose of losing money does not make sense. The best thing you can have going for you in dealing with Canadian feature films is the people involved with them. Make sure their track record is good enough to allow you to bet on them with a reasonable hope of making a profit.

OIL AND GAS EXPLORATION FUNDS

The mechanics and mathematics of tax shelters based on oil and gas drilling funds have been affected most significantly by changes in government's attitude toward the relative merits of tax incentives in the open marketplace and government grants. In this regard, 1980 and 1984 are watershed years. It was in late 1980 that then federal Energy Minister Marc Lalonde introduced the National Energy Program (NEP). Then in late 1984, after the Progressive Conservatives had toppled the Liberals from power, Energy Minister Pat Carney announced repeal of the NEP.

Tax Incentives in Oil and Gas

As a tax shelter opportunity, oil and gas drilling funds offer three major attractions:

- A 100% writeoff against any kind of income for expenses incurred in drilling "wildcat" or exploration wells where oil and gas have not been discovered before.
- A 30% writeoff against any kind of income for expenses incurred in drilling development or "stepout" wells in an area where at least one successful well has been drilled already.
- A 33⅓% "depletion allowance" against oil and gas revenues only; i.e., a

writeoff of ⅓ of revenue as recognition of the fact that the oil and gas reserves from any well will eventually be depleted.

Sharing Oil and Gas Revenues and Expenses

The typical syndicated drilling fund provided for sharing of revenues and expenses between investors and operators is as shown in Table 9.1.

Typically, the large public funds offered by full prospectus through brokerage firms with high-powered advertising campaigns call for the biggest share of revenue to the operator. On the other hand, they are more accessible to the average investor because minimum units are as low as $10,000.

Private placements, where money is raised with no costly advertising, lower sales commissions (often nil) and less formal documentation, typically offer the investor a bigger slice of the revenue pie. But the minimum investment unit is at least $100,000, thus ruling out this type of investment for many investors.

Table 9.1
Sharing of Revenues and Expenses in a Typical Syndicated Drilling Fund

Item	*From/To Investor*	*From/To Operator*
Exploration expense	100%	Ø
Development expense	50%-80%	20%-50%
Revenue — exploration wells until original investment recovered	90%	10%
Thereafter	60%-80%	20%-40%
Revenue — development wells	60%-80%	20%-40%

Flow-Through Shares

A recent development in the area of resource exploration, flow-through shares address the problem of lack of liquidity and access to a potentially appreciating asset. These shares provide equity participation as with any other common-share investment, but they also offer the purchaser a very interesting tax-deduction situation. Let's look at an example.

The X Mining Corporation has an exploration budget for 1986 of $2,000,000. They offer to the public investors 200,000 common flow-through shares of X Mining Corporation at $10.00, raising the required $2 million. The corporation then spends the entire amount on exploration in 1986. That entire expenditure flows through to the purchasers of the flow-through shares as a personal deduction on their individual tax return for 1986 at rates as high as 133% of the actual expenses.

Key Points

1. Investor John Doe buys 1,000 shares of "Z" at a cost of $10,000.
2. John Doe then deducts from his taxable income for 1986 the expenses incurred for exploration of 133% of $10,000.
3. Assuming John Doe's marginal tax rate is 50%, his after-tax cost of the 1,000 shares is now $3,333, or $3.33 a share ($10,000 – 50% of $13,333).
4. For tax purposes (capital gains tax), his "adjusted cost base" on the 1,000 shares is "zero."
5. If he subsequently sells the 1,000 shares at, say, $10,000 (no market gain or loss), he incurs a capital gain of $10,000, $5,000 of which is taxable, and would pay $2,500 tax on the sale. If the capital gain falls within his lifetime capital gains exemption, he pays no tax.
6. Assuming no interest costs, etc., he would be ahead $4,167.

Flow-through shares can be a very interesting vehicle, if you feel the underlying security is worth your actual out-of-pocket cost. You should be aware, however, that these shares yield no tax deductions until such time as the relevant expenses have been incurred by the issuing corporations. Initially, you buy a non-transferable unit and the actual common shares are not delivered until the funds raised have been expended to the satisfaction of the tax department.

Evaluating an Oil and Gas Drilling Fund

Petroleum engineers are often referred to as "earth scientists" and, indeed, the theory and practice of finding oil and gas has all of the complexity that name suggests. In addition, no one outside the petroleum business can develop a "feel" for an oil and gas play the way all of us might have a strong hunch about a real estate location — or even a movie plot — developing into a winner.

As a result, the best you can do as a potential investor is check the track record of the people running the operation, particularly their track record *as a team*. All-star teams are notoriously bad at playing well together, and it can happen in business as well as sports.

Other points to look for:

- How diversified is the program? Is everything being bet on a few holes or will a dozen or more be drilled? Is there a spread of probability among the different plays — some high risk with big potential rewards, others low risk but with a strong possibility of achieving some results?
- What are the relationships among the drilling fund and the operators and their private interests? Sometimes it seems clear that the prime motive for raising money is to provide a make-work program for equipment which otherwise might be idle.
- What are the relative chances of hitting oil vs. gas? Oil can be sold; gas often has to be shut in because of a glut in the market.

Mining Exploration Funds

The "flow-through" share is also being used to raise capital for exploration for mineral resources, an area of investment which has become much more interesting from a tax shelter standpoint.

In the April 1983 Budget, stimulus was provided to direct investment in mining exploration by the introduction of tax writeoffs as high as 133% of expenses incurred. If you are in a 50% tax bracket or higher, this would mean your tax refund would be ⅔ or more of your investment and your net investment at risk less than ⅓.

To sum up, unless you know and trust someone in the petroleum or mining business — or are desperate to get a direct piece of the action — you would be wise to stay away from this type of investment and buy shares in an energy-related mutual fund or a major integrated oil and gas company. If you insist on a tax-sheltered investment in resources, look for a play which offers flow-through shares. If you can satisfy yourself that the shares have not been diluted too much in terms of underlying assets and realistic prospects, they could offer you the all-important advantage of ready marketability in good times or bad.

MULTIPLE UNIT RESIDENTIAL BUILDINGS (MURBs)

We've all heard about, or perhaps even met, durable hypochondriacs who, despite dire predictions of their imminent demise, live long enough to inter all their physicians.

The Canadian MURB tax shelter program has been like that. It was introduced for one year from November 18, 1974 to December 31, 1975 to offset the adverse effects of so-called federal tax reform measures introduced in 1972 and provincial rent control programs; given a new lease on life until December 31, 1979; rendered extinct from January 1, 1980 to October 27, 1980; and then resurrected on October 28, 1980, ostensibly until December 31, 1981.

Creeping MURB Death: The November 1981 Budget

On November 12, 1981, then Finance Minister Allan MacEachen rose up in the House of Commons and, in one fell paragraph, smote the MURB program *immediately*. That was on a Thursday. By the next day, across Canada, millions of dollars of development had ground to a halt. On the weekend, a hastily assembled group representing the Canadian real estate development community travelled to Ottawa to try to talk some sense into the Minister. On Monday, he rose up again in the Commons to announce that an extension would be granted until December 31, 1981 on projects substantially agreed to in writing before Budget date.

On December 19, he granted a further extension of certain tax concessions on projects for which footings were in place by May 28, 1982.

Finally, in August 1982, the new Finance Minister, Marc Lalonde, announced a concession of crucial, practical importance to the availability of fully qualified MURBs in 1983 and, to a lesser extent, in 1984. Previously, there had been a requirement that for a project to qualify for full MURB "soft costs" and capital cost allowance writeoffs, progress on construction had to be continuous from January 1, 1982. On this basis, many sites for which MURB certificates had been obtained "on spec" before the December 31, 1981 deadline would have failed to qualify because no work had been done on them for many months in 1982.

Lalonde's announcement breathed new life into the program, and as late as December 1985 there were still available on the market examples of a species that was deemed endangered in 1975, became officially extinct in 1979, was resurrected in 1980, hammered unconscious again in 1981, and finally resuscitated enough to keep breathing through 1985 until its likely demise in 1986. MURB resales, however, are starting to happen and there are likely to be more of these on the market than original MURBs. Resales differ from the original MURBs in two ways: (1) the soft costs are not deductible; and (2) they are likely to be more competitively priced.

The moral of this story: don't rule out MURBs as a tax shelter investment just because someone says the program is going to be terminated.

From a social standpoint, it has produced an enormous amount of useful rental accommodation across Canada — development which would not have taken place otherwise. And it has produced some excellent results for investors as well. It has also produced some bad results.

What Is the MURB Advantage?

To understand the MURB advantage, let's compare a MURB and a "non-MURB" investment. Here are the specs:

Type of unit: Condominium townhome

End Price: $100,000 (land, $33,000; building, $52,000; appliances, $3,000; soft costs, $12,000)

Financing: Downpayment: $25,000; 1st mortgage for $75,000 @ 12% amortized over 30 years = $755 per month

Rental income: $750 per month net of rental fee

Operating expenses: $50 per month (renters pay their own utilities)

Taxes: $110 per month

Total expenses, including debt service: $915

Revenue: $750

Pre-tax operating deficit: $165

After-tax net loss (in 50% tax bracket): $82 per month, or $984 per year.

Why would anyone invest to run a deficit? There are two reasons: first, debt service charges, the biggest single expense, will remain level for five years. If, in that time, rents can be increased by $165 per month or more, the investor will be in a break-even position in the sixth year and should start to enjoy net income thereafter. Second, if inflation continues to force up land and building costs, the market value of the townhome may increase substantially, allowing a sale for a capital gain.

With a qualifying MURB, there would be a third reason: tax deductions for "soft costs" and capital cost allowance (CCA) or "depreciation." The impact of such deductions on the net cash position of the investor are shown in Table 9.2

Table 9.2
Tax Deductions on a MURB

Year	*1*	*2*	*3*	*4*	*5*
Rents[1]	$9,000	$9,360	$9,734	$10,124	$10,528
Operating expenses:					
Maintenance[2]	(600)	(648)	(700)	(756)	(816)
Taxes[2]	(1,320)	(1,426)	(1,540)	(1,663)	(1,796)
Income before debt service	7,080	7,286	7,494	7,705	7,916
Debt service	(9,060)	(9,060)	(9,060)	(9,060)	(9,060)
Cash flow (deficit)	(1,980)	(1,774)	(1,566)	(1,355)	(1,144)
Repayment of principal	225	375	425	450	475
Soft costs	(2,400)	(2,400)	(2,400)	(2,400)	(2,400)
CCA	(3,200)	(2,950)	(2,730)	(2,536)	(2,364)
Loss for tax purposes	(7,355)	(6,749)	(6,271)	(5,841)	(5,433)
Tax reduction @ 50%	3,678	3,374	3,135	2,920	2,716
Net profit (expense)	1,698	1,600	1,569	1,565	1,572
Net profit (expense: cumulative)	1,698	3,298	4,867	6,432	8,004

[1]Rents increase at 4% annually.

[2]Operating expenses and taxes increase at 8% annually.

On a qualifying MURB, then, the purchaser would have decreased his or her after-tax investment in the property by $8,004 while creating a deferred tax bill on soft costs and capital cost allowance, ranging from $5,882 to $8,882, depending on whether or not capital gain on half the amount of soft costs would be exempt.

What About a Non-MURB?

The same operating budget on a property which did not qualify for MURB treatment would produce a much different result from a tax standpoint – and therefore a much different result in terms of net cost.

Capital cost allowance deductions would be eliminated altogether, since there was an operating deficit throughout the period.

Soft costs (except for landscaping) would have to be added to building cost and written off at 5% per annum. However, because the project operated at a deficit, these writeoffs would not be available, as was the case with CCA writeoffs on the basic building cost.

The overall result would be that total tax writeoffs would decrease by $23,763 cumulative, and there would be a net after-tax cost of $3,878 instead of a profit of $8,004. On the other hand, there would be no deferred tax bill.

In other words, the "numbers" come out about the same in either case. The difference is mostly in the *timing* of the cost. On the MURB, the tax cost would be deferred until you actually sold the property. On the non-MURB, you would have to cover the added cost each year out of your current after-tax savings.

The longer you hold the qualifying MURB, the bigger this advantage becomes.

Sale of a MURB: Capital Appreciation vs. Deferred Taxes

But the biggest attraction in a MURB investment, as with most real estate investments, is potential *capital appreciation*.

Suppose, in our example, that the market value of this type of housing increased at 6% annually over the five-year period.

Let's look at what net proceeds would result:

Gross sale price based on original value of $88,000 ($100,000 less soft costs)		$117,764
Less: Sales commission @ 6%		(7,066)
Net pre-tax proceeds		$110,698
Capital gain (i.e., $110,698–$88,000)	$22,698	
Taxable gain	11,349	
Tax @ 50% (if gain non-exempt)		(5,674)

Recaptured CCA (building only)	11,763	
Tax @ 50%		(5,882)
Net after-tax proceeds		$ 99,142
Less: 1st mortgage balance		73,050
Net proceeds		$ 26,092
Original investment		$ 25,000
Less: Net profits		8,004
Net cost		$ 16,996

Net after-tax return on investment (cumulative): 53%
Net after-tax return on investment (annual): 9%
Note: If capital gain were exempt, net return would increase by $5,674 and rate of return to 13% after-tax.

Obviously, if the market value had increased at a rate higher than 6%, the result would be more favourable. In addition, the longer you held the property and it continued to increase in value, the better the result would be. Generally you should not buy a MURB unless you feel confident that the property is capable of enjoying capital appreciation at a rate of 6% or higher and that you can hold the property for at least ten years. Otherwise, invest your money elsewhere.

When considering a MURB investment, look at the following:

1. Location. Is it attractive in the short and long run? Who will want to rent it?
2. Quality of construction. Will the building maintain its value throughout a long period of time (15–20 years)?
3. Management. Will tenants be happy and will the project be filled?
4. Track record of MURB sponsors. Have they done other projects before? Have they been successful? Are earlier investors happy with results so far?
5. Does the project compare favourably in price with other MURBs in the same area? Does it compare favourably in price with similar buildings that are not MURBs, allowing a reasonable (say 10–12%) premium for MURB advantages?
6. Is the economy of the community strong? Are vacancy rates in the community low and are they projected to remain so in the future?
7. Have increases in housing prices in that community kept pace in the past with inflation increases?
8. Will you have freehold or condominium title to the individual apartment or townhouse units? These forms of title allow you to sell to a user as well as to an investor. They also are easier to sell than a MURB in which you are a limited partner.
9. Are there any rental or cash-flow guarantees that put the developer at risk?

Try to inspect the site before it is built on and look at similar projects by the same developer. While you are there, close your eyes and ask yourself: "Will a couple or a family want to buy it and live in it in ten years' time—when the difference between shoddy and quality construction and poor and proper upkeep will come home to roost?"

If you can answer yes to all or most of these questions, your MURB investment should prove to be a winner.

Generally speaking, of all the various tax deferral schemes, the MURB program offers the best risk-return ratio for the conservative investor. But like all investments it should be carefully analyzed, not only by a tax consultant or accountant, but by someone who has a good feel for the underlying value of real estate.

The ideal MURB investor, we believe, is an employed executive or self-employed professional—doctor, dentist, lawyer, or private company owner whose corporation pays a high rate of tax—whose income is $100,000 a year or more. Normally we advise that a MURB investment be financed with borrowed money; cash should be placed in areas offering less risk, or used to fund income-splitting loans where possible.

INVESTING IN A FARM

If you own and operate a farm, and are not merely "hobby farming," the government lets you deduct the first $2,500 and up to half of the next $5,000 of your operating loss. That means if you lose $7,500 you'll have a tax writeoff of $5,000 against your other income. If you are in a 50% tax bracket, you'll save $2,500 in taxes.

Your operating loss can include depreciation of a barn as well as expenses.

In order to take advantage of this tax shelter, the farm has to be run as a farm. It has to generate some income—and the income can't include rental revenue from a farmer who leases your land. This does not mean you have to do the farming yourself. You can form a partnership with a neighbouring farmer, where you share the costs of seed, fertilizer etc. The farmer contributes the labour and sells the crop, then pays you a share of the proceeds.

Using your country land for farming purposes also may entitle you to a property tax reduction, depending upon which province you live in.

Farmland can be a profitable investment, particularly if the land is near an urban centre. These tax shelter provisions make it even more attractive because taxes are substantially lower than on an investment that is not tax preferred.

SELLING YOUR FAMILY HOME

The biggest tax-free profit you will make in your lifetime (unless you win a lottery) may well be the profit you make when you sell your family home.

Capital gains on your principal residence are *not* taxable. If you decide to move to a smaller house after retirement, a portion of the money you'll need for retirement can be generated from the sale of your larger home.

It's important to remember that the interest you pay on your mortgage is *not* tax deductible. Therefore one of the wisest investments you can make is to pay off your mortgage as fast as possible.

TAX SHELTERS AND THE ALTERNATIVE MINIMUM TAX

Before you make a major tax shelter investment, check with your financial or tax adviser to make sure your tax advantage will not be eroded by the effect of the Alternative Minimum Tax (AMT) calculation.

If you earn salary, pension and/or interest and non-Canadian dividend income (so called "non-preference income items"), the chances of your being adversely affected by the AMT are remote; but if you feel you might be affected, take the time to double check.

INVESTMENT LOAN INTEREST

Don't forget that interest you pay on a loan for a business or investment purpose, including major tax shelter investments, is tax deductible. But remember that interest on a new loan to fund a contribution to a RPP, DPSP or RRSP is *not* tax deductible.

REDUCING SOURCE DEDUCTED TAX

If you want to get immediate advantage from a tax shelter investment, apply to your District Taxation Office to have your source deducted tax reduced in anticipation of reduced taxable income because of tax shelter and investment loan interest deductions.

It beats waiting until half way through the year after the tax year in question to get a refund of your overpayment of tax.

DO'S & DON'TS

Do Adopt a positive attitude toward tax shelters. They're legal, ethical, and even patriotic. The tax you don't pay gets invested by the private sector of the Canadian economy, instead of getting spent by the Canadian government.

Do Remember, too, that the advantage of tax shelters is a lot greater than our tax vocabulary would suggest. If you pay $1,000 tax on $2,000 of income, we say you're in a 50% tax bracket. Yet the tax you pay is equal to 100% of what you have left. If you can save the tax by using a tax shelter you *double* the money at work for you. Are you in a 50% tax bracket, or a 100% tax shelter bracket? Think about it!

Do Make your RRSP contributions as early in the calendar year as possible to minimize taxable interest.

Do Use a spousal RRSP to balance income in retirement.

Don't Let tax shelter advantages blind you to underlying weaknesses in the proposed investment.

Don't Get into a MURB or other real estate tax shelters unless you're prepared to hold for 10 years or more.

CHAPTER 10

Sorting Out Your Insurance Priorities

Insurance is not as complicated as most of us think. To use it wisely requires just two things: that your total insurance program leaves no major risks uncovered, and that there is a logical and consistent relationship between the amount you pay for a particular kind of insurance and the amount of protection you're getting.

IDENTIFYING YOUR PRIMARY INSURANCE NEEDS

The first insurance most of us buy is forced on us by our creditors — fire insurance to cover the mortgage on the family home, or collision and comprehensive insurance on the car we've bought with borrowed money. Most of us also contribute to group insurance plans subsidized by our employers, and insure our tangible property such as homes, summer cottages, or boats. Almost everyone buys life insurance. Some of us even buy disability insurance, although most don't — a serious oversight, because omitting it from our insurance planning invites trouble and prevents us from getting the best value for our insurance dollar.

How do you establish priorities among the many different insurance coverages you need?

The answer is simple: your biggest need is for insurance protection on your assets and property that are most valuable; you also must have protection against hazards that pose a relatively high risk of liability for losses by other people. Your first need is to insure the things you find most difficult to replace, or the liabilities that are most onerous to discharge. Ask yourself, "How much could the loss I'm insuring against cost me?" and, "How likely is such a loss?"

Unless you're a millionaire about to retire, or you already are disabled, the biggest financial asset you have is your life. You can't earn money if you're dead. So you begin by insuring your life for an amount that would permit your family to maintain the standard of living they now enjoy, even if you're not around to share it with them. If you have no dependants, you may still want insurance to cover debts, or to fund bequests to parents, siblings, special friends, or favourite causes.

Another primary need is disability insurance. You can't earn money if you can't work; but even if you're permanently disabled, with disability insurance there can be enough money coming in to preserve your standard of living.

There is one other primary insurance need: to insure yourself against the greatest liability you can attract — causing someone else's death or disability. Most of us routinely carry public liability coverage on our cars, but too many Canadians fail to cover their liability in other high-risk activities such as boating or snowmobiling. And we forget to add to our car insurance coverage for things like campers and house-trailers.

The financial implications of death or permanent disability caused by your negligence, or that of some member of your family, can be overwhelming. Your third primary insurance objective should be to protect yourself against any liability that could result from your own negligence.

Remember, your insurance priorities begin with your three primary needs: life insurance, disability income insurance, and public liability insurance.

IDENTIFYING YOUR SECONDARY INSURANCE NEEDS

What comes next? Apply the same two common-sense factors: How much will a loss cost me and what is the probability of such a loss?

Begin with things that are expensive but have a low probability of loss, such as your house. It isn't very likely that your house will burn down. However, if your house *should* be destroyed by fire, the costs of replacing it could be crippling. Insuring your house is therefore a leader among your secondary insurance needs — not just to cover the mortgage, but to protect your equity as well. At the same time you also should think of insuring the contents of your house, your summer cottage or other secondary residence, and its furnishings.

Next, look for things that are relatively inexpensive but could easily be damaged or destroyed, such as a boat or a car. Apply common sense here as well.

If your car is worth only a few hundred dollars, don't bother insuring it; if it is brand new, that's a different story. The same goes for boats. If you have a $300 rowboat that is already six years old, forget the insurance; if your boat sleeps eight and has a mahogany bar in the galley, make sure it's covered.

The same standards apply to liability coverage for damage to property or for bodily injury or death caused by you or your family in low-risk activities such as owning and maintaining a house or having a pet dog. These things are not very likely to happen but, if they did, they could cost you a great deal. Because they *are* unlikely, the insurance premiums for protection against them are relatively low.

The last of your secondary insurance needs is the all-risk coverage you ought to buy for valuable possessions such as jewellery, furs, antiques, or art. They attract thieves, are easily mislaid, and can be burdensome to replace.

DON'T PLAY THE ODDS

Perhaps you are thinking, "Why spend money to protect myself against things that will likely never happen?" Most of the financial disasters insurance could have prevented have their roots in that kind of thinking.

Sure, the possibility of you killing a swimmer or water-skier with your boat is fairly remote. But if it does happen, the ensuing lawsuit and legal costs could ruin you.

The cardinal commandment of intelligent insurance planning is this: ask not what the odds are that it *will* happen, but what it could cost you if it *did* happen. Remember, the odds will always be reflected in the premiums. If the hazard isn't likely to occur, you won't have to pay much to insure it adequately.

Consider your car insurance, for example. Many people have only $300,000 public liability coverage. The possibility of your being successfully sued for any more than that is unlikely. As a result, you may only have to pay 5% more to increase your coverage from $300,000 to $500,000 and only another 5% to increase it to $1,000,000 – a sum which is not excessive given recent court judgments in serious injury cases. That's a bargain when measured against the disastrous consequences of an uninsured judgment against you for more than $300,000.

The same principle applies to your secondary insurance needs – your coverage against accidents on boats or in and around your home. It is unlikely that anyone will be injured or killed as a result of your negligence in maintaining your residence. As a result, the extra premium to increase your coverage from the automatic $100,000 to a more realistic $500,000 would probably be less than $5 per year; and to $1,000,000, only an extra $10 per year.

REDIRECTING YOUR INSURANCE PREMIUM DOLLARS

Canadians buy a lot of insurance, but not all their buying decisions are wise. Ask yourself a few questions about your own coverage. You may discover that changing some of your decisions will make dollars available to buy products that better suit your needs.

Start with your car insurance. Do you really need a deductible of only $25 or $50 on your collision coverage? Couldn't you afford to "self-insure" damages up to $250? If you can handle these amounts out of your cash flow, it would have quite a striking effect on your car insurance premiums.

For example, if you're a thirty-year-old driver in Toronto, have been accident free for five years and drive a medium-priced, late-model car to and from work, you can save up to $75 a year by opting for $250 deductible collision and $25 deductible comprehensive coverage, rather than for $25 deductible "all perils" coverage. That $75 used elsewhere could allow you to:

(a) increase your public liability limit from $300,000 to $1,000,000 at an extra cost of only $10 *and*
(b) add five-year renewable, convertible term life insurance for about $28,000, or
(c) add $200 monthly of non-cancellable guaranteed renewable disability income coverage, or
(d) buy special coverage to protect you against the under-insured person who may run into you.

Don't these alternatives offer much better value for your $75?

Most proud parents like to "take out insurance on the baby," but do you really need life insurance on your children as badly as they need disability income insurance on you? Buying insurance policies for your children is a good thing to do; it is a relatively painless way of saving and guarantees them at least *some* life insurance protection if they run into health problems later. But if it is an either-or situation, insure your earning power first. It's more important to you and to them. Or, if you think you are adequately covered, insure your spouse, whose death would be a real economic loss to the family unit.

Check your life insurance policies for accumulated dividends. Those same dividend dollars might be more wisely invested in term insurance, disability-income coverage on you, life insurance on your spouse, or increased liability limits.

TAKE THE INITIATIVE

Remember that no one cares as much about your insurance priorities as you do. Don't expect your insurance advisers to volunteer to do the "fine tuning" on the allocation of your total insurance dollar. Don't expect your general lines agent to get excited about helping you reduce your premium outlay on car insurance to make dollars available to help pay for disability income coverage. Even if one person handles all your insurance business, both life and general, remember that he or she is probably busy with more customers than he or she has time to serve properly. Your adviser will become concerned if he or she thinks you are concerned, and will answer questions you ask. But do not expect him or her to take this initiative. That is your responsibility.

A CLOSER LOOK AT LIFE INSURANCE

Given a working life of sufficient length, most of us will accumulate a large enough estate — in the form of real estate, pension funds, savings, etc. — to guarantee financial security for our families. Two problems, however, make life insurance essential: first, none of us is *guaranteed* a long enough working life to build that kind of security; second, the normal kind of estate is difficult to turn into money quickly.

Life insurance creates instant cash — capital to ensure there will be no time-gap in your family's income. It can guarantee your family the right to continue enjoying things such as your home and summer cottage, instead of having to sell them for cash.

A monthly premium of as little as $20–$25 can create an instant estate of $100,000 or more, depending on your age, your health, and the type of policy you select.

So life insurance does make sense, but just how much life insurance makes sense for you?

Don't Let the Lump-Sum Value Go to Your Head

Most life insurance policy death benefits are expressed as lump sums. Because you are sure to have some lump-sum obligations, such as debts and taxes, measuring life insurance benefits as lump sums makes sense, up to a point.

On the other hand, the most important job your life insurance will likely perform is to replace your income so that your family can continue to enjoy the standard of living you have built for them.

If you had saved $50,000 and were continuing to earn your income, that $50,000 would be a lot of money. A savings account of $100,000 for a person earning a good income would seem to be a small fortune. But just how much income could either amount generate? With no other source of income available, it would not be enough to keep your family at their current standard of living for more than a few years.

So while you shouldn't forget your lump-sum obligations, don't let them blind you to the real job of your life insurance: *replacing your income.*

Start by Adding Up All Your Lump-Sum Obligations

Adding up your lump-sum obligations is the first step in calculating your life insurance needs. Do not forget to include a provision for "final expenses" — funeral, burial, uninsured pre-death medical expenses, taxes. Plan for enough to pay off *all* your debts, including any mortgages on your home or resort property.

Then, Make Sure There is Enough Money Left to Provide an Income Equal to at Least 50% of Your Current Income

Without you, your family will not need as much income. Look back to the chapter on budgeting where you calculated how much it cost to earn your income. That amount came right off the top of what you really had to spend. You added a lot to the grocery, clothing, and entertainment bills; you needed "walking around" money. If you are not walking around anymore, all of these areas of expenditure can be reduced. Clearing debts, including mortages, with the lump-sum portion of your insurance also will reduce family living costs substantially. So if you provide an amount large enough to generate 50% of the income you are now bringing in, your family should be solvent and independent.

Some insurance people argue that the survivor benefits available from the Canada Pension Plan or the Quebec Pension Plan should be considered as part of that 50% income (1986 scale – CPP: $291.67 [over 65] for a widow, $91.06 for each child regardless of number; QPP $291.67 [over 65] for a widow, $29.00 for each child regardless of number). Others suggest that these benefits should be stacked on top of the 50% income generated from your private insurance program, especially because children's benefits drop off when they get married or reach age eighteen (or age twenty-five if they remain full-time students).

To illustrate the 50% "capital needs" formula, suppose you have developed the following specs on your life insurance needs and resources:

Liquid Assets		*Liabilities*	
Cash in bank	$ 3,000	Mortgage	$40,000
Canada Savings Bonds	$ 7,000	Consumer credit	$ 3,000
Group life insurance	$ 50,000	Total	$43,000
Personal life insurance	$100,000		
Total	$160,000		

Current earned income: $36,000

Objectives at Death:
1. Pay off mortgage and other debts – $43,000
2. Final expense fund – $10,000
3. Education fund – $20,000 (2 children × $10,000 each)
4. Emergency fund – $5,000
5. Provide income of 50% of current income (based on an estimate that the capital sum will provide 6% net interest *after taxes*).
   This is in addition to CPP or QPP survivor benefits.

How much more life insurance, if any, would you need? Here is how to calculate it:

Cash objectives at death	$ 78,000
Capital to generate $14,000 a year from 6% net interest	$235,000
Total needs	$313,000
Less liquid assets	$160,000
Net additional insurance required	$153,000

Of course, once you have decided how much insurance coverage you need, you still have to decide what kind of policy to buy. That decision really isn't as simple as a lot of people would have you believe.

"Buy Term and Invest the Rest" Makes Sense—if You Do Invest the Rest and if Your Investments Work Out Well

Whole life insurance provides permanent protection for a level premium. As a result, the initial premium outlay is higher than for term insurance, which provides protection for a limited period of time only.

Endowment insurance is more expensive than whole life or term because, for a level premium, it guarantees not only that the face amount will be paid at death, but that a certain amount – usually the same as the face amount – will be paid at a specified date (in twenty years, at age sixty-five, etc.). In other words, it is an insured savings plan, and it should be used only where a savings objective takes priority over the need for insurance protection.

Unfortunately, a lot of confusion has surrounded the nature of the whole life contract because most life insurance sales people have been trained to explain it as a contract that is split into a protection portion (the death benefit) and a savings portion (the cash surrender value). It is true that a cash reserve is created to meet the commitment to provide permanent protection for a level premium. But that cash reserve is available to you *only if you give up all or part of your protection*, either permanently or temporarily.

Term vs. Permanent: The Line Blurs

Fortunately for the insurance-buying public, the gulf between "temporary" term insurance and "permanent" whole life insurance has been bridged by the development of new forms of insurance which combine aspects of both term and whole life.

The new hybrids go by different brand names – "perma-term," "term to age 100," "term plus," etc. – but they share common characteristics:

- Protection is available to actuarial absolute ages like 100 or 105 – as "permanent" as any whole life policy.

- Premiums can be *graduated* as in five-year renewable, convertible, or *level* as in term to 100. Premiums can also be prepaid over a relatively short period of time — typically from five to ten years. This "Flex-term" approach is designed to maximize tax-free interest discounts without making the policy "non-exempt" under the new tax rules (dealt with later in this chapter).
- *Paid-up values* are available as an option on many policies; i.e., you can stop paying premiums at some future date having fully paid for part or all of the original death benefits or "face amount."
- *Cash values* are *not* required to make the policies permanent — a fact that makes coverage less expensive than whole life.

Universal Life: Protection and Savings

Another interesting new product development sounds more like a religious cult than a financial instrument. It's called Universal Life. Simply stated, it segregates the protection (death benefit) and the savings and investment (cash values) features of the old whole life or endowment policy.

Universal Life is different, however, in that it typically offers a range of savings and investment alternatives — guaranteed as well as equity — and it allows changes in the relative proportion of the premium dollar being applied to provide death benefits on the one hand and savings and investments on the other.

With Universal Life the investment gain is used to buy the insurance. This feature can be attractive, as there would be no tax on the investment gain used to buy the insurance. If, for example, instead of buying a Universal Life policy your savings were used to buy a GIC, the gain other than the first $1,000 of investment income would be taxable at top marginal rates.

Caution is advised in considering Universal Life, however. Remember that you could create the same combination of ingredients using totally separate insurance vehicles and savings and investment vehicles. There's convenience in buying them at the same "store," but just make sure you're not paying too much for the convenience in the form of commission dollars to the agent, reflected in inferior returns on investment or uncompetitive pricing of the death benefit portion.

You may be able to obtain a better return for your investment dollar by paying off your non-deductible debt, maximizing your RRSPs, and investing in property which could give rise to tax-free capital gains.

Non-Smoker Rates

The definition of "non-smoker" is a person who does not smoke and who has not smoked a *cigarette or cigarillo* in the 12 months previous to his or her application for insurance. With most companies, pipes and cigars are permitted.

If you qualify as a non-smoker, insist on getting non-smoker rates, and shop around. Considerable rate differentials exist between different companies, even on a non-smoker basis.

Table 10.1 illustrates the value of shopping around. Policy B offers higher paid-up values and lower premiums than Policy A.

Table 10.1
The New "Hybrid" Life Insurance Plans:
A Comparison of Level Annual Premiums
Term to Age 100 with Paid-Up Values
(Male; Age 40; Standard Rates; Non-Smoker)

Company	*A*	*B*
Paid-Up Values		
5 years	Nil	Nil
10 years	$16,500	$20,000
20 years	$37,300	$55,400
At age 65	$46,000	$68,700
Annual Premiums		
First year	$ 1,100	$ 980
Thereafter	$ 1,100	$ 980

Table 10.2 dramatizes the severe premium penalty you pay for the luxury of smoking cigarettes. What's the hidden cost of your cigarette habit? Even for only $100,000 death benefit — not a king's ransom these

Table 10.2
"Money Up in Smoke":
Comparison of Smoker's Premium Rates
(All Policy Details the Same as in Table 10.1)

Company	*A*	*B*
Annual Premiums		
First Year	$ 779	$ 929
Thereafter	$ 779	$ 929
Present Value 25 Years' Premiums (discounting @ 8%)	$8,980	$10,709
% Penalty for Smokers (compared to non-smoker rates in Table 10-1)	66.8	77

days – the extra cost is almost 50¢ a day. These figures are for term to 100. The initial outlay for five- or ten-year convertible and renewable term would be substantially less, and for a 40-year-old non-smoker it could be as low as $250 per year for $100,000 worth of coverage for the first five years.

Obviously, there's a high price to pay for not shopping around, and an even stiffer penalty for continuing to indulge your cigarette habit. Why not start shopping, quit smoking, and invest the savings? After all, it's *your* health and money!

TAXATION OF LIFE INSURANCE AND ANNUITIES

Time was when taxation of life insurance cash values was relatively simple. If and when you cashed in your policy for more money than you had paid in premiums, the difference was taxed at regular income tax rates subject to the $1,000 interest deduction, if applicable. Non-insured annuities received the same tax treatment.

With the demon Budget of November 1981, however, the plot thickened, the waters became muddied – and according to some more acid commentators, the cream may have curdled.

What follows is a highly concentrated summary of the effect of changes threatened in November 1981 and finally passed into law in March 1983 as part of Bill C-139:

1. We now have to distinguish between "old" and "new" policies, depending on the date they were originally issued or last subject to a change considered a "reacquisition."

   Old policies are all those issued or "last acquired" *on or before December 1, 1982*. New policies are those issued or "last acquired" after December 1, 1982.
2. "Old" policies will be subject *only* to the old taxation rules illustrated in Table 10.3

Table 10.3
Taxation of Life Insurance: "Old" Rules Applied to an Old Policy
($25,000 Whole Life; Non-Par; Male; Age 40; Smoker)

Annual premium	$ 672.50
Accidental death	33.75
Disability Waiver of Premium	18.75
Total	$ 727.50
Taxation and cash surrender at age 65	
Proceeds on surrender	$14,800.00
Total premiums ($727.50 × 20)	14,550.00
Taxable gain	$ 250.00

3. New policies will be subdivided into "exempt" and "non-exempt" categories.

   The distinction is based on the ratio of cash values to death benefit at different ages. The benchmark is a policy called "20 Pay Endowment at Age 85." If the cash value of a "new" policy is greater at any time than the amount which would accrue in a 20 Pay Endowment at Age 85, then it is non-exempt. If the cash value is always *less* than the amount which would accrue in a 20 Pay Endowment at Age 85, then it is exempt.

   Special rules have been developed to cover situations where exempt policies may become non-exempt, and include grandfathering and anti-abuse rules, which are complex and beyond the scope of *It's Your Money*. However, it is worth noting that a policy, once it has lost its exempt status, can never regain it. This suggests great caution in choice of policy, especially if it contains a cash surrender value.

Taxation of New, Exempt Policies

New policies which qualify as exempt will be subject to tax only on disposition, as will be the case with old policies. Unfortunately, however, for new exempt policies the formula for calculating the amount of taxable gain has been adjusted to eliminate all components of premium not attributable to the buildup of cash values; i.e., the death benefit portion or "pure protection element" and the cost of additional protection features such as disability waiver of premium and "double indemnity" for accidental death. Over a period of several years, this can add up to thousands of dollars in increased taxes.

Table 10.4 illustrates the effect of the new formula.

Table 10.4
Taxation of Life Insurance:
Modified "Old" Rules to Apply to a "New Exempt" Policy
(Same Policy Details as in Table 10.3)

Taxation on Cash Surrender at Age 65

Proceeds on surrender		$14,800
Total premiums	$14,550	
Less: "Pure protection cost"*	(5,550)	
Accidental death	(675)	
Disability Waiver of Premium	(375)	
Adjusted Cost Basis		$ 7,950
Taxable gain		$ 6,850

*"Pure protection cost" figure is an estimate, not a precise actuarial calculation, as it would be in a real-life situation.

Taxation of New, Non-Exempt Policies

"Non-exempt" has an ominous ring, and the tax realities confirm that impression. New, non-exempt policies are subject to two levels of tax: the modified "old" system illustrated in Table 10.4, and a tax every three years on "accrued income" as defined.

Accrued income is calculated as the amount by which the accumulating cash value fund (generally equal to the cash surrender value) exceeds the adjusted cost basis of the policy.

The two levels of tax are integrated in that income brought into tax every three years is added to the adjusted cost basis in determining the amount of taxable gain when the policy is finally "disposed of" on surrender for its cash value.

Tables 10.5, 10.6, and 10.7 illustrate the effect of this tax treatment of "non-exempt" policies.

Table 10.5
Taxation of Life Insurance:
"New" Accrual Tax Rules on a New "Non-exempt" Policy
($25,000 Ten-Payment Whole Life; Female; Age 40; Smoker)

Annual Premium Breakdown		
Total annual premium	$ 896	
Less: Pure protection cost	(150)	
Accidental death	(46)	
Disability Waiver of Premium	(8)	
Net adjusted cost basis		$ 692

Taxation at Death

New, non-exempt policies will be subject to tax at the death of the insured. Tax is calculated as if the insured had disposed of the policy immediately before his or her death (i.e., cashed it in for its cash surrender value). Essentially, the amount subject to tax at death will be the income accrued since the last three-year accrual reporting date — the same as if the insured had cashed in the policy the day before he or she died (in Table 10.7, $500).

Non-Individually Owned Policies

Policies owned by entities other than individual persons (e.g., corporations, trusts, partnerships) are subject to somewhat different rules.

The major difference is that accrued income on non-individually owned, non-exempt policies *must* be reported *annually*, not every three years.

This is an option for individual policy owners but not mandatory.

Table 10.6
Three-Year Accrual Tax Calculation
(25 Years—Age 40 to Age 65)

End of Year	*Cash Surrender Value*	*Total Net Premiums*	*3-Year Accrual Gain*	*Cumulative Net Taxable Gain**
3	$ 1,875	$2,076	$ (201)	—
6	4,875	4,152	723	$ 723
9	8,300	6,228	2,072	1,349
12	10,300	6,920	3,380	1,308
15	11,400	6,920	4,480	1,100
18	12,200	6,920	5,280	800
21	13,100	6,920	6,180	900
24	14,300	6,920	7,380	1,200
25	14,800	6,920	7,880	500

*Cumulative Net Taxable Gain = Total gain less gains previously taxed; e.g., at year 15, $4,480 − ($723 + $1,349 + $1,308) = $1,100.

Table 10.7
Final Tax Calculation on Surrender at Age 65

Proceeds of disposition		$14,800
Less: Total net premiums	$ (6,920)	
Gains previously taxed	(7,380)	
Adjusted Cost Basis		$(14,300)
Terminal taxable gain		$ 500

Planning Implications of the New Tax Rules

How should you respond to these confusing new tax rules in your personal life insurance planning? Here's a list of questions to ask yourself to help simplify decision making:

1. Do I own any policies issued before December 2, 1982? If so, do they have any cash values?

   If the answer is yes to both questions, you should be very careful about any suggestion that you cash in such policies because, as "old" policies, they enjoy highly favourable tax treatment.

   If your "old" policies are term insurance with no cash values, you can deal with the question of replacement more pragmatically, comparing premiums and benefits on available new policies with what you're paying already. But you should recognize that, if you convert an "old" term policy to a cash-value policy after December 1, 1982, the cash-value policy is deemed to be an "old" policy for tax purposes.

This should make you think twice before replacing an "old" term policy with a "new" one, especially if rate differences are marginal or you think that a future conversion to a cash-value policy is a strong possibility.

2. Do I own any "new" cash-value policies? If so, which are exempt or non-exempt?

   On this point, you should consult an expert — your life insurance agent or financial planner, or the head office of the insurance company.

   If you find you have a non-exempt policy and want to exchange it for an exempt policy, contact your agent or planner or the head office for advice on how to proceed and any possible tax implications. It is worth noting that 85% of new cash value policies in force are "exempt," including popular forms such as whole life and life paid up at age 65.*

Taxation of Annuities

The new three-year accrual tax rules apply equally to non-insured deferred annuity contracts. This has seriously reduced the attractiveness of such accumulation plans from the standpoint of tax deferral.

Taxation of Individually Owned Annuity Contracts

For purposes of tax treatment, annuity contracts must be divided into two broad categories:

1. *Deferred* annuity contracts, in which value is *accumulating* through new deposits and/or interest on previous deposits and no payments are being made out of the contract; and
2. *Immediate* annuity contracts, from which payments are being made to an annuitant, into which no new contributions are being made, and in which interest is being earned, but on a reducing capital balance.

Deferred Annuity Contracts

Under the old rules, taxation of deferred annuity contracts mirrored closely the treatment of cash-value life insurance policies. In fact, you could think of them as cash-value policies without the "mortality gain" at death.

---

*This statistic was provided by the Institute of Chartered Life Underwriters of Canada (CLU), an affiliate of the Life Underwriters Association of Canada (LUAC), whose Action Committee Taxation lobbied vigorously and successfully to modify the severe tax penalties originally announced in the November 1981 Budget.

Under the new rules, this analogy holds true but, unfortunately, any new annuity contracts are automatically considered *non-exempt* with a few exceptions. In other words, accumulating values will almost always be subject to the three-year tax on accrued income — seriously reducing their attractiveness.

Some good news, however: consistent with the rules for traditional income-producing investments, the new legislation permits the deductibility of interest on funds borrowed to acquire annuity contracts.

Exceptions From the Accrual Tax

The following individually owned annuity contracts are not subject to the accrual rules:

1. A contract "last acquired" before December 2, 1982 under which annuity payments have commenced before the date (including a settlement option under a life insurance contract).
2. A "locked-in" deferred annuity contract acquired before December 2, 1982 and where no change can be made in the original timing and terms of payments out of the contract.
3. A "prescribed" annuity contract; i.e., essentially one in which payments have already commenced to a person over age 60 (unless permanently and totally disabled) and where the payments are for a fixed term or the lifetime of the annuitant (and the annuitant's spouse, if desired) and where guarantee periods cannot extend beyond the annuitant's age 90.

Taxation During the Accumulation Period

All other individually owned contracts will be subject to tax on accrued income as follows:

- For those issued in December 1982 or after, income must be reported first in 1985.
- For annuity contracts acquired before December 2, 1982, the three-year intervals are counted from December 31, 1984; i.e., the first reporting of accrual income will be on December 31, 1987. At that time, all income accrued after 1981 must be reported.

After these initial reporting dates, tax will be levied on growth at the end of each third calendar year.

Unallocated income accrued before 1982 will be taxed at the time of disposition of the contract (as with cash-value insurance if cashed in a lump sum; as described below if annuity payments are elected).

Taxation During Payout

The following rules apply:

- When payments begin, there is no deemed disposition of the contract.

- For contracts not subject to the new accrual rules, taxation of payments will follow the old rules; i.e., each payment will be divided into a taxable "interest" portion and a non-taxable "return of capital" portion, and the dollar amount of the respective portions will remain *constant* throughout the payment period.
- Annuity payments subject to the accrual rules will be divided into interest and return of capital portions. Their respective dollar amounts, however, will vary from year to year in much the same way as with blended mortgage payments, where the taxable interest portion starts out high and gradually decreases over time — and vice versa for the non-taxable return of capital portion.

  This means that more tax will be paid in the early years than under the old formula and less later on, obviously reducing the overall value of tax deferral.

Non-Individually Owned Annuity Contracts

Generally, the rules are the same as for individually owned contracts, except that accrual tax must be reported annually.

Planning Implications of the New Tax Rules

1. If you are within three years of retirement, investigate whether there may be some advantage in investing in a deferred annuity contract now and either cashing in the lump sum or starting annuity payments after your retirement, when you can control your tax bracket through rollovers of pension to RRSP or rolling RRSP income to another RRSP (to December 31, 1989).
2. If you foresee high income for a period of years followed by a period of low income (e.g., if you are close to retirement), consider borrowing to buy an annuity and deducting interest from your high current taxable income. Even if you are more than three years from retirement, there could be advantage in the fact that interest is deductible annually, while income is taxed only every three years. Make sure, however, that net income exceeds net interest cost.

   As with cash-value life insurance, consult your agent or financial planner or another adviser before making moves in this new and complex environment.

WHAT? ME NEED DISABILITY INSURANCE?

This most neglected of all forms of insurance is one of your primary insurance needs. If you think disability can't happen to you, examine the odds. How many people become disabled and for how long? Table 10.8 gives the answers.

Table 10.8
Relative Chances of Disability

Age	*Chances of Disability versus Death*
30	2.7 to 1
40	2.3 to 1
50	1.8 to 1
59	1.6 to 1

If you still think disability isn't as serious a hazard as death, consider the figures in Table 10.9.

Table 10.9
Relative Length of Disability

Age	*Disabled for 6 months*	*Disabled for 1 year*	*Disabled for 2 years*	*Disabled for 5 years*
25	34%	27%	22%	15%
30	33	26	22	15
35	33	26	21	15
40	32	25	21	15
45	30	24	20	14
50	28	23	19	14

When you look at the odds closely they are pretty frightening. But most Canadians don't know that, so they ignore the need for disability insurance. And too many life insurance agents don't try to sell disability coverage—either because they don't know enough about it, or their company doesn't have a good product, or because disability premiums might reduce the number of dollars available to buy high-commission life insurance.

If you still think the other person is the one who'll get disabled, and say, "It can't happen to me, I never get sick," look at the tables again; 22% of the people aged twenty-five who say that will be proven wrong to the tune of two years' income.

The Case for Individual Disability Income Insurance

Disability coverage is available to all of us through government plans and to most of us through group coverage at work or through a professional association. Before you decide you don't need individual coverage, consider the following hard facts:

The amounts paid through Canada and Quebec Pension Plan benefits are inadequate for most people. For instance, on the 1986 scale the maximum benefit for a disabled contributor with three minor children is $729.82 a month under CPP and $684.96 under QPP. Try to build a budget on that! Besides, the definition of disability under CPP and QPP regulations is so stringent that, in effect, you have to be permanently and irreversibly disabled to qualify for benefits.

Unemployment Insurance pays disability benefits, but they last for only fifteen weeks. What do you do after that?

Workers' Compensation covers you adequately only for disabilities from on-the-job accidents or occupational diseases. But what about weekend driving on the highway, or the coronary that had nothing to do with dust levels in your factory?

Most employer group plans are non-portable. Your group long-term disability coverage stops thirty days after you leave the company, and is *not* convertible. If you leave your present job to go out on your own or into a company without adequate group disability coverage, you will have to hope that your health is good enough to allow you to buy individual coverage. If it is not, you could be out of luck.

Most association group plans can be cancelled by the insurance company. If that happens and you are uninsurable, you could be out in the cold.

The only totally portable benefits are available through your own personal disability coverage. It is the one plan you can tailor to suit your needs and pocketbook – and keep as long as you need it.

When you are buying disability income coverage, it pays to be paranoid. Disability income contracts can be more complicated than life insurance policies because of the problems of defining disability, duration, recurrence, and partial disability. To make sure you are getting a top-quality product, ask the following questions:

1. Is the policy non-cancellable and guaranteed renewable to age 65 or longer?
2. For what period of time is disability defined in terms of your occupation rather than in terms of "any occupation for wage or profit"? (This is most important for specialist professional practitioners.)
3. Is loss of speech, hearing, sight, or the use of two limbs considered to be total disability under this policy?
4. What about waiver of premium? Does it continue beyond the benefit period? Are premiums paid during disability refunded when the waiver does come into effect?
5. Does the sickness definition refer to manifestation of symptoms rather than the illness itself commencing during the contract period?
6. Is the contract free of time limitations between date of injury and beginning of disability?

7. Is the policy incontestable after two years regardless of any claims?
8. Is the only policy exclusion an act or accident of war?
9. Are options available for increasing income benefits in the future, without evidence of good health?
10. Does the policy provide benefits during a period of rehabilitation or retraining?
11. Are benefits indexed for inflation?

If you get a "yes" answer to all these questions, the policy you're getting is among the best available.

How Much Is Enough Disability Insurance?

Don't lose sleep over this one. The insurance companies have solved it for you. Because benefits from personal disability coverage are tax free as you receive them, and because the companies like to keep a gap between what you were making while working and what they'll pay you while you're disabled, you are restricted to insuring 60% to 70% of your gross income minus any benefits already in force.

Your agent can give you details on how your group and personal benefits may be integrated with benefits from government plans but, boiling it all down, the message is simple. Take as much personal disability income coverage as the insurance company offers you. If you have fully disclosed all sources of benefit available to you, they will not offer you more than you need.

SUMMING UP

The objective is to use insurance properly and to get the best value for your insurance dollars.

First, get your priorities straight. Unless you are already rich, disabled, or very close to retirement age, your biggest asset is your own ability to earn income. It is also your most vulnerable asset. People do die or become disabled, so insure yourself against both eventualities. Make sure you are adequately protected against liability for the lives and physical health of others. Since this is the most potentially crushing risk, provide for it realistically.

Second, find good advisers. Remember, if you have chosen well, they will be good advisers; so treat them accordingly — not like snake oil peddlers. You will hear more about this in the chapter on choosing professional advisers.

Insurance isn't much fun, but it is crucially important to you and to the people who depend on you for their financial well-being. Combine one bad insurance decision with a little bad luck, and an uninsured claim could wipe out the fruits of years of careful budgeting, saving, and investing.

DO'S AND DON'TS

Life Insurance

Do Check beneficiary designations in your life insurance policies to make sure they comply with the terms and objectives of your will.

Do Use an automatic monthly bank withdrawal system to pay your premiums. The extra cost is only about 7% and it makes it easier for you to budget.

Do Review your insurance needs at least once every two years and whenever significant changes take place (marriage, new baby, new job, new home, going into your own business, adding a partner).

Do Figure out how much protection you need and how much you can pay, and then decide what kind of insurance you should carry.

Do Add valuable riders such as total disability waiver of premium, guaranteed insurability options, mortgage insurance (reducing term), family insurance (on spouse and children).

Don't Buy an "education" endowment on your new baby unless you are satisfied that both you and your spouse are adequately covered. If the child dies, you lose the family allowance cheque; if you or your spouse die, the child loses a lot more.

Don't Buy whole life as a savings plan.

Disability Income Insurance

Do Insist on a non-cancellable, guaranteed renewable contract.

Do Check to see if "step rate" coverage is available to keep costs down for five or ten years till you can afford level premium coverage.

Don't Assume you are covered at work. Check to make sure. How much? For how long? Is it portable?

Car Insurance

Do Apply the money you save by taking a higher collision deductible and use it to increase your public liability coverage to $500,000 or $1,000,000.

Do Check with your agent to make sure your car insurance company will give you at least one "free" accident before they start charging you extra because you have lost your accident-free premium credits.

Don't Get talked into $25 or $50 deductible collision coverage and no deductible comprehensive coverage. If you cannot afford to pay $100, $250 or even $500 to put your car back on the road, reread Chapter 2 on budgeting and/or get a new job.

Don't Assume your house-trailer is covered automatically for public liability under your regular car insurance policy. Only two-wheeled "utility" trailers are covered.

Don't Assume that clothes and cameras you leave in your car are covered under the theft coverage on your car. They are not, and if they are stolen from an unlocked car, they won't be covered under the "off premises" coverage on your Homeowner or Tenant's Package policy. Always lock the car!

Boat Insurance

Don't Cover the boat for physical damage only.

Don't Assume it will be covered for liability under the comprehensive personal liability coverage attached to your Homeowner or Tenant's Package policy. Without extra premiums most companies will not cover boats powered by outboards of more than 25 hp and inboards of more than 50 hp. Investigate separate liability coverage on the boat, if necessary.

Contents Insurance

Do Keep receipts for major purchases in a file at the office or in your safety deposit box, not at your residence.

Do Make an inventory of the contents of your apartment or home and keep it in the same place off the premises.

Do Insure valuables such as jewellery, furs, firearms, cameras, sporting equipment, art, antiques, and stamp and coin collections on a separate schedule for "all risk" coverage, including "mysterious disappearances" (i.e., loss as opposed to theft) and on a "valued" basis (i.e., with no reduction for depreciation). If you can't afford this kind of coverage, put small items in your safety deposit box and buy an inexpensive SDB bond to protect you in case the bank is robbed.

Don't Assume the insurance company will accept your lump-sum guess if you attempt to list from memory everything you have lost.

House Insurance

Do Insure to 100% of replacement cost (new for old) and insist on an "inflation escalator" clause to protect against increases in replacement costs.

Do Ask your agent to do an evaluation of replacement cost on your home, rather than guessing at it yourself.

Do Increase your coverage if you make substantial improvements or additions to your house.

Do Make sure the contents of your home are covered for replacement cost, i.e., new for old.

Do Make sure extra hazard liability exposure such as a swimming pool, domestic servants, tenants occupying a basement apartment, draft or saddle animals are covered under the comprehensive personal liability coverage.

Do Be sure, if you live in a condominium, that the management company has adequate insurance on the building itself plus special coverage on the interior walls and fittings in your unit, which usually are not covered in the basic building policy.

Don't Assume you can get by with partial coverage because you will never have a total loss. Even if you suffer only a partial loss, the "optional settlement" clause may mean that you will recover only part of your partial loss unless you are insured to at least 80% of value.

Don't Forget to add voluntary compensation coverage for occasional servants. Why get cleaned out financially because your cleaning woman breaks her leg on your icy driveway?

CHAPTER 11

Retirement: Is There Life After Work?

Answer the following questions quickly:

1. How much income will you need to live on after your retirement?
2. How much income can you count on from all sources, including government pension plans?
3. What changes do you intend to make in your lifestyle after retirement?
4. What financial implications will these changes have?

Few Canadians under age 50 can give anything but vague answers to these four questions — and that's unfortunate.

Not that retirement should be a source of financial panic for middle-income people in Canada: all of us will receive certain retirement benefits from the government. Many of us belong to private pension plans. Even more have stored money in RRSPs. And by the time we want to retire, almost all of us will have accumulated some private assets that can be converted into income, if necessary.

But like every other financial problem we face, the question is, "Will it be enough?" We can deal with reduced income at retirement more easily and effectively if we do a little realistic planning — starting a long time before we retire. After all, one purpose of good financial management is to eliminate worry about money, and that should apply to your retirement finances too.

As a first step in projecting your after-retirement financial requirements, ask yourself, "How do I want to live after I have retired?" Then draw up a list of lifestyle options you hope to enjoy at that time.

LISTING YOUR LIFESTYLE OPTIONS

A lot more than money is involved when we stop working. By the time we finally retire, our raises and promotions have been one important way to measure our own worth. Most of us will have been getting up and going out on the job for almost forty years. And the challenges we have faced and met have had a lot to do with our self-respect. Our jobs have helped us meet people, and among them are some of our closest friends who have a great deal in common with us. And, perhaps just as important, our jobs have taken a great deal of time off our hands.

At retirement we have not only that time to fill, but emotional and social vacuums as well. Social adjustment to retirement is not easy. That is why retirement is no time to have financial problems to add to your anxieties. And that is why more and more companies are offering counselling to older employees, and community colleges, the YMCA, and others are offering courses designed to help us fill those forty hours a week that are suddenly empty.

Obviously, you can't predict what you might want to do every day of the year. But you know your own tastes, and you know what you have always wanted to do but have never quite got around to. These unfulfilled ambitions should go on your list of lifestyle options. They're not things you're necessarily going to do, just things you want to be able to do.

For instance, what about travel? During our active careers, most of us travel a lot less than we'd like to. Maybe you'd like to go on one long trip around the world. Or you might like to winter in the sun every year. Perhaps you'd like to spend most of each year in one place, where you have friends and family, and the rest travelling to new and different places.

What about hobbies? A personal plan could include gardening, and that could mean buying a house with a bigger lot so you have room to operate.

Where do you want to live? Do you want to keep your house, or would you rather move into an apartment, where fewer things will need fixing.

What about family obligations you'd like to meet? Sending your granddaughter to medical school if she wants to go, or financing a trip to Europe for her before she settles into a job — these might be some of your priorities.

Your answers to questions like these should go down on your list of retirement lifestyle options. The next step is to get some sense of how much these things will really cost.

How Much Income Will You Need?

Inflation makes it impossible to predict the exact amount of money you will require upon retirement. However, you can come close by starting with what you will need in current dollars. For example, if you feel that $20,000 will cover all your expenses in 1986, and that inflation will continue at the rate of 5% for the 25 years from now until you retire, you will need $67,720 (20 × $3,386) per year on which to live; at 10% inflation you will need about $217,000 (20 × $10,834). (See Table 11.1.)

Remember, too, that these figures are after-tax. To get an idea of how much pre-tax income you'd need, you should "gross up" the after-tax figure by anywhere from 20% to 60%, depending on what your average tax rate is likely to be.

That's the bad news — let's look at the good news.

Table 11.1
Inflation Equivalents of $1,000

Years	*Annual Inflation Rate*				
	3%	*5%*	*7½%*	*10%*	*12%*
1	$1,030	$1,050	$1,075	$ 1,100	$ 1,120
5	1,159	1,276	1,435	1,610	1,762
10	1,344	1,629	2,061	2,593	3,105
15	1,558	2,079	2,958	4,177	5,473
20	1,806	2,653	4,247	6,727	9,646
25	2,094	3,386	6,098	10,834	17,000

When You Retire You'll Have Some Major Reductions in Living Costs

You'll have the obvious savings — that portion of your income you had to spend to earn the income itself. Your clothing bills, for instance, should decline.

Chances are your mortgage will be paid off by then, so you will realize a big reduction in your living costs. But don't make the mistake of assuming that you'll have to pay nothing for your housing. Remember the operating costs of your home such as heat and electricity. Taxes on real property probably will go up with general price levels. Maintenance costs will increase, because as you grow older you may not be able to do as many things for yourself. You may even need to make some health-related changes to your residence to make sure it is safe and comfortable.

On the other hand, your grocery bill will probably be lower since your children will be on their own by then. And you'll probably find yourself spending less on furniture, because you will have accumulated just about all you'll need.

In addition, you won't have to contribute to Unemployment Insurance, Canada Pension Plan, or a private pension plan.

If you were to enjoy reductions like these *now* at your current income level, you probably would find that your living costs are reduced by 30% or more. The amount of income required to cover these costs would be reduced further because marginal tax rates decrease as total income decreases.

As a result you'll probably find you could get by on 50%-70% of your inflation-adjusted current income.

Part of this income will be provided by Canada Pension Plan and Old Age Security, both of which are indexed to increases in the Consumer Price Index (CPI).

As a result of all these allowances for reduced costs and additional sources of income, your personal retirement objective could be as low as 40%-55% of your total retirement income need — based on a straight inflation-adjusted projection of your total current income between now and when you retire.

Be Capital Conscious

Your pension income in retirement will be just that — a stream of monthly payments, from government and employer, which will last at least as long as you live, and perhaps longer if you've opted for survivor benefits under your private pension plan.

To generate private income, however, you first have to accumulate capital and then convert it to income in the form of interest, dividends, rents, annuity payments, or some combination of these components. For instance, if you determine that you'll need $30,000 pre-tax from private sources, and you want to earn it from dividends at 8%, you'll have to accumulate $375,000. If, on the other hand, you're prepared to "trade in" your capital for a life annuity of $30,000, you'll need a lot less (e.g., at age 65, approximately $250,000).

Tax treatment is a factor as well. For instance, interest income, and income from RRSPs, is fully taxable (at least over $1,000), but income from rents, Canadian dividends, and "non-registered" annuity payments all enjoy a measure of advantage which reduces the net impact of income tax. Therefore, if you want to do a more detailed calculation, you should estimate how much of your total retirement income will come from these different sources.

Once you have decided how much capital you'll need in retirement, it is time to start evaluating the financial arrangements you're already making. By doing this you can see just how much money you are going to have when you retire.

ACCUMULATING SUFFICIENT INCOME

We are often asked, "How much should I save every year to make sure I have sufficient income upon retirement?" Earlier in the book we suggested you pay yourself 10% of your income. If you follow this suggestion faithfully as your income rises, you should have accumulated sufficient assets to turn into income. If, however, you have started late in the savings game or are self-employed, or want to retire early, you may want to increase this to 15% or 20% of your income.

Let's be more specific about some sources of retirement income. These include government benefits, your company pension plan, and your own investments.

Government Benefits

You start off knowing you're going to be entitled to certain government benefits. Canada Pension Plan will pay you 25% of the average income you earned during your final three years of employment, up to a maximum that will be equal to the average wage in Canada. In 1986 this maximum income is $25,800 and is indexed to remain at that level in "constant dollars."

Everyone over sixty-five gets Old Age Security. In 1986 it is $288.34 a month and is adjusted every three months for inflation as measured by the Consumer Price Index.

Table 11.2
Income from Government Plans 1986 Level, Starting at Age 65

CPP/QPP	*Old Age Security*		*Total for a*
	Husband	*Wife*	*Married Couple*
$486/mo.*	$288/mo.	$288/mo.	$1,062/mo.

*This assumes that your earnings over the three years preceding retirement exceed $25,800 each year, and that only one spouse qualifies for CPP.

Private Pension Plans

Your major source of retirement income will probably be your pension plan, but just what kind of pension plan is it? If you already belong to a pension plan, you can't calculate the additional income you'll need until you know just how your plan works and what kind of income it will generate.

If you're in the happy position of being able to choose between two or more pension plans – if you're considering job offers from several employers or if your employer just now is establishing a pension plan for you – it helps to know how the various plans work.

All pension plans have the same objective: they help you and your employer take income you earn now and store it to provide you with an income after you retire. In Canada, both you and your employer can deduct contributions to pension plans for tax purposes. (In the United States only the employer can make such deductions, so it is normal for only the employer to contribute to the plan. In Canada most plans call for contributions from the employee as well.)

Your employer gets several benefits from operating a good pension plan. Most employers really are concerned about the people who work for them, and setting up an adequate pension plan is a good way of making sure they won't run into financial troubles later. Since pension plans normally return their greatest benefit only to employees who retire, a good plan will encourage greater work force stability for the employer. Also, a good plan can help an employer compete for good employees.

Types of Pensions

There are only two basic structures for a company- or union-operated pension plan. The first is called a Defined Contribution Plan. The amount contributed by both employer and employee is fixed, and the benefits paid by the plan will be whatever can be bought at retirement when the accumulated value in your account is converted to an annuity. The type of plan is also referred to as a Money Purchase plan. A typical Defined Contribution Plan would call for both the employer and the employee to contribute 5% of the employee's annual salary to the plan. A common alternative would be for the employer's share to be, for instance, 2% plus a special contribution to be determined each year. Union plans may call for contributions in relation to the number of hours worked.

The actual pension provided will vary with the size of the contribution made and the income earned by investments over the years the money is in the plan. If the contribution is made many years before retirement, there will be more investment income than if contributions have been made only a few years before retirement. As interest rates or other investment factors change, the level of investment income earned in the pension plan also will change.

Pension income can be guaranteed now through the purchase of an insurance company deferred annuity, or the money can be accumulated in a fund until retirement and the accumulated value used at that time to purchase a pension from an insurance company (immediate annuity).

In either case, you can't predict what your pension will be. A realistic basis for your own planning will be to assume that the total amount you save will yield about 8% per year, and that annuity rates will remain at or near current levels.

The second kind of pension plan is the Defined Benefit Plan. In this plan, a clear formula is set out for the amount of income the plan will deliver at retirement – usually based on a combination of earnings and years of service. Then it's up to the employer to make sure there's enough money in the plan to deliver benefits at that promised level.

Provincial laws require the employer to make his or her contributions to the plan adequate to pay for the promised benefits. This assures that the plan really will be able to deliver the predetermined benefit.

Obviously, in this kind of plan the employer has a vested interest in keeping administrative costs low and investment income high. But once you as an employee have made your contribution, your worries are over. By applying the benefit formula and estimating your future income, you can measure approximately how much income the plan will generate for you. Then you know what private arrangements to make to supplement government and company pension benefits.

All this makes the benefit formula very important. Basically there are three types.

The first is the *Flat Benefit*. It usually is found in union-sponsored plans for hourly paid workers. The benefit is expressed as a flat monthly income multiplied by the number of years worked. For instance, if the basic benefit is $25 per month, a retiring employee with twenty years' service would receive a pension income of $500 per month. A variation of this formula would set the benefit at $500 a month and require twenty years' service to qualify. For less than twenty years of service, there would be proportionate reductions in the income provided.

The second is the *Career Average Benefit*. This is very popular with medium-sized employers. Here your pension is expressed as a percentage of your average annual income over your whole career multiplied by the number of years you've worked. For example, the formula might offer 2% of the average income for each year worked. In that case, if you had worked for twenty years, you could retire with an income equal to 40% of your average earnings over your whole career. Note that this will inevitably be less than 40% of the employee's income at the time of retirement because early, low-paid years will pull down the average.

The third formula—and the most attractive to the employee—is called the *Final Average Benefit*. Here the pension is based on the average salary over a short period of time immediately before retirement. The most common periods are the last five years of employment, or the last three years. In any case, the formula will provide for a given percentage of the average salary over this final period multiplied by the number of years worked. For instance, if the formula provides for an income equal to 2% of the final period average for each year worked, and you have twenty years' service, you will receive an income equal to 40% of your income over this final period, which is almost always the period of highest average income as well.

Defined Benefit RPPs are subject to maximum benefit amounts—2% of salary to a maximum of $1,715 multiplied by number of years of service to a maximum of 35 years. For higher-paid executives with long service, these maximums often reduce pension below what otherwise would be payable under the company formula.

Example 1
Company formula: 2% of final 3-year average salary × # of years of service
Employee final 3-year average salary: $100,000
Years of service: 37

Pension from company formula = $100,000 × 2% × 37 = $74,000
Pension from government formula = $1,715 × 35 = $60,025

Example 2
Company formula: Same as in Example 1
Employee final 3-year average salary: $110,000
Years of service: 25

Pension from company formula = $110,000 × 2% × 25 = $55,000
Pension from government formula = $1,715 × 25 = $42,875

Many employers are moving to prevent this arbitrary reduction in retirement benefits by introducing a supplementary retirement income benefit to make up the difference between the amount payable under the company formula and the amount payable under the government formula.

Funding of the plan is similar to that for deferred compensation; that is, no deductible contributions can be made, but company accounting procedures should recognize a contingent liability. The *payment* of the benefit is different, of course, in that a stream of income payments is made rather than a lump sum.

Arrangements can be made to provide a broad range of annuity options similar to those under the basic pension plan or, alternatively, have some paid out as a lump sum retiring allowance and transferred to an RRSP.

Which Plan Will Work Best for You?

As protection against inflation, a Final Average Benefit Plan is best for you. If you are lucky enough to be in such a plan you can predict your retirement income by projecting your salary based on an inflation assumption.

It's worth noting that under certain conditions other kinds of pension plans can be very advantageous to employees. For instance, although a Defined Contribution or Money Purchase Plan gives benefits that don't necessarily relate to your income, contributions made at younger ages (under forty-five years old, for instance) will earn greater pension value than you might receive under a Career Average Plan. In fact, if you are a long-term employee and if there is little or no inflation, it is possible for you to end up with a pension that actually *exceeds* your final salary.

The Flat Benefit Plan assures you the same benefit for each year you work, regardless of your length of service or your salary. In occupations where income actually declines in the last few years before retirement, this can be an advantage.

The drag-down effect of your low-paid early years on the pension paid by a Career Average Plan doesn't necessarily apply these days. In the face of severe inflation, many employers are considering extra contributions to upgrade the pension benefits to make sure the retiring employee will receive a realistic benefit. This is often done by "dropping off" earlier, lower-income years from the career average calculation. When you are evaluating your own plan, check to see whether or not your company has done this over past high-inflation years.

No matter what kind of pension plan you are in, measure the probable benefits you will receive as a percentage of your final earnings just before retirement. This will give you an idea of the additional income you will need to enjoy the lifestyle options you want for your retirement years.

If You Change Jobs, You May Lose Substantial Pension Protection

In many pension plans, if you leave the company before retirement, you receive only your contributions to the plan plus interest. Alternatively, you may leave a deferred pension entitlement sitting in the fund.

Benefits are said to be "vested" if you have a right to your employer's contributions even if you leave the company before retirement. Some plans provide no vesting for the first ten years in the plan, then provide 100% vesting after ten years' service.

Another common system is called partial vesting. Here the company might vest 10% of the employer's contributions after one year and add a further 10% for each year thereafter. Under this formula, an employee with ten years' service would have 100% vesting.

Other pension plans offer conditional vesting. Here the employer's contributions are available to the employee only if he or she leaves his or her own contributions in the fund. This way the employee is encouraged to preserve his or her right to a retirement benefit rather than take the cash and spend it.

In several provinces and in industries regulated by the Federal Employment Standards Act, 100% vesting is required when you reach age forty-five, provided you have ten years of service. All contributions from both employer and employee must be left in the plan to provide a retirement benefit, although there *is* a provision that allows the employer to permit 25% of the benefit to be taken in cash when employment is terminated. In some provinces, vesting must take place before ten years. In Ontario, starting in 1987, vesting must take place after two years.

Keep in mind that any money you take out of a pension plan — except for the first $1,000 — will be taxed as income in the year you take it. One alternative is to move the cash into another registered plan such as an RRSP. Also consider that if you do take out your contributions you may receive a very low rate of interest on them because pension plans are designed to deliver pensions, and those who leave before the pension starts often get only minimal benefits.

The Path of Pension Reform

In February 1984, the Liberal government introduced sweeping changes in the rules governing pension contributions, benefits, and portability of such benefits. The proposed legislation never became law because Parliament was prorogued to pave the way for the September 1984 election, and the reform measures died on the order paper.

Then, in May 1985, the newly elected Progressive Conservative government introduced proposals similar to what had been introduced in 1984. Most obvious were increases in the tax-deductible contribution

Table 11.3
The Proposed New RPP[1], DPSP[2] and RRSP[3] Contribution Limits

	RPP		DPSP	RRSP[3]		
Year	*Def. Ben.*	*Def. Con.*	*(Employer)*	*In Def. Ben. RPP*	*In Def. Cont. RPP or DPSP*	*Not in RPP or DPSP*
	$	$	$	$	$	$
1985	3,500[4]	3,500[4]	3,500	3,500[5]	3,500[5]	5,500
1986	3,500[4]	3,500[4]	3,500	3,500[5]	3,500[5]	7,500
1987	9,500[6]	9,500[6]	4,750	2,000[7]	9,500[8]	9,500
1988	11,500	11,500	5,750	2,000	11,500	11,500
1989	13,500	13,500	6,750	2,000	13,500	13,500
1990	15,500	15,500	7,750	2,000	15,500	15,500
1991	15,500[9]	15,500[9]	7,750[9]	2,000	15,500[9]	15,500[9]

Notes:

Unless otherwise noted, contribution limits are the *lesser* of the dollar limit indicated and 20% of qualifying income in 1985 and 1986, 18% thereafter.

The definition of qualifying income is scheduled for restriction in 1987 and thereafter. Net rental income, pension, and RRSP income will be eliminated from the list of qualifying sources, leaving only employment, self-employed and business income on the list.

[1]Employee contributions.
[2]Employer contributions.
[3]Employee (personal) contributions only.
[4]Less any RRSP contribution.
[5]Less any RPP contribution.
[6]Less employer DPSP, or employee RRSP contributions; ditto for 1988 and subsequent years.
[7]$2,000 limit will probably be increased depending on the assessment of the particular Defined Benefit RPP against the benefit levels in a "profile plan."
[8]Less employer RPP or DPSP contributions; ditto for 1988 and subsequent years.
[9]Contribution limits will be indexed to the average wage in 1991 and thereafter.

limits to Registered Pension Plans (RPPs), Deferred Profit Sharing Plans (DPSPs), and Registered Retirement Savings Plans (RRSPs). In addition, measures were introduced to restrict the ability of members of Defined Benefit pension plans to make voluntary contributions to RPPs or RRSPs.

Of more concern to employers was the proposal to reduce maximum vesting delays to two years. There was some discussion of minimum inflation indexing requirements.

By early 1986, two-year vesting had been introduced, although the requirement of minimum indexing was not introduced. It seems clear, however, that the path of pension reform will continue in the direction of greater portability and flexibility of contribution formulas — good news for you in your quest to provide adequate income in your retirement.

VOLUNTARY PENSION CONTRIBUTIONS

Whether or not you are in a good company pension plan, it is wise to maximize your RRSP contributions. One alternative to RRSP contributions is that of past service contributions to a pension plan. If you have worked for an organization and at some stage during your employment with them you did not contribute to a pension plan, you may at some later date contribute up to $3,500 to make up for each year you did not contribute. If you add this to your current service contributions you may contribute up to $7,000 in one year, all of which is tax deductible. If you make maximum current service and/or past service contributions, you will not be able to make a deduction for an RRSP in the same year. You should note, however, that you will not be able to make voluntary current service contributions after 1986.

Assuming you are eligible to contribute for past service, there is another element to consider. You should make voluntary past service pension contributions only if you are fairly certain you will stay with the employer until retirement or that your contributions will earn a competitive rate of interest. This can be accomplished by setting up a segregated fund for employee voluntary contributions, with a choice of guaranteed and equity funds.

To supplement pension and RRSP contributions, follow the savings and investments ideas outlined elsewhere in this book. They will help you accumulate the amount of money you need for retirement.

WHAT TO DO WHEN YOU RETIRE

Don't discard the idea of a part-time job when you retire. You have experience and ideas that can be put to good use. It will provide you with extra income, and help you retain a feeling of self-worth that's vital. Whether you work or not, make your money work harder by using the following ideas on tax deferral and reduction.

1. When you retire do not create any more taxable income than necessary. As a hedge against further erosion of the dollar due to inflation

we think about 20% of your assets should be invested to produce deferred income.

2. Remember, you may transfer into an RRSP income received from Canada Pension Plan, your company pension plan, and Old Age Security. These transfers may be made in addition to your regular RRSP contributions, but only until December 31, 1989. If you receive a lump sum retiring allowance, remember you can defer tax on an amount equal to $2,000 multiplied by your years of service with the employer by "rolling" it to an RRSP.
3. You and your spouse may both receive $1,000 of private pension income tax-free at age 65. If your spouse is not earning any income, contribute to an RRSP for your spouse an amount large enough to produce an annuity of at least $1,000 per year to commence at age 65.
4. Several different income options are available when you convert your RRSP into income. These include life annuity (with different contingent guarantees to spouse and/or for a minimum number of payments), term certain annuity to age ninety, and Registered Retirement Income Fund (RRIF) to age ninety. Choose your options carefully, because mistakes can be costly.
5. When you're in the market for an annuity, get several quotations. Table 11.4 illustrates the variation in annuity rates among companies.
6. Remember that you must convert all RRSPs into income no later than the end of the year in which you turn 71.
7. Even if you are over 71, you can still claim a deduction for a contribution made to an RRSP on behalf of your spouse, until the end of the year your spouse becomes 71.
8. As you get closer to retirement, invest more conservatively. As a general rule, switch from equity to guaranteed investments to avoid losses

Table 11.4
Annual Income for Life (Guaranteed as Indicated)
From a Fund of $20,000 For a Male Age 65

Company	*Guaranteed 10 Years*	*Guaranteed 0 Years*
A	$3,401	$3,770
B	3,135	3,430
C	3,126	3,126
D	3,070	3,360
E	3,068	3,371
F	2,986	3,217
Difference between Best and Worst	14%	17%

from which it would be difficult to recover when you are close to retirement.

However, if you require additional income, as an alternative to an annuity, you may want to turn over some of your non-registered money to a mutual fund and withdraw a certain amount each year. Experience has shown that with many reputable mutual funds a withdrawal of up to 15% over a period of time has actually kept the fund operating, and in some cases the capital has increased. When withdrawn, a portion of the income is treated as dividend income, a portion as capital gain, and a portion as your original capital. Hence the tax payable on such an arrangement is usually not substantial.

Our Advice Is Based on Conservative Assumptions

Every guideline we have described here is based on fairly pessimistic assumptions. It's better to "overprepare" for retirement than find yourself short on income and long on insecurity because inflation continues to rob you of hard earned savings.

Planning your retirement finances is like planning the rest of your finances. You are not building a straitjacket, you are trying to make reasonable decisions to ensure financial freedom and security for yourself in the future. That's why retirement planning is especially important, because it can help you prepare for all the non-financial changes you will have to cope with. And it is never too early or too late to start!

DO'S AND DON'TS

Do Plan to provide, on your own, for the difference between the total income you'll need and the amount of income you'll receive from government and company pension plans, using RRSPs and other accumulation vehicles.

Do Review the above regularly to make sure your plans change along with your changing wants and needs.

Do Figure out the income you will need for lifestyle options after retirement, as well as for necessities.

Do Keep at least 20% of your assets in deferred income forms of investment when you retire and use tax-deferral plan opportunities available to you at that time.

Don't Write off the importance of small amounts of savings. Regularity and persistence is the key to success—it builds the momentum called compound interest.

Don't Procrastinate. The dollar you don't save or shelter from taxes today is the one with the biggest growth potential between now and retirement.

Don't Gamble with your retirement funds. If you insist on doing some high-risk investing, don't do it with your RRSPs.

CHAPTER 12

Estate Planning

You've worked hard for a long time, saved a little money, acquired some investments. You own a summer cottage, you've just about paid off the mortgage on your house, and you've bought a quarter of a million dollars worth of life insurance by the time you add up all the different plans and policies you own.

Now answer this quickly: What would have happened to all these things you've worked so hard for if you had died last night?

Unless you've reviewed your will and your entire estate plan recently, you probably can't answer that question. A large number of Canadians don't have a will at all, let alone one that is up to date.

Estate planning is simply what you do before you die to make sure the people and things you care about are taken care of after your death. Estate planning is also the part of personal financial management that causes more procrastination than all the rest combined.

It's not that any of us really doubts we're going to die some day. It's just that very few of us accept the possibility it might be soon. So we put off planning for it.

Who is there to persuade you to face the prospect? Estate planning experts from the traditional professions — lawyers, chartered accountants, trust officers — are all prevented by their professional codes of ethics from pursuing you aggressively.

The person most likely to press you about estate planning is a life insurance agent. But, however competent and well intentioned he or she might be, you know he or she makes a living selling life insurance, not providing advice about estate planning. Over the years, we've all become pretty good at deflecting insurance agents — not always for our own good.

So how do you get around to planning your estate? Start by examining what will happen if you don't.

WHAT HAPPENS IF YOU DON'T LEAVE A WILL

Most of us have a number of reasonable-sounding assumptions about what happens to our property when we die. Most of those assumptions are wrong. Consider these five things that won't happen if you don't leave a will:

If you die without a will, your spouse does *not* automatically inherit all your property.

If you die without a will, your spouse does *not* have the right to decide how your property should be divided up among your children, or even to decide when they should get their shares.

If you die without a will, your spouse does *not* have the right to pick the person who will be responsible for handling all the arrangements for dividing up your property.

If you die without a will, your next of kin do *not* have the right to decide together how to divide up your estate.

If you die without a will, the whole thing is *not* brought before a judge who will decide how the property ought to be shared on the particular merits of your case.

What *does* happen if you die without a will is that your assets are frozen (with a few exceptions we'll talk about later) while the courts appoint someone to supervise the winding up of your affairs, and the payment of your debts. Your remaining estate is then divided up according to rigid rules set down in your province's intestacy laws. Intestacy means the state of dying without a valid will. No matter how needy your surviving spouse may be, your estate has to be divided according to the law, even if that means the bulk of your estate is tied up in a government-administered trust until your children reach the age of majority.

Any property other than money or liquid securities will be sold for the best price as soon as possible by the court-appointed administrator who will then invest the proceeds for maximum safety of principal. If you have long-term growth investments or business interests, this kind of quick sale can reduce the value of your estate dramatically. On top of all this, the legal bills involved in an intestacy may be higher than in cases where there is a will.

Table 12.1 shows what the laws are in the various provinces.

Table 12.1
Distribution of Estates by Law (Intestacy)

In British Columbia	
Spouse only	All to spouse.
Spouse and one child	First $65,000 to spouse. Remainder: one-half to spouse; one-half to child.
Spouse and children	First $65,000 to spouse. Remainder: one-third to spouse; two-thirds to children, divided equally.

Children and children of a deceased child	Equally to the children, and children of deceased child take share of their deceased parent.

In Alberta

Spouse only	All to spouse.
Spouse and one child	First $40,000 to spouse. Remainder: one-half to spouse; one-half to child.
Spouse and children	First $40,0000 to spouse. Remainder: one-third to spouse; two-thirds to children equally (with the children of any deceased child to take their deceased parent's share).
No spouse or children	All to father and mother equally, or to the surviving parent.
No spouse, children, or parent	Equally among brothers and sisters (with the children of any deceased brother or sister to take their deceased parent's share).
No spouse, children, parent, brother or sister	Equally among nephews and nieces (per capita).
No spouse, children, parents, brothers, sisters, nephews, or nieces	Next of kin.
Descendants and relatives conceived but unborn	If born alive after your death, they inherit as if they had been born during your lifetime.

In Saskatchewan

Spouse only	All to spouse.
Spouse and one child	First $40,000 to spouse. Remainder: one-half to spouse; one-half to child.
Spouse and children	First $40,000 to spouse. Remainder: one-third to spouse; two-thirds to children, divided equally.
Children and children of a deceased child	Equally to children. Children of a deceased child take their parent's share.
No spouse or children	All to parents or the surviving parent.
No spouse, children, or parent	Brothers and sisters equally. Children of a deceased brother or sister take their parent's share. If only nephews and nieces survive, they would share in the estate equally without representation (per capita).
Descendants and relatives conceived but unborn	If born alive after your death, they inherit as if they had been born during your lifetime.

In Manitoba

Spouse only	All to spouse.
Spouse and one child	First $50,000 to spouse. Remainder: one-half to spouse; one-half to child.
Spouse and children	First $50,000 to spouse. Remainder: one-half to spouse; one-half to children, divided equally. Children of a deceased child take their parent's share.
No spouse or children	Entire estate to parents or the surviving parent.
No spouse, children, or parent	Brothers and sisters equally. Children of a deceased brother or sister take their parent's share. If only nephews and nieces survive, they would share the estate equally (per capita).
Descendants and relatives conceived but unborn	If born alive after your death, they inherit as if they had been born during your lifetime.

In Ontario

Spouse only	Entire estate to spouse.
Spouse and one child	First $75,000 to spouse. Remainder: one-half to spouse; one-half to child.
Spouse and children	First $75,000 to spouse. Remainder: one-third to spouse; two-thirds to children, divided equally. Children of a deceased child take their parent's share. If only grandchildren survive, they would share the estate equally (per capita).
No spouse or children	Entire estate to parents or the surviving parent.
No spouse, children, or parent	Brothers and sisters equally. Children of a deceased brother or sister take their parent's share. If only nephews and nieces survive, they would share in the estate equally (per capita).
Descendants and relatives conceived but unborn	If born alive after your death, they inherit as if they had been born during your lifetime.
Children born outside marriage	Same rights to share in estate as children born in marriage.

In Quebec

Spouse and brother and sister	One-half to spouse; one-half to brother and sister equally.

Spouse and parent(s) and brother or sister	One-third to spouse, one-third to parent(s); one-third to brother or sister.

In New Brunswick

Spouse only	All to spouse.
Spouse and one child	Personal chattels to spouse. Remainder: one-half to spouse; one-half to child.
Spouse and children	Personal chattels to spouse.* Remainder: one-third to spouse; two-thirds to children divided equally. Children of a deceased child take their parent's share.
Children and children of a deceased child	Equally to children. Children of a deceased child take their parent's share.
No spouse or children	All to parents or to surviving parent.
No spouse, children, or parent	Brothers and sisters equally. Children of a deceased brother or sister take their parent's share. If only nephews and nieces survive, they would share in the estate equally (per capita).
Descendants and relatives conceived but unborn	If born alive after your death, they inherit as if they had been born during your lifetime.

In Nova Scotia

Spouse only	Entire estate will go to spouse.
Spouse and children	First $50,000 plus accrued interest from date of death of intestate to spouse; if only one child, one-half the remainder to spouse and one-half to child; if more than one child, one-third the remainder to spouse and two-thirds to children, divided equally. If the intestate owned and occupied a home, spouse has option of electing to receive the home and contents as part of $50,000, or in lieu thereof if the value of home exceeds $50,000.
Children and children of a deceased child	Equally to children of intestate with children of deceased child taking their parent's share equally.
No spouse or children	All to parents equally or to surviving parent.

---

*An Act to Amend the Devolution of Estates Act clearly defines "personal chattels."

No spouse, children, or parent	Brothers and sisters equally. Children of a deceased brother or sister take their parent's share. If only nephews and nieces survive, they would share in the estate equally without representation (per capita).
Descendants and relatives conceived but unborn	If born alive after your death, they inherit as if they had been born during your lifetime.

In Prince Edward Island

Spouse only	First $50,000 plus interest from date of death of the intestate to spouse. Remainder: one-half to spouse, one-half to next of kin of the intestate.
Spouse and child	One-half to spouse and one-half to child.
Spouse and children	One-third to spouse and two-thirds to children. Children of a deceased child take their parent's share.
Children and children of a deceased child	Equally to children. Children of a deceased child take their parent's share.
No spouse or children	Entire estate to parents divided equally or to surviving parent, if only one.
No spouse, children, or parent	Brothers and sisters equally. Children of a deceased brother or sister take their parent's share. If only nephews and nieces survive, they would share in the estate equally (per capita).
Descendants and relatives conceived but unborn	If born alive after your death, they inherit as if they had been born during your lifetime.

In Newfoundland

Spouse only	All to spouse.
Spouse and child	One-half to spouse and one-half to child.
Spouse and children	One-third to spouse and two-thirds to children divided equally. Children of a deceased child take their parent's share.
Children and children of a deceased child	Equally to children. Children of a deceased child take their parent's share.
No spouse or children	Entire estate to parents divided equally or to surviving parent, if only one.

No spouse, children, or parent	Brothers and sisters equally. Children of a deceased brother or sister take their parent's share. If only nephews and nieces survive, they would share in the estate equally (per capita).
Descendants and relatives conceived but unborn	If born alive after your death, they inherit as if they had been born during your lifetime.

COMMON MISTAKES IN ESTATE PLANNING

When the provincial legislators passed the various intestacy laws, they were trying to set up a system that would be as fair as possible. But their method of dividing up your estate may not reflect your wishes. In fact, it may actually disrupt and reduce the value of your estate. To prevent this you have to plan your estate. Make sure you avoid the most common mistakes.

First, don't try to do it all yourself. Estate planning is complicated. You will need help and advice to make sure your plans are realistic.

Second, don't leave major decisions to your advisers. They're *your* decisions. Basically, you decide what you want to achieve with your estate plan; your advisers can only tell you how to do it. Making provisions for the people you love isn't something you should leave to anyone else.

Third, don't decide to spare your spouse the discomfort of talking about your death. Make sure your wife or husband is involved in the planning and knows as much as possible about your wishes. That's the best way to make sure your wishes will be carried out.

Fourth, don't forget that changes in your estate or in your family may call for changes in your estate plan. If you get a lot richer, if you have a baby or adopt a child, or if you become widowed or divorced, you will probably want to alter your estate plan. Right from the start, review your plan regularly to make sure it continues to reflect your desires. Changing an estate plan is a lot easier than most people think.

Finally, and this happens more often than you think, don't lose the plan. Don't take it for granted that it will be easy for your survivors to lay their hands on all documents and information that make up your plan. Make a record of the location of all important documents and leave copies with your spouse, your lawyer, and possibly a grown-up child.

WHO SHOULD BE INVOLVED IN ESTATE PLANNING?

Even if your estate is relatively modest, involve at least four people in your plan: you, your spouse, the lawyer who's going to draw up your will, and your life insurance agent or personal financial adviser. If you're highly paid or own your own business or professional practice, you'll probably want to add your accountant as well. If you decide that you want to include trust arrangements in your will, you may wish to consult a trust company planning officer.

DRAWING UP YOUR ESTATE PLAN

Start by deciding just what you want your estate plan to achieve. Sit down with your insurance agent or personal financial adviser and make sure your spouse is present. (If you don't have an adviser, read Chapter 15, which describes how to choose a financial adviser; even if you are financially astute, his or her services can be very useful.)

Draw up a detailed inventory of your assets and liabilities. State your objectives and then convert them into dollars and cents. (A sample, detailed personal profile form can be found at the back of this book.)

As a next step, draw up a rough plan showing how you'll use your property to meet the objectives you've set for your estate plan. Who will get what? Which assets should be sold to produce cash? Which should be held to produce income or capital appreciation?

SEEING A GOOD ESTATE PLANNING LAWYER

Estate planning is a specialized branch of law. Don't assume that the lawyer who helped you buy your house is qualified to plan your estate. Ask around, and when you have found someone who specializes in this area, call to request an interview.

Before the interview send in a copy of your rough plan so that when you and your spouse arrive at the lawyer's office he or she won't have to waste billable time finding out how to spell your middle name.

The lawyer is an expert, but he or she will be able to do a better job for you if you've already made some of the major decisions about what you want done. So have the answers to the following questions ready before the interview:

What Do You Want Done in the Event of a Common Disaster?

What if you and your spouse die simultaneously or within a few weeks of each other? Who should get your property? If you want it to go to your minor children, do you want them to get it as soon as they reach the age of majority, or do you want it held in trust until they're older? If so, who should act as *trustee*? If your children are too young to take care of themselves, who should act as their *guardian* until they reach the age of majority?

Have You Thought About Setting Up Trust Provisions for Your Spouse?

Is your spouse unable or unwilling to handle large amounts of money?

You can protect him or her against bad financial advice and fortune-hunting second spouses by setting up trust funds to provide an income and even a limited right to use the principal to support himself or herself and your children. The main amount will then be safeguarded; it can continue producing income for your spouse until he or she dies and then be divided among your children.

What if Your Spouse Remarries?

If you leave your estate in trust for your children and provide a life income from the trust for your spouse, you may be in for problems if you have no "remarriage clause" in your will. It's possible that your spouse may marry again, not need the income from the trust, and live to be eighty-five. Your children will not be able to take possession of their money until the death of the spouse. That's not what you intended when you drew up the will. It's not the best possible arrangement for relations between spouse and children – but it can happen.

A remarriage clause could terminate your spouse's rights on remarriage; but an excessively tough remarriage clause can be destructive. Suppose your will dictates that your spouse loses all support from your estate upon remarrying. You either restrict the choice of future partner to someone who is well off, or force your spouse into an arrangement less formal than marriage so that he or she can avoid being "cut off" from trust income. Whatever purpose you had in mind when you drew up such a tough remarriage clause, it undoubtedly was not to increase the pressure that could be put on family relations if your spouse should choose such an arrangement.

Consider, too, what happens if there is an extra-tough remarriage clause and your spouse makes a mistake in choosing a second mate and ends up divorced. Or what if the second mate dies without making adequate provision for your former spouse? Was it really your intention that there'd be no independent income available from your estate?

In planning your estate you'll have to find a reasonable middle ground. One good system provides the spouse with an income until remarriage and with a lump sum settlement at that time. The spouse, then, will have enough capital to make arrangements for his or her own future security, permitting the rest of the estate to be distributed among your children as specified in the will.

The question of a remarriage clause is serious, especially when you intend to use trust funds to provide a lifetime income for your spouse and have the capital ultimately go to your children. This is the kind of question that can be delicate if it comes up for the first time when you and your spouse are sitting in the lawyer's office. So talk it over before the interview.

CHOOSING AN EXECUTOR

In your will, you will have to name an *executor*. This is the person, persons, or trust company you want to handle all the arrangements called for in the will — paying off your debts, protecting your assets from loss, and distributing them in accordance with your instructions.

You may wish to name your spouse as your executor — and that's not a bad idea. But be realistic about the skills your spouse can bring to the job. Unless you're sure he or she will be fully competent to handle all the details — even under the kind of pressure and difficulty that will follow your death — it's a good idea to consider appointing one or more co-executors to help with the work. A grown-up child, an old family friend, or a trusted business associate may be a good choice. Appointing two co-executors can prevent a deadlock if there is disagreement about any aspect of your will.

Remember that executors are as mortal as you are. They can die too, and if they do, their executors succeed them unless you have provided otherwise. It's a good idea to appoint contingent executors in case your first choice is unable or unwilling to act when the time comes.

Duties of an Executor

1. Locate and examine last will of deceased.
2. Make funeral arrangements.
3. Consider immediate financial needs of family.
4. Review personal papers of deceased to become familiar with estate assets and liabilities.
5. Notify beneficiaries.
6. Employ suitable lawyer.
7. List contents of deceased's safety deposit box.
8. Open estate account and rent safety deposit box if necessary.
9. Compile inventory of estate assets and liabilities.
10. Protect estate assets and business interests.
11. Cancel subscriptions or credit cards.
12. Obtain grant of letters probate from Surrogate Court.
13. Advertise for creditors and settle claims for and against deceased's estate.
14. Prepare and file income tax return for year of death and any previous year, if required.
15. Apply for Canada Pension Plan benefits, if entitled.
16. Settle valuation problems with taxing authorities. Pay outstanding duties and obtain transfer consents for assets (Quebec only).
17. Gather assets.
18. Prepare and file estate's income tax return.
19. Obtain clearance certificate from income tax department.
20. Establish any trust funds as directed in will.

21. Pay legal fees, funeral expenses, and debts.
22. Pay cash legacies and distribute bequests of personal property.
23. Prepare and submit accounting of administration to beneficiaries and obtain their releases, or pass estate accounts before judge of Surrogate Court.
24. Make final distribution of remaining assets to named beneficiaries.

NAMING A TRUSTEE

When funds are to be held in trust, you'll need to appoint a trustee—someone to control the funds for the purpose spelled out in your will. It may be one or more of the executors of your will, another individual, or a trust company. Trust companies emphasize their specialist knowledge in the field, their continuity, impartiality, and diversity of administrative and investment facilities. On the other hand, they tend to be overly conservative in business management and investments.

The key question to ask yourself is how long you intend the trust to run. The longer it is to run, the more sense it will make to appoint a trust company instead of an individual. You know that whenever you die, they'll still be there.

An alternative to naming a trust company as an executor and trustee is to suggest to the individual executors and trustees that they appoint a trust company as *agent* for them to carry out the trust provisions in your will until your estate is totally distributed. There could be substantial savings in fees, and your family can still utilize the professional expertise of the company.

Arrange Your Affairs to Take Advantage of the Judgment of Your Executors and Trustees

You may have strong feelings about certain investments. You may think that certain ways of handling some of your assets are better than others, and you may be right — today. But you can't be sure things won't change.

Write your will so that it allows your executors and trustees to use their discretion when carrying out your wishes. You select these people because you trust their judgment — give them the chance to use it.

If you do have preferences about certain assets or investments, express them in an informal estate-planning letter that can be kept with your will. It will let your executors and trustees know what you want, yet give them the freedom to respond sensibly to changing circumstances.

THE COMMON PITFALLS OF DIVIDING YOUR PROPERTY

The lawyer or notary who draws up your will knows *how* things are done. He or she may well be reluctant, however, to question *what* you want to do about dividing up your estate — after all, it's your money and you're the boss. But keep in mind some common-sense considerations to make sure you're not signing a will that may defeat your own purposes.

If you want to leave all your property to one person (a universal legacy), there's no problem. On the other hand, if you want to divide your estate among a number of people, you'll have to decide whether you want to leave it in fractions (general legacies) or specify particular sums of money or particular assets for certain individuals (particular legacies). Then you'll have to decide what you want to do with the "residue" of your estate – the total that's left after satisfying all the particular legacies.

You should be aware of some of the problems that can arise depending on the kind of legacy you choose.

Let's say you opt for particular legacies and decide, for example, to leave specific sums of money to each of your children with the residue going to your spouse. What happens if, at your death, the value of your estate is considerably less than it was when you drew up the will? It's possible that the value of some of your investments may drop and the particular cash legacies may use up so much of your estate that your spouse ends up with little or nothing. You can avoid this situation by stating clearly in your will that your children are to receive specific sums of money *only* if these sums do not exceed a certain fraction of the total value of the estate.

Consider also what would happen if the cash and liquid assets in your estate are not great enough to cover all the specific cash bequests. In that case, your executors would have to sell other assets to raise the required funds and, once again, there could be a significant reduction in the value of your estate as a result of losses incurred in liquidating these assets. To avoid this problem, make sure there is enough cash available, either by buying life insurance to cover the bequests in your will or by arranging for the sale of certain assets at fair market value. Buy-sell agreements between partners in a business or a professional practice are an excellent way of doing this, especially if they are funded by life insurance.

ASSETS THAT PASS DIRECTLY TO YOUR HEIRS

Even when you've drawn up a legally valid will, the assets that come under the administration of your executors will be tied up for a while. They will be subject to the claims of your creditors and possibly to claims from government for taxes due at death. So it makes sense to pay particular attention to assets that will pass directly to your heirs.

Any property held in joint tenancy with right of survivorship will pass directly to the surviving owner. Usually this applies to real estate – your family home or summer place. If your house is registered in your name only, it might make good estate-planning sense to change the ownership to include your spouse's name as well. (In Quebec, jointly owned property held under the marital regime of community property or its replacement since 1970, Partnership of Acquests, is not affected by the terms of your will and passes directly as called for in the law.)

Death benefits from life insurance policies and annuities and from retirement savings vehicles, where a specific beneficiary has been named, will pass directly to that beneficiary. If you have no will or if your will leaves everything to one person and your insurance policies name your estate as beneficiary, you would be wise to change them to name that particular individual as beneficiary instead.

Any business assets or interest you hold (whether shares in a corporation or assets of an unincorporated sole proprietorship or partnership) which are subject to a buy-sell agreement will be disposed of as called for in the agreement. The proceeds from the sale will be administered with the rest of your assets, but the price or formula in the agreement will often protect the particular asset from a forced sale at a loss, especially if the agreement is funded by life insurance.

WHAT TO DO AFTER YOUR WILL IS DRAFTED

If you've answered all the questions in your meeting with the lawyer, you'll be ready to ask him or her to draft your will. Once the draft is prepared and you've had a chance to go over it with your spouse, you'll have to make a list of things to do to make sure your property is arranged so that the will can work. This is the time to think about how your property is registered. It is also the time to sit down with your partner to talk about a buy-sell agreement, and to take a hard look at your life insurance coverage.

First, look at the cash requirements that will be counted against your estate. Will there be enough cash to meet all of them without forced sale of assets? If not, you may wish to change the beneficiary of some of your life insurance coverage from an individual to your estate. If you want to leave your spouse a lifetime interest in your estate instead of leaving him or her cash, you may do the same thing – make your estate the beneficiary of life insurance policies.

If you want to leave your spouse cash, it may be a good idea to name him or her as the beneficiary of life insurance policies. This way the money will go to him or her directly instead of being tied up in the administration of your will. You can use other policies to create other cash bequests as well.

You can also use insurance to set up trust provisions by creating an *inter vivos* trust. This is a trust between living people who can own insurance policies on your life. Get professional advice on how to transfer funds to pay insurance premiums properly to minimize income tax.

The *inter vivos* arrangement protects the money from claims by your creditors, provides the safety of a trust arrangement and also offers complete confidentiality. At your death the operation of such a trust is not subject to the kind of publicity that will mark the administration of your will. Because of this last feature, it is often used to create legacies for lovers or for married people living with someone other than their legal spouse.

This review of your life insurance may lead to nothing more than changing the names of a few beneficiaries. It's also possible that it will indicate the need to purchase additional coverage. In any event, identify your requirements clearly, then ask your insurance agent to review alternative policies to help find the most economical solution.

Next, write a covering letter to accompany your will. It should be addressed to your executors and beneficiaries, and should summarize any philosophies, concerns, or strong views you have about different kinds of investments or the handling of certain assets. You can also add any other information that may help your executors carry out your wishes more effectively.

With the letter, include a summary list of all the documents and pertinent information related to your estate plan, including the location of all documents. A sample of such a summary sheet appears in the Personal Financial Profile at the back of this book.

ESTATE PLANNING AND SINGLE PEOPLE

Single people, young and old, tend to ignore estate planning. The rule for single people, however, is the same as for married people: take a look at what will happen to your estate if you die without a will. If it meets with your approval, fine. If not, make one.

The intestacy laws will divide up your estate, but they'll provide nothing for anyone who is not related to you. No lover, long-time friend, school, or charity you may want to help will benefit from your estate if you die without a will. And don't forget that most of us do have a significant estate if only from the group life insurance we carry at work.

ESTATE PLANNING AND WIDOWED PEOPLE

If you're widowed, you probably have already inherited the bulk of your spouse's estate and with it your spouse's estate plan. But that plan may not be right for *you*. Ask yourself the following questions:

1. How well did my deceased spouse's administrators and advisers do their job?
2. Did they seem interested?
3. Would I be more comfortable with people of my own choice?
4. Have I rearranged my assets so that they are producing maximum income and growth, according to my requirements?
5. Am I filing my personal income tax return properly, taking advantage of all available deductions?

6. And what about my own estate planning?
7. Will there be sufficient cash at my death for tax on capital gains, regular income tax, and last expenses? Because there will be no property passing to a spouse tax free, your estate may be exposed to greater tax liability than your spouse's was when you inherited it.

ESTATE PLANNING AND DIVORCED PEOPLE

If you're divorced, support payments can stop with the death of your ex-spouse. If you have custody of the children from a marriage that ended in divorce, and are receiving alimony and support payments, make sure there's a provision for your ex-spouse's death. If you can't win voluntary agreement from your ex-spouse to provide legacies, at least for the children, you ultimately may have to buy life insurance policies on him or her yourself.

What about a guardian and trustees for the children if you die? Have you made arrangement for that?

ESTATE PLANNING AND COMMON-LAW MARRIAGES

The union of couples living together who are not legally married to each other will not be recognized as a common-law marriage unless they hold themselves out to the community as being married. Generally speaking, common-law spouses have no status under the intestacy laws, though children are recognized.

The rights of common-law spouses are not likely to prevail against those of a legal spouse, although illegitimate children will share equally with legitimate children unless provisions are established in the will to exclude them. Anyone involved in such a relationship should check carefully with provincial authorities or competent legal advisers to establish exactly what their status is. From a planning standpoint, the most foolproof method of providing for lovers, common-law spouses, and children born out of wedlock is through an *inter vivos* trust, often funded largely by life insurance.

ESTATE PLANNING IN QUEBEC

Certain institutions that affect estate planning are unique to Quebec; they may affect you, even if you don't live in Quebec. If the husband was living in the province of Quebec at the time of his marriage – regardless of the fact that the marriage may have taken place outside the province or that the couple has lived elsewhere for years – you may come under some or all of the Quebec requirements. It's worth checking.

Quebec has codified marital regimes that pool certain assets of the two spouses unless a specific marriage contract has been drawn up to provide for separate ownership of property. These arrangements probably are a good idea, but they may or may not reflect your wishes and those of your spouse.

First, see if you come under any of these laws. If you do, the best way to avoid having them interfere with your wishes is to agree on a marriage contract.

ONTARIO FAMILY LAW ACT

The Ontario Family Law Act, which came into force in March 1986, is viewed as being a prototype for similar legislation in all provinces except Quebec. It establishes a new foundation of law for marriages; it repeals or significantly alters several acts which previously governed relationships among husbands, wives, and children, creating a new regime of property rights between spouses based on the equal position of spouses as individuals within marriage. It recognizes marriage as a form of partnership, and also provides for an orderly and equitable settlement in case of breakdown of the partnership.

It is important to note that the act covers only formal marriages whether or not they began before the act came into force. Separation of property will continue to be the norm; however, in the event of death or divorce there will now be community of property rules which entitle each spouse to 50% of all property with the exclusion of:

- Property owned before marriage.
- Property, other than the matrimonial home, that was acquired by gift or inheritance from a third person *after* date of marriage.
- Gifts or inheritances.
- Court awards and settlements for personal injuries.
- Proceeds or a right to proceeds of a life insurance policy as defined in the Insurance Act.

If you're concerned about the possibility of marriage breakdown, consider drawing up a marriage contract to provide for an equitable division of property values. Even if you're not concerned about marriage breakdown, remember that the Family Law Act provisions apply at the death of a spouse. Be sure to review your will in light of this new legislation, because it could affect the distribution of your property, and also your spouse's position as an executor or trustee of your estate.

DEATH AND TAXES: THE TAXES GO ON LONGER

Even if your estate is small, you can't afford to ignore taxes. Tax planning at death can be complex, so all we can do here is deal with a few bread-and-butter issues.

Naming a Specific Beneficiary

Unless you name a specific beneficiary for your pension plan, DPSP, or RRSP, the proceeds will be taxed as a lump sum, either in your income tax return for the year of death or in your estate. If you name your spouse as beneficiary on any pension plan, DPSP, or RRSP, he or she will be able to defer taxes on amounts not needed for immediate use by rolling the proceeds into his or her own RRSP. If you have named a dependent child or grandchild* to receive the pension plan proceeds or a DPSP, he or she will be able to pay tax on amounts received at his or her rates. So be sure to choose your beneficiary carefully. The alternative is to pay a lot of extra dollars in taxes.

Capital Gains

Remember that property and investments on which a non-exempt capital gain has accrued will be taxed as capital gain — that is, one-half of the total gain will be taxed as income. This tax is payable by your estate and cannot be deferred. There are, however, two important exceptions worth noting.

The first is that there is no capital gain tax levied on a principal residence.

The second exception applies to property left to your spouse. Here the capital gains tax is *deferred*, unless an election is made to pay tax. It's not collected when you die, but it *is* collected if your spouse disposes of the property during his or her lifetime or when your spouse dies. When that happens, the tax bill can be a whopper, so you may be wise to purchase "joint and last survivor" insurance policies to pay the taxes. These policies insure both spouses, but the benefits are payable only on the death of the second spouse.

As noted above, an election to pay tax on capital gains at death may be made when property is passing to a spouse. This would make sense where the deceased spouse had not "used up" his or her lifetime capital gains exemption.

Another reason might be uninsurability of the surviving spouse which would rule out insurance on his or her life.

Tax on "Recapture": Depreciation Coming Back to Haunt You

Remember that any depreciable property such as buildings is subject to income tax on the full amount of capital cost allowance (depreciation) which is deemed to be "recaptured" at death, as well as on half of deemed non-exempt capital gains. If the property is transferred to the deceased's spouse or to a trust created solely for the spouse, tax will be deferred until his or her death or until he or she sells or gifts the property during his or her lifetime.

If the property is transferred at death to someone other than a spouse or spouse trust, the value of depreciable property for tax purposes is estab-

---

*Note: RRSP proceeds paid to a child or grandchild who at the time of death was financially dependent on the planholder will be taxed at the beneficiary's rates on amounts equal to $5,000 × the number of full years under age 26 if his or her income for the year preceding the year of death exceeded $5,000.

lished at the mid-point between its actual market value at that time and its depreciated value for tax purposes, known as its undepreciated capital cost. This undepreciated capital cost is the difference between the original cost and the total amount of capital cost allowance (depreciation) written off during the deceased's lifetime. If this mid-point value is equal to or greater than the original cost, all depreciation will be recaptured and full tax paid on it, and tax will be payable on half the difference between mid-point value and adjusted cost base (often equal to original cost). If the mid-point value is less than original cost, the depreciation will be deemed to have been recaptured only back to that value and not to the original cost.

If the owner's will does not leave the property to his or her spouse or to a spouse trust, provision should be made in estate planning for sufficient cash to take care of full income tax on recaptured depreciation and taxable capital gains. Often the best practical way to arrange such cash is through the purchase of appropriate amounts of life insurance.

Taxes from Self-Employment

Self-employed business people and professionals who report income on an accrual basis should allow for the impact of income taxes on their accounts receivable and the value of work in progress at the time of their death. These tax effects can be alleviated through elections under sections 70(2) and 70(3) of the Income Tax Act, and you should make sure your executors are given freedom to make such elections in your will. Other categories of employment and forms of income are subject to tax relief through these sections: employed executives on deferred compensation awards, salespeople on deferred or renewal commissions, and farmers on crops and livestock.

Back Taxes

Keep in mind that when you die, your estate must pay any back taxes that are due. Too often people overlook tax arrears when they're evaluating their life insurance programs. (This happens particularly to self-employed taxpayers, who often are allowed to fall several years behind in their tax deposits and payments because of lax policing of obligatory quarterly tax deposits.) Don't let this happen to you — or if it has, *allow for it* and buy extra insurance to cover the liability.

People with large estates often try to limit the growth of their estates by transferring growth assets to other people — usually to children, or to trusts, or to holding companies set up for the purpose. If you're not careful, you may inadvertently trigger income or capital gains tax or even recapture of capital cost allowance. You can avoid that by "roll-over" transactions such as those permitted under sections 85 and 97 of the Income Tax Act, or by making a term loan rather than a demand loan, or a combination of the two, on the transferred asset. In that way you can spread the impact of tax over five or ten years, depending on the relationship between lender and borrower and whether the transaction involves shares of a Canadian-controlled private company.

Estate Planning Is Planning for People

If you feel strongly enough about it and are willing to spend the money, you can buy expert help in the art of "tax karate" at death. But remember —you're planning for yourself and for the people you love, so don't let tax reduction be the only factor to consider.

There are almost no tax problems at death that you can't avoid or limit if you're prepared to divest yourself of large amounts of money and assets by gift or sale, in return for non-interest-bearing promissory notes or non-growth preferred shares. But do you really want to do that? Do you think you'll be happy dismantling the estate you worked so hard to build? Do you really want to give up control? What about inflation? What will it do to a fixed income? Are you sure your children are ready to handle the property you're giving up? And, in an era when marriage breakdown rivals the common cold in frequency, just how much property should you be transferring to your spouse?

Pay close attention to your liquidity. If you die and there's no money available to pay taxes, a forced sale of your assets will be necessary unless you have adequate cash and life insurance to meet the requirements on your estate.

By all means, arrange your affairs to minimize your tax liability. But be realistic and remember that people are what make the process worthwhile and that you—with your ability to build an estate—are as deserving of generous treatment as any of your beneficiaries.

G. K. Chesterton said of religious faith, "It's not that it was tried and found wanting, but that it was tried and found difficult." Estate planning is like that. It is difficult. If you put it off, however, it gets more difficult.

Start now with a comprehensive plan. And then review the plan every two years or so to make sure it stays up to date and adequate.

It really is worth doing.

DO'S AND DON'TS

Do Believe you're important enough to make a will. The only qualification is caring about someone or something.

Do Leave a written record of your thoughts about your estate plan and the location of important documents.

Do Talk over your plans with your executor and principal beneficiaries.

Do Review your estate plan regularly.

Don't Put off drawing up your will.

Don't Wait for someone else to prod you into planning your estate. If you have an adviser you trust, call him or her; if not, check with people you trust to recommend someone.

Don't Forget that only legal spouses can count on recognition under the law of intestacy. If you love someone you're not married to, get a will done to protect that person.

Don't Let the tax-reduction "tail" wag the people-priority "dog." Keep flexible and protect yourself and your spouse, not just your children and grandchildren.

CHAPTER 13

Women and Financial Planning

"Husbands can earn, but only wives can save," the old proverb states. Obviously, it's an old proverb because women are earning and saving — and investing — in unprecedented numbers. They're also taking the initiative in buying the services of professional financial planners, and other financial service specialists. Their ranks include career women, widows and divorcées who have to do their own planning. They also include married women who have stopped being diffident about their own ability to manage money — and started being realistically irreverent about their husbands' gifts in this regard.

Unfortunately, many women continue to abdicate responsibility where money is concerned. If they're married, they cede the area to their husband. If they're on their own, they adopt a kind of financial fetal position, never venturing into anything more aggressive than a Canada Savings Bond or a credit union term deposit.

If that describes you — read on. It's time to take control of your financial destiny, even if that means nothing more than challenging the decisions of your male partner. You never know when you might find yourself on your own.

PLAN YOUR FINANCES AS IF YOU'RE SINGLE

Even if you're not single, get involved in the financial planning process as much as you'd have to if you were. It's the first step toward developing the knowledge, experience and confidence you need to be independent.

Group Programs

Some of the cheapest and most effective financial management vehicles are group programs from employers: group life insurance, major medical expense coverage to supplement government plans, dental insurance, disability insurance to cover you if you're sick, pension plans, and other tax-deferral vehicles such as Deferred Profit Sharing Plans (DPSPs).

The rule for working women is the same as for everyone else: use these low-cost vehicles to build financial stability for yourself. Read your company's handbook on benefits. Evaluate your need for them realistically. It's easy to say you don't really need life insurance. But using your group life plan often can assure you of the ability to buy life insurance coverage later should you need it — at minimal cost. Group disability coverage also is quite reasonably priced. Weigh its cost against the prospect of being unable to work for two or three months, a year, or even longer.

Make sure you use the coverage you are entitled to. Many employees never bother to claim prescription drugs which could have been paid for at work. Keep your receipts. Make sure you apply for reimbursement. Insurance companies don't pay money unless you make and prove your claim. Keep your receipts for all prescriptions — they can go a long way toward using up the $25-per-year deductible clause in many plans.

Savings

Just because you're a woman doesn't mean that saving makes no sense. Living from payday to payday is a dead end. So make savings a first financial priority — not just for short-term luxuries like vacations, but also for long-term goals like retirement income or a home of your own. Otherwise you'll never achieve financial stability and independence.

Preparing a Budget

Review the budget and banking system described in Chapter 2. The logic is sound and provides a means of controlling your money. Take a look at your income, and for one month keep a detailed record of every expenditure you make. Include everything from major items such as rent right down to bus tickets and cigarettes. And, of course, note the luxuries you buy as well.

Once you've recorded everything for a whole month, you may well discover areas where you could reduce your expenditures and save some money. Be realistic. You're not trying to put yourself in a straitjacket, you're just trying to control your spending. This will inevitably help you save more for sudden emergencies, unexpected bargains, or investment opportunities.

BUILD AN INDEPENDENT CREDIT RATING

Until very recently getting credit was much more difficult for women than for men. But it's not that difficult any more. Part of the reason is that governments have intervened. Several provinces have passed laws that require any credit granter to apply the same rules to women as to men. The change probably would have come anyway, laws or no laws. The people who grant credit make money doing it. Today more and more women are credit-worthy in their own right, and credit granters want a share of your business.

The best time to build an independent credit rating is before you are married. Once you're married, it is harder to establish one. Typically, credit-reporting agencies lump your history in with that of your husband. If your husband turns out to be a bad risk, your ability to borrow money or charge purchases may be impaired. If you don't want your file to be lumped in with your husband's, visit your credit bureau and request separate files.

Should your marriage end in divorce or widowhood, and you have no independent track record as a borrower, it will be that much harder to borrow money when you need it.

Credit Cards

Start to establish your independent credit rating by applying for a bank card such as Visa or Mastercard. Then use it. It's the first step in building your credit record. But be sensible: pay the balance promptly at the end of each month.

Credit Unions

If your place of employment has a credit union, seriously consider joining it; but before you do, satisfy yourself that it is stable financially. Often these institutions will offer lower-interest loans and preferential treatment to people who work for the employee group sponsoring them. You may wish to consider joining a credit union in the community as well.

Know Your Bank or Credit Union Manager

Take the time to introduce yourself and talk to the manager of your bank or credit union. Then if you do decide you need funds and want to negotiate a loan, you won't be dealing with a complete stranger. Prepare for this meeting with the strategy set out in Chapter 3.

GET EDUCATED

One of the most important things you can do is to educate yourself about money. You can do this by reading a book like *It's Your Money*, taking a course, or reading the financial section of a newspaper. But the best way is to handle money in all its forms. As a starter, write down your answers to the following questions:

- What are your financial objectives?
- What are your monthly budgetary needs?
- What is your gross income?
- What is your take-home pay?
- How much income tax do you pay?
- How much do you pay for group insurance plans?
- What are the group insurance benefits?
- How much do you pay for Canada Pension Plan?

- What are your benefits under Canada Pension Plan?
- How much do you contribute to your company pension plan(s)?
- What are the benefits under the company pension plan(s)?
- How much personal life insurance do you have?
- What type of insurance?
- Does this fulfill your needs?
- What does your general insurance cover?
- Do you understand how a bank works?
- Do you know the type of bank account(s) you have and how much is in each account?
- How much money is in your RRSP(s)?
- What other investments do you have?
- What amount and type of investments?
- What are some investment alternatives?
- What are the terms of your will(s)?
- How much money do you owe?
- How much interest are you paying?
- How much will you need to live with dignity in your old age?
- Where are your financial documents located?
- Who are your financial advisers and how well do you know and trust them?

FINANCIAL MANAGEMENT AND MARRIAGE

How you and your husband handle your financial affairs can determine the kinds of financial problems you will face if you find yourself single again. If your husband oversees all the finances and you just assume that things get paid, you'll have a difficult time. And on top of the grief of widowhood or the disorientation of divorce, financial problems are the last thing you need. Keep in mind, also, that too much money can be just as difficult to handle as too little. If you play a full part in your family's financial management now, you won't be caught by surprise later.

Many women have detailed knowledge and responsibility for the "pay-out" side because they take charge of household bills — utilities, dry cleaning, furniture bills, and so on. But these are day-to-day things. It's important for married women to have an extensive overview of the family's finances. What about life insurance coverage? Is there enough of it? Has your husband made a will? Have you? What about the family's total indebtedness? Is it big enough to gobble up the total value of your husband's estate if he should die? What kind of investments have your family made? Would their value be destroyed by quick forced sale in the event of your husband's death? If your husband owns part of a business, is it covered by a buy-sell agreement with the partner?

It is important for you to know the answers to these questions — and making sure you know them is *not* morbid. In fact, your active interest in these areas will help your family's financial management by making certain that your own plans and objectives fit in with your family's overall financial needs.

Conversely, make sure your husband knows how the household budget works. If something should happen to you, he could be floored by such things as weekly shopping and monthly bill paying.

A WIFE TOO HAS FINANCIAL RESPONSIBILITIES

If you are married and not earning an income, insist on receiving a realistic amount of money to cover the expenses you are best able to handle. The types of expenses should be spelled out clearly, and the allowance should include "walking-around" money to spend on discretionary personal matters without first having to obtain a dispensation from your husband. Perhaps even more important in the long run, insist on a say in your husband's life and disability and retirement income programs. If he dies or becomes disabled you will probably have to — and want to — work yourself; but a supplement to your earnings may be necessary to maintain a reasonable standard of living.

Knowing your husband's financial affairs will go a long way to relieving the anxiety associated with not having enough money, particularly if you are afraid of being old and poor. To help you know where you are now and where you will be in the future, fill in the financial recorder in the appendix. It represents a complete summary of all your financial records, including the location of valuable documents.

If you are married and earning income, develop with your husband a realistic budget that calls for a fair allocation of your income among various expenses and savings. For instance, share fixed expenses such as rent or mortgage payments, debt reduction and insurance, as well as discretionary items such as gifts and vacations. If you don't, your husband may resent being an involuntary Scrooge in the eyes of your children, while you play the generous heroine, dispensing luxuries. In your deliberations, you should also deal with the allocation of savings money. It is important that both spouses contribute as much as possible to RRSPs and pension plans. Give considerable thought to additional savings. Both spouses can earn $1,000 of investment income. If your husband saves all the money, then you will waive your right to $1,000 tax-free, while your husband, if his investment income exceeds $1,000, will pay tax at his top marginal rate. If you are in substantially different income tax brackets, allocate most of your savings to the lower income spouse. The most important item, though, is open communication. As many marriages flounder because of money disputes as for any other reason.

MARRIAGE CONTRACTS

The best time to make a marriage contract is before you're married. Have the contract drawn by a competent lawyer experienced in this area of the law. However, before you meet with the lawyer, discuss the following items:

- Home — do you want to allocate this to one spouse or the other?
- Review property brought to the marriage as well as inheritances that may be received during the marriage.
- Discuss any businesses which either spouse may own or run. This is bound to be a difficult area for both parties. In many cases, the business may be a very large percentage of a family's net worth. In Ontario, for example, if a marriage breaks up the non-owner spouse could have a claim on the other spouse's shares of a corporation. This might be a fair arrangement in some circumstances; however, it could create severe operational problems in the business, particularly if the marriage break-up was a bitter one. If you do not think this would create problems, ask yourself how you would like to do business with your ex-spouse's new spouse's lawyer. Terms of the contract regarding title to a business property should be coordinated with partnership agreements and, of course, your will.

Don't overestimate what a marriage contract can do. It is not magical. It cannot avert all the heartbreak and hassles in a divorce or the death of a spouse. It can, however, guarantee certain financial rights for each individual to protect his or her right to assets, save a lot on lawyers' fees, and avoid painful arguments later.

WHO'S GOING TO TEACH YOUR CHILDREN TO MANAGE THEIR FINANCES?

Teaching children about money is a responsibility that often falls to their mothers. Unfortunately, many mothers know very little about money, and as a result feel inadequate to teach their children about it — so they do nothing. In today's changing world, girls will need to know as much about money as boys will. It's important that children realize this, so that the young women of today will not have the problems dealing with money that many of their mothers have. And the best way to impress this on children is by example — let them see both parents involved in the family's financial decisions and planning, and in teaching the children. For those who wish to pursue the subject in detail, Chris Snyder's book *How To Teach Your Children About Money* (Toronto: Macmillan, 1982) is filled with practical ideas, including games and activities. A brief outline follows.

Allowances

Provide your children with a predictable allowance — don't just give them money every time they ask. Give them weekly sums paid on a regular day and make it their responsibility to live within those means. Spell out the general guidelines of what the money is meant for and tell them that if they run out it's *their* problem. They have to learn to live with it—or without it.

Savings

Teach your children to develop the habit of savings at an early age. A child needs a specific goal in order to save—one which reflects the child's stage of development. For instance, a nine-year-old is unlikely to be motivated to save for university, but might be motivated to save for a bicycle.

You can encourage savings by a dollar-matching plan. If your child wants a bicycle, set a realistic savings target out of his or her allowance. Once that amount is saved, you can make up the difference to buy the bicycle. Not only will the bike mean a lot more to the child that way, but he or she will have acquired the habit of saving. Alternatively, teach children to save 10% of their allowance.

Working

One of the best ways for children to learn about money is to earn some income themselves. By the age of 11 or 12, girls and boys should be old enough to take on a job outside the home, such as a paper route. Once your children become teenagers, more opportunities for part-time work will be available to them—for example, in stores or restaurants.

Experience with handling their own money at an early age should help children develop sensible and responsible attitudes toward it.

Being a Good Consumer

Many young people have a lot of money at their disposal but have never learned to be wise and careful shoppers. Teaching children to budget and to prioritize their spending helps them develop the discipline and skill to use their money for the items they really desire, making it go further instead of wasting it.

Investing

Children can learn about the "real" world of finance even when they are very young. Even if you do not invest in stocks, show your children how. In the process, take the time to explain how a company works, why it needs to make profits, and what it does with the profits. To make this type of investment meaningful, choose a company in which the child has some interest—a computer company, the local bank, or the company a family member works for. An especially creative investment lesson for children is buying a stock such as Irwin Toy. At Irwin Toy, children actually become the shareholders and attend the shareholders' meeting in Toronto each year with their parents. They get a taste for big business, get to vote on new toys going on the market for that year, and they can attend the free shareholders' meeting luncheon (where hot dogs and ice cream are served, of course).

A young person's investment program should have four objectives: (1) to teach the child, first to save regularly, then to invest; (2) to earn a reasonable rate of return; (3) to be tax effective for the parent and/or child; and (4) to be educational for the child.

SUMMING UP

If you are a woman, the best kind of financial management is establishing financial independence. Abdicating your financial responsibilities is giving away your independence and, over a long period of time, even your capacity for independence. It also means shirking your responsibilities inside the family. That's why this book applies as much to women as to men.

DO'S AND DON'TS

Do Work toward financial independence.

Do Begin to establish your financial foundations during your first income earning years.

Do Prepare a realistic budget. This is the first step toward gaining control of your money.

Do Authorize an automatic transfer each month from your chequing to your savings account.

Do Take the time to evaluate the benefits available from your employer.

Do Establish an independent credit rating.

Do Coordinate your financial affairs with your spouse.

Do Be aware of your family's financial affairs.

Do Communicate with your spouse on all financial matters.

Do Consider drawing up a marriage contract.

Do Teach your children about money.

Don't Use revolving credit cards. Set up a line of credit at the bank instead.

Don't Abdicate your financial responsibilities. "I'm just no good when it comes to money" is an excuse you could live to regret.

CHAPTER 14

Changes

One lesson seems vividly clear: change carries a physiological price tag with it. And the more radical the change, the steeper the price.

— Alvin Toffler, *Future Shock*

This chapter explores the financial dimension of changes we all may have to face at some time in our lives — a move across the country, dismissal from a job, separation and divorce, the death of a spouse. None are pleasant to experience or even to contemplate, and all can be expensive as well as traumatic. What follows is designed to keep expense to a minimum by helping you prepare for these eventualities if and when they occur.

MOVING

Moving can be a painful experience. It can cost you old friendships, current conveniences as you leave a familiar home and neighbourhood and, in most cases, a lot of money. On the other hand, it can be a time to make new friends and take on exciting new job responsibilities. It can also be a great opportunity to do some positive financial planning. Unfortunately, financial aspects of a major move often get lost in the physical confusion. Here are some hints to help you.

1. The time of year you move can be very important. If you establish residence in another province before a calendar year ends, you may find that your income tax will be significantly changed. For example, if you move from Montreal to Calgary and establish residence in Alberta before the end of the year, your income tax bill on an income of $50,000 could be reduced by up to $4,000. A move from Calgary to Montreal could cost you $4,000 more.

   When you sell your home is important. Try to sell at a time when its most attractive features show to best advantage, or when buying activity is traditionally at its peak. In most of Canada this means spring or early summer.
2. Before selling your home, spend a little money improving its appear-

ance, even if it's only a new paint job. The better impression it will make on buyers can increase the price more than enough to return your investment on the improvements.

3. Surveys indicate that 80% of people who move use professional movers. The cost of movers and the quality vary considerably. Talk to several moving companies before you move and ask your friends for references. Also be sure to check your insurance — and the movers'. Even the best break things.
4. Don't forget to advise everyone you deal with of your change of address. This includes banks, financial advisers, insurance companies, and various other organizations who provide you with services, such as phone, electricity, etc. It is especially important to notify your insurance company of a change of address if you are paying by automatic bank withdrawal. If you do change accounts and don't notify the insurance company, your policy could lapse if it has no cash values to finance automatic premium loans. Of course, this will apply particularly with term insurance coverage.
5. Review your wills. Different provinces and countries have different rules. Recruit a local lawyer and check out any differences in legislation as soon as possible after you get settled.
6. When you sell your home you may be asked to take back a mortgage on it. If you do, all interest you receive on the mortgage will be taxable, with the possible exception of the first $1,000. If you are asked to take back a mortgage, borrow the money from the bank, then lend it to the buyer who will pay it back to you as an increase in his or her downpayment. Charge him or her the same rate as you are paying at the bank. This makes the cost of borrowing tax deductible and offsets tax on the interest income you receive from the buyer. If you take back the mortgage directly, you will pay more tax than you have to.
7. When you buy a new home, put as much cash into it as possible. If you must get a mortgage consider paying a little more to keep it open. Most mortgages are arranged through large financial institutions such as banks, trust companies, and insurance companies. These institutions tend to be inflexible in their terms, so you might consider other sources, such as your parents. Don't be embarrassed to borrow from members of your family; most parents would rather lend money to their children to help them buy a house than give it to a financial institution and in turn provide mortgage money to some stranger. Besides, your parents would deal directly with you. You can pay them a better rate than they would get with a financial institution, in the form of a guaranteed investment certificate, yet still strike a better bargain for yourself. When looking for money to finance the purchase of a home, don't forget your employer. The difference between the

interest charged on the loan by the employer and the "normal" rate* of interest established by the federal tax authorities will be a taxable benefit. Nevertheless, employee loans remain one of the less costly ways of obtaining mortgage money.

MOVING OUT OF THE COUNTRY

More and more people are being transferred out of the country. If this happens to you, get professional advice before leaving Canada to help you make the right decisions. If possible, get your employer to pay the cost of this service for you. The following are some of the more important considerations.

1. Determine whether you will be considered a Canadian resident or non-resident for tax purposes. As a general rule, you cannot count on being considered non-resident unless you will be out of Canada for two years or more. Certain people, such as members of the armed forces, federal or provincial government employees, and people who work for Canadian International Assistance Programs, are considered Canadian residents even though they may be living abroad all year round.

   With proper planning, being a non-resident for several years can be financially rewarding, although it is now more difficult to arrange. Effective January 1980 the Income Tax Act was amended so that Canadians employed abroad for six months or more under a Canadian contract for the exploration or exploitation of natural resources, or working in the construction, agriculture, or engineering business, or seeking contracts for a Canadian employer, will still be considered Canadian residents for tax purposes. If you are in this category, 50% of your employment income to a maximum $50,000 will be exempt from tax.
2. Contact your District Taxation Office at least ten days in advance of your departure from Canada, so that your income tax records can be adjusted. Tax must be paid by April 30 in the year following departure.
3. Review your investments before you leave the country. On the one hand, interest rates in Canada are high compared to the rest of the world and you may wish to keep your money invested here. On the other hand, if you are uncertain about the future of the Canadian dollar, you may want to liquidate your various holdings. Some countries have exchange controls, and once the money is in the country you might have difficulty getting it out.

---

*This rate is determined quarterly in advance and is based upon the 91-day treasury bill rate. The rates for the four quarters of 1985 were 12%, 10%, 10%, and 9% respectively. The deemed rate for Quebec was 11% for all of 1985.

Before you leave Canada, check to see if you pay tax on your world income in the country to which you are moving, including investment income earned in the country to which you are moving and investment income earned in Canada.

At the same time, determine if interest payments being made for investment loans in both Canada and your new country are deductible against income in your new country.

Because of tax treaties between Canada and other countries, it may still be worthwhile to continue with your Canadian investments — on the other hand, the difficulty of managing them from a distance might suggest selling them.

Timing, too, is important. It may be worthwhile to wait until after the end of the year you leave to sell the investments. Most investment income paid out of Canada to a resident of another country will be subject to a 15-25% withholdings tax, depending upon the country to which you are moving. This tax will be credited against tax payable in another country if there is a tax treaty between the two countries. If your investment situation raises a lot of questions, make sure you obtain professional help.

4. If you have Canadian pension, DPSP, or RRSP income, you can make an election under section 217 of the Income Tax Act to have all or part of your income from these sources defined as Canadian income, and you can have it taxed in Canada even though you are resident in another country.

   For example, if your standard Canadian deductions totalled $7,000, the amount ($7,000) of income could come to you tax free. The size of the deductions will vary (for details see Chapter 8; note that the deductions could include such things as ongoing MURB write-offs). Tax will be withheld on the income you received, but you will be able to claim it back from Revenue Canada on the tax-free portion of your income. The balance of the tax will be treated as a tax credit on your foreign return.

5. Remember that an organization that sends you pension payments, dividends, or other types of income from Canada to an address outside the country will be required to withhold tax at source. The rate of tax withheld is between 5% and 25%, depending on the type of payment you receive and the country where you have become a resident. You can obtain a complete list of withholding tax rules and rates from Revenue Canada.

   If you are retired, certain income is exempt from non-resident withholding tax. Included are payments from the Canada or Quebec Pension Plan, Old Age Security, and pension plans for service during a year in which you were not a resident.

6. If you are transferred by your company outside Canada, make sure

you settle in advance all details concerning group insurance and pension arrangements. Also ask about provisions for housing, tax equalization programs, hardship allowances, and home leave.
7. When you arrive in the new country of residence, locate a competent adviser who can help you with financial planning. Ask questions such as: Is mortgage interest tax deductible? How do income tax rates compare with those in Canada? How should I be paid? In other words, is there an advantage in taking certain non-cash forms of compensation as opposed to cash or bonus? Are there exchange controls if I invest my money in a new country and then move on again either to another country or back to Canada? What about my wills? Will they have effect in the new country or should I have new wills drawn?

TERMINATION

Most people assume they will never be dismissed from a job. When it does happen the shock is so severe that many people make unnecessary financial errors. The fact is that being dismissed often can be a blessing in disguise; among other things, it represents an ideal time to do some creative financial planning.

Every employee has certain minimum rights. They are set down in the Employment Standards Act. The actual entitlement upon dismissal is dictated by common law. For example, the Employment Standards Act says that if you have been with a company for from two to five years you are entitled to two weeks' notice in writing or two weeks' pay in lieu of notice as a termination allowance. In practice, payments can be as much as two years' salary or more. What a person is entitled to depends on what is deemed to be reasonable under the circumstances. Such factors as age, length of time employed, promises made upon hiring, conditions under which the person was dismissed, and opportunities in the job market help to determine what is reasonable.

These payments, sometimes called severance pay, can be made in the form of:

1. A continuation of salary for a predetermined period of time.
2. A retiring allowance (payment) in recognition of long service, loss of office, or loss of employment.

The way you receive your severance payment can have a major effect on the net amount you will have left after tax. Since continuing salary represents no change, this has natural appeal. However, in most instances, a retiring allowance is more appropriate.

If your salary is continued, it will be taxed in the normal fashion; i.e., all of the income will be taxable. This could create serious tax problems, if you relocate quickly and have income from two jobs.

With a retiring allowance, the money is usually paid in a lump sum, thus giving you the use of the money. Furthermore, many relocation counsellors feel making a clean break with your former employer has a positive emotional impact.

As outlined, a retiring allowance can be paid either in a lump sum or in regular instalments. Certain amounts can be transferred to an RRSP — $2,000 for every part or whole calendar year you have been with your employer plus, for 1985 and previous years, $1,500 for every part or whole calendar year you have been with your employer for which there is no vesting of employer contributions to a Registered Pension Plan or Deferred Profit Sharing Plan.

For example, if you joined a company in November 1967 and left in October 1985, and five years' pension credits were vested, you would be entitled to 19 years × $2,000 + 14 years × $1,500, or $59,000.

It is proposed the amount that can be transferred to an RRSP from a retiring allowance will be as outlined above for the years prior to 1985, and then only $2,000 for each year after that date. You will, however, be able to make additional contributions to an RRSP under the proposed new contribution limits.

Your former employer can transfer funds directly to the RRSP with no withholding tax, or the employer can pay you directly subject to withholding tax (10% under $5,000; 20% between $5,000 and $15,000; 30% over $15,000); however, you can recover this withholding tax to the extent you contribute to an RRSP by March 1 of the year following receipt of the income.

The best route to take for you, the employee, will depend on many things, including personal debt and the time it takes you to relocate. You should note, however, that amounts of termination payments "rolled" to an RRSP will be included as income for purposes of calculating the minimum tax you must pay under the new Alternative Minimum Tax.

When you lose your job your employer is obligated to treat you properly and fairly unless you have given him or her just cause for immediate dismissal. If there is any question in your mind whether you were properly dismissed, or are being offered proper compensation, we suggest you consult your lawyer promptly. He or she will be concerned with preserving your rights. Avoid making statements or signing documents that could prejudice your case.

It is worth noting, too, that if you leave a job of your own accord it is your responsibility to provide proper notice. A sudden departure can be expensive to the company and you could conceivably find yourself on the wrong end of a lawsuit.

If you are dismissed or leave on your own accord, we suggest you take the following steps:

1. Immediately go to the personnel department and review with them your various employee benefits.

a) *Group life insurance.* You will be covered under the group life insurance program for thirty-one days after your termination date. You have the option of continuing your group coverage on your own, regardless of your health, by purchasing term insurance which will cover you for one year, after which time if you wish to continue with the insurance you must convert to permanent insurance (whole life or endowment coverage). Some plans allow you to purchase level term insurance to age sixty-five that may be converted at any time before age sixty-five, or you may purchase permanent insurance. The least expensive method is to purchase the one-year term insurance. However, you must remember that if you want to continue the insurance beyond one year it will be necessary to convert it to more expensive permanent coverage. Before you sign up, determine what the premium will be from the group plan, then check with your insurance agent on the price for alternate forms of term insurance. If you are in good health, and particularly if you are not a cigarette smoker, chances are the insurance agent will be able to provide the coverage for less than your group plan, and you will be able to continue it on a term basis for a much longer period of time. You should determine your insurability within thirty-one days, because the option of continuing with your group insurance at standard rates expires thirty-one days after you leave the company.

b) *Disability coverage.* Your disability coverage will cease the day you cease employment. Since it is extremely difficult to purchase this type of coverage when you are unemployed, this is an exposure you may have to live with.

c) *Major medical and dental coverage.* This coverage normally ceases the day you leave. You can buy major medical coverage on an individual basis through Blue Cross. If you are fortunate enough to live in the province of Manitoba you may purchase dental coverage on an individual basis as well through Blue Cross. Both plans are subject to high deductibles and high co-insurance. However, this coverage should be worth purchasing if you are going to be unemployed for some time or if no group insurance is available at your new job.

d) *Provincial medical insurance plans.* The provincial medical insurance authorities should be notified immediately of your departure, and it will be up to you to pay any required premium on your own.

e) *Pension Plan.* Depending upon your age and length of service with the company, you may be able to take the money accumulated in your pension plan as income, or transfer it into a Registered Retirement Savings Plan. But before you blow the money in your pension plan on that new piece of furniture, remember the purpose of your pension plan is to help you save for retirement, so generally you should try to transfer as much as possible into an RRSP.

If you think you may need the pension money for your living expenses, transfer your pension to several RRSPs, then systematically collapse the RRSPs one at a time, but only if you really need the money. Make sure the underlying RRSP investment is liquid.

If the amount surrendered is less than $5,000, the amount of tax withheld is 10% at the time, but additional tax will be levied up to your marginal rate when you file your tax return.

An alternative, if you need the money, is to take the pension in cash and then transfer it to an RRSP later. If you do, the following steps could be taken:

i. Have the money paid to you in cash (there will be a withholding tax of up to 30% of the amount in the pension plan).
ii. Use the amount received in cash to pay your non-deductible interest expenses such as the mortgage on your home, or use it to help create $1,000 of tax-free investment income.
iii. Before the first of March in the year following receipt of the money from the pension plan, deposit an amount equal to the pre-tax pension proceeds into an RRSP. Borrow it if necessary. Other things being equal, the amount of tax withheld will be returned to you, and could be directed toward the payment of the mortgage on your home.
iv. If you have no personal debt, you would be wise to transfer the money directly into an RRSP.

Before you withdraw your pension money, however, determine whether you are eligible to make a past service contribution to your pension plan. If you are eligible you may contribute $3,500 to the past service portion of your plan plus $3,500 for current service contributions for a total deferral of $7,000. The past service contribution can be made even after you have left the company. However, it must be done by the end of the year in which you leave and before taking any money out of the plan. The contribution for the current year (current service) must be made before you leave. This may be the only chance you ever get to contribute for past service and it could add substantially to your pool of tax-sheltered retirement funds. Note that based on recent proposals you will not be allowed to make voluntary past service pension contributions for any year after 1986.

2. People who have been dismissed are normally very anxious about where the money will come from to meet ongoing expenditures. A budget at this time is vital. Sit down with your family and work out the money needed. As mentioned earlier, money coming from a termination allowance can be deposited into a series of short-term RRSP deposits to help provide the monthly income you require.

3. Unless your company had a policy in force prior to December 31, 1984, you will not be eligible to receive unemployment insurance payments until after the "time value" of your company-paid severance payments has expired; e.g., if you receive three months' severance, UIC considers this as income and hence you will not be eligible for payments until after three months. Unemployment insurance also considers as income for these purposes other payments such as a car, and effective January 1, 1986, pension income. You should review this with you personnel department to determine when you can expect to receive unemployment insurance.

SEPARATION AND DIVORCE

Marriage breakdown is an increasingly common and socially accepted hazard of modern living. Society has begun to respond to the phenomenon. Counselling services and social clubs have been organized to help the ex-married through the emotional trauma and social dislocation of a separation or divorce. Despite increased interest in the problems of separated spouses, many remain confused and uninformed about the legal, financial, and tax aspects of separation and divorce settlements.

Marital Property Regimes

All provinces in Canada now have established statutory marital regimes which, among other things, dictate property rights between spouses when their marriage breaks up. It is defined in some of the provincial statutes, and implied in others, that marriage is an economic and financial partnership.

With the recent changes in family law in several provinces, anyone getting married, whether for the first time or not, would be wise to consider a marriage contract.

While the rules vary from province to province, the general trend is to distribute all of the property equally between spouses, with the exception of property brought to the marriage or inherited during the marriage. This distribution includes business interests as well as personal assets.

It is possible to contract out of these arrangements, and couples should discuss this openly when they are on good terms and not when they are on the brink of separation or divorce. This could eliminate considerable trauma and costly valuation and legal fees if the marriage breaks down.

Wherever you live in Canada, if you are involved in separation or divorce or are seriously contemplating it, you should obtain competent legal advice on what your rights are to a share of property of all kinds, regardless of who owns it or who paid for it. Starting from that base, you can work out details of a legal settlement involving distribution of other property and arrangement for maintenance payments.

Tax Planning and Divorce

Perhaps because of guilt or emotional trauma, tax planning is often neglected. The biggest single problem in most divorce actions is that there isn't enough money to go around. For that reason, effective planning to minimize taxes can considerably ease financial problems.

Capital Settlement

A capital settlement involves payments of a lump sum of money — either in cash or equivalent property value — as a partial or total substitute for making regular maintenance payments. It is the simplest solution to the financial problems of divorce and in many circumstances is most attractive to both parties because it allows a quick and clean financial break. It is important to note, however, that capital settlements are not tax deductible, although you may save enough in maintenance payments through the capital settlement to offset this disadvantage.

Typically, the most valuable capital asset owned by either spouse is equity in the family home. Understandably, a spouse may quibble about handing over his or her most valuable financial asset. However, to retain an interest in a house where your spouse will continue to reside can lead to a number of problems:

1. You may have to wait a long time to realize your share of the proceeds.
2. As a result, your maintenance payments will be higher in the meantime.
3. If you buy a new house and designate it your principal residence, your interest in the old family home becomes subject to tax on capital gains when it is sold, subject to the terms of the lifetime capital gains exemption.
4. Paying your share of the mortgage on the family home directly could be a non-tax-deductible payment. If you give up your equity in the home, and include an element for the mortgage payment in your maintenance payment, the total amount will be tax deductible.

A capital settlement can also be attractive from the receiving spouse's standpoint. It provides outright ownership of the family home, an opportunity for tax-free capital appreciation, and freedom from concern about the ex-spouse keeping up maintenance payments.

Maintenance or Support Payments

Often, equity in the family home is not sufficient to make a complete settlement from that source alone. It is far more common for settlement to require regular monthly maintenance payments in lieu of or in addition to a capital settlement.

Tax Planning and Maintenance Payments

Many divorce actions have been made even more acrimonious because of resentment at what is considered unfair tax treatment of maintenance payments and receipts.

Here are some hints on the tax aspects of maintenance payments:

1. Get a formal separation agreement as soon as possible. Voluntary payments are not likely to be tax deductible, but payments under a formal agreement are.* While lawyers are necessary, try to work out an agreement yourself, then have the lawyer formalize it.
2. Include all possible items in the regular maintenance payment. The paying spouse can receive tax relief only on payments which are taxable income to the receiving spouse. Payments to third parties are deductible provided they are pursuant to a formal agreement, are periodic, and are made to or for the benefit of the spouse or the children in custody of the spouse.
3. Split maintenance payments between spouse and children eighteen or over. This minimizes tax in their hands by making a full personal exemption available to the spouse and each child to write off against income received. If you are the paying spouse, apply to the source deductions branch of Revenue Canada for a reduction in tax at source, in anticipation of deductions for maintenance payments.
4. If you are the receiving spouse, make sure you take advantage of the "equivalent to married" extra personal tax exemption as long as you remain unmarried.
5. Pension benefits should be discussed. They are often large and it is understandable that a receiving spouse would want to share in them.

As a substitute for a share of pension benefits if they turn out to be unavailable, provide long-term protection with life insurance or a reversionary annuity. The latter guarantees that if the paying spouse dies before the receiving spouse, regular income payments will be made to the receiving spouse for life. Remember, too, it is now possible for a spouse to get a share of the other person's Canada Pension Plan benefits after divorce.

Marriage Contracts and "Domestic Agreements"

It is said that the best defence against heart disease is a good set of parents. In recent years, more and more couples contemplating marriage, or those who are already married, as well as couples who contemplate living together but not marrying, have realized that the best way to avoid fighting over separation or divorce settlements is to draw up an agreement before entering into a relationship, or at least before it starts to break down.

---

*Payments made prior to a formal agreement being signed are also deductible, but not until the agreement is signed, and can be deducted retroactively only to the first of the year in which the agreement was signed or when the separation occurred, whichever comes last.

For many, a marriage contract is a new idea. Anyone considering one should seek expert advice from a lawyer, but make sure the lawyer you choose is indeed an expert in this area. Ask for references and ask a lot of specific questions about his or her experience before hiring him or her to work for you.

Financial Planning for Your Future

Separation and divorce create two financial units where there was only one before. In most marriages, the burden of financial management rests with one spouse. The spouse who hasn't had that responsibility before is faced with learning a whole new set of skills — budgeting, balancing bank accounts, making decisions about saving and borrowing, and arranging various forms of insurance. It is a rare person who can handle this effectively without help. The spouse with experience in family finance may be able to help if communication hasn't broken down. If he or she can't or won't, outside expertise will be required.

Even the spouse with experience in handling money may need help dealing with the unfamiliar burdens of maintenance payments, along with the separate cost of accommodation, transportation, vacations, etc. He or she may well have less disposable income to work with than ever before, and both personal discipline and outside expertise may be required to make a go of it.

Those who need help should read Chapter 15 to find out how to choose a financial adviser. The time and money spent to acquire a team of competent people is the best investment that can be made for financial security and peace of mind.

WIDOWHOOD

"When Martin died, I lost so much — lover, confidant, companion, counsellor — he was a thousand things to me. And at the same time, the money stopped."

— Lynne Caine, *Widow*

What to Do When Your Spouse Has Died

Of the changes in our lives that can jar us, none is more traumatic than the death of a spouse. Unfortunately, it is often made more devastating by the financial and legal problems that inevitably ensue. Chapter 12 deals with the process of preparing for death in the family. Here we present a checklist for the widow or widower as she or he sets out on what may be a totally new, confusing, even terrifying solo flight into the realm of money management and financial planning.

The first thing to remember is to not make any immediate moves, such as selling your home. It takes time to get over the death of a spouse, often as long as a year or more. So wait until emotions have calmed down before risking major changes. Some things, however, must be done right away.

Immediate Concerns

1. Locate and read the last will. There may be instructions that must be carried out immediately in order to prevent losses — for example, options for the purchase of shares, or assets that can be exercised only in a short fixed period of time from date of death.
2. Employ competent advisers to help with estate administration — a law firm, trust company or financial adviser. Trying to do it yourself to save money will probably cause mistakes and will cost you extra legal fees to undo the damage. The outline in Chapter 12 of the duties of an executor should be helpful.
3. Make sure property insurance on cars, home, and other real estate, and tangible possessions will continue in force.
4. Make sure you understand your rights under the intestacy and family law acts. There may be alternatives to taking your share under the will that will yield a better result for you; but, typically, there's a deadline for making the decision.
5. File life insurance claims promptly, and apply for Canada or Quebec Pension Plan death and survivor benefits. If you are the beneficiary of pension benefits, RRSPs, or DPSPs, check to see what options are available to you regarding deferrals, rollovers, or forms of cash payments.
6. Do some serious estate planning of your own (see Chapter 12). Do you have a will? Does it meet the needs of your present situation? Are trustee and guardian appointments required because of minor children? What about life insurance? Do you have enough? Do you have any? If you die, will your children be orphans? Consider granting a general power of attorney to a key adviser in case you become physically or mentally incompetent to handle your own financial affairs. This will, for instance, allow the disposal of assets to provide for your maintenance.
7. Do some aggressive tax planning to maximize take-home income and net return on savings and investments. Try to generate at least $1,000 of interest or dividend income to use up the $1,000 deduction. Make maximum RRSP contributions, if possible. If your income is large enough, consider other tax shelters.
8. Recruit financial and investment advisers to help you set planning priorities, and to help you decide the investments best suited to meeting those objectives. For instance, if you anticipate substantial extra expenses or tuition fees within a year, it would be wise to invest the sums required in short-term deposits rather than lock them into five-year GICs or equity investments.

9. Work out a budget based on your new situation. What sources of income have been lost? Have any new ones been created? Have any major expenditures been added or eliminated? Be realistic. If you're a widow who will be working for the first time in many years, be sure to incorporate your *take-home* pay into the budget. Don't forget to include extra expenses you may have to incur — gas and oil, car maintenance, a better wardrobe, domestic help, etc.
10. Many widows and widowers remarry. But many, in the emotion of the event, neglect to talk about money. As with any marriage, there are financial questions to discuss, such as: Who pays for what? Who looks after the bills? Who is responsible for the cost of the children's education? What happens to the assets in the event of death? Don't forget your obligations to your children. Many families have been torn apart after the parents have remarried and the family treasures have ended up in the hands of a step-parent or step-sibling. Talk about this with your own children, even if they are on their own and are financially independent. Make sure you draw up a new will, and consider a marriage contract as well.

An existing will is null and void if you remarry. If you do not draw up a new will, your new spouse will have automatic rights, as outlined in Chapter 12, but they may bear no resemblance to what you both want.

A FINAL WORD

Don't cop out. Don't hide behind a facade of false modesty. Or if you really don't know, take time to learn about money. "I'm spastic when it comes to money," may sound cute, but if you are a pawn in the hands of advisers or con artists, you are doomed to anxiety about your financial position and probably to less disposable income. Even the best advisers do better when challenged by an alert, discerning client.

DO'S AND DON'TS

Moving

Do Consider the timing of your move, if possible, and allow time to prepare for it properly.

Do Take advantage of your move to make the best mortgage arrangements. If you move internationally, get financial help in both countries.

Don't Forget to review wills and notify the various financial advisers and institutions involved of your move.

Termination

Do Know your rights upon dismissal. If you have any questions, check with a competent lawyer.

Do Review your employee benefits.

Do Take advantage of this time to work out a budget and do other financial planning.

Do Make sure you have your severance payments clearly defined.

Don't Thoughtlessly cash in your pension plan or other tax deferral plans.

Divorce

Do Seek expert advice early — to deal with available money in the most tax-effective way.

Do Consider working out a marriage contract to settle property questions while relations are good and negotiations can be carried on amicably.

Do Consider a capital settlement — particularly the family home.

Do Pay attention to financial and tax considerations.

Do Plan for the future — you still have one.

Don't Let guilt feelings make you defensive about standing up for your financial rights.

Widowhood

Do Locate and read the will immediately.

Do Make sure homeowner and car insurance stays in force.

Do Seek competent advice and take advantage of rollover provisions from tax-deferral plans.

Do Educate yourself in financial matters and your property rights under the law.

Don't Forget your own estate planning, including insurance on your own life.

Don't Make any major moves until your emotions have stabilized.

Don't Neglect to discuss your financial affairs with your new spouse and your children if you remarry.

CHAPTER 15

Professional Advisers

"Free advice is worth exactly what it costs."

— Eliot Janeway

To get competent professional advice, both financial and legal, you must learn how to recognize and take advantage of competence in your adviser.

RULES FOR FINDING AN ADVISER AND USING HIS OR HER SKILLS

Rule 1: Remember Professional Advisers Are in Business To Make Money

Advisers make their money by providing a service for you, the buyer. It is possible, therefore, that an adviser may provide you with services you do not require. An adviser can be as prone to create excessive fees as a salesperson can be to oversell. In other words, don't automatically identify a fee with objectivity.

Rule 2: Take the Time To Find the Adviser Who Is Right for You

Ask someone whose business judgment you trust to recommend someone to you. Make sure this recommendation is based on personal experience. Ask about the adviser's strong points, then call the person to arrange an interview. The purpose of this interview is to help you decide whether or not *you* want the adviser, not vice versa.

Ask about qualifications, education, practical experience, and areas of expertise. Listen to his or her approach and make sure your personalities don't clash. Ask for names, occupations, and phone numbers of a few clients, and get permission to call them. Check these references immediately.

Rule 3: Find Out How Your Adviser Is Paid

Before deciding, get an estimate of cost and how the adviser expects to be paid. Remember, the lowest price is not necessarily the best bargain.

Rule 4: Know What You Want the Adviser To Do

Take the time to think about your plans. In the long run you'll save time and money — and you'll get better advice. For example, if you have put together all your income and expense documentation before you ask your accountant to do your income tax return, the time he or she saves will mean money in your pocket. The same applies to will planning with a lawyer.

Rule 5: Be Honest with Your Adviser

Tell your adviser about your objectives, and don't try to second-guess. A good one will work out a plan that is best suited to your lifestyle.

Once you have chosen an adviser, trust his or her judgment. If you have an insurance adviser, for example, do not call six other agents and ask each of them to quote a price. It is your own adviser's job to get the best price for you.

Rule 6: Don't Expect Your Adviser To Be an Expert Outside His or Her Specialty

Many financial advisers have a good working knowledge of areas outside their specialty. However, they are rarely able to keep up with current specifics in other fields — recent amendments to legislation or new products available. Don't ask a mortgage broker to do your income tax, or your accountant to pick your investments.

Rule 7: Review Your Situation Yearly

Establish a regular date each year when you will get together with your adviser to review and update your program. This is absolutely essential, not only because of changes in the economic or legislative environment, but also because of inevitable changes in your attitudes, priorities, family, and career situations.

INSURANCE AGENTS

Most of us have at least two insurance agents — the one who sells life insurance and the one who insures our cars and homes.

Insurance agents are paid according to the type of policy sold. This could vary anywhere from 1% on an annuity, to 15% on car insurance, to 100% or more on the first annual premium of a life insurance policy. The commission on life insurance is highest the first year; commissions for subsequent years are designed to compensate the agent for attending to a client's needs beyond the first year. Most "general lines" agents who sell insurance other than life insurance are paid the same rate of commission each year the policy is in force.

Find out if your prospective agent has a strong bias toward any particular type of insurance. An agent who wants to sell only higher premium whole life may have trouble getting you enough protection for what you can afford to pay. Arrange to interview the agent at his or her office, where you can learn about the kind of operation he or she runs. Some first-rate agents refuse to see people in their homes in the evening.

Ask how long the agent has been in business. Many work in the industry for a year or two and then go on to something else. While it is nice to help young people get started, it is more important to know that your agent will be there to give you service when you need it. Chances are an agent who has survived in the business for five years will still be in it five years from now.

When you ask about your agent's professional qualifications, find out whether he or she has or is on the way to getting an FIIC (Fellow of the Insurance Institute of Canada) or CLU (Chartered Life Underwriter) designation. These designations are awarded by insurance associations only after an agent has completed an intensive course of study and passed certain examinations. Many competent agents do not have these designations, but having them implies that an agent takes his or her responsibilities seriously.

If your prospective adviser is a life agent, make sure he or she asks you a lot of questions before recommending a particular insurance plan. If he or she fails to mention disability coverage or tries to sell you a whole life policy on your three-year-old before getting around to mentioning disability income insurance, get another agent.

Make sure your prospective agent is interested in the size of your account, no matter how small. Some competent agents sell millions of dollars worth of insurance a year, and may not be interested enough in a small account to allow you to benefit from their superior knowledge and skills.

Find out, too, if the agent works for only one company or sells the products of a variety of companies. An agent who sells many different products may be better equipped to select the right company and product for you.

LAWYERS

A lawyer is primarily a legal adviser, not a business adviser. Many people feel their lawyer is the source of all wisdom and, unfortunately, some lawyers do nothing to dispel that illusion. A good lawyer will admit his or her limitations; a poor one will not. Most lawyers know no more than the average layperson about such things as stocks, bonds, or insurance.

Lawyers are trained to look at the legal aspects and consequences of financial transactions and draft documents like wills, trusts, business agreements, real estate contracts, and divorce and separation settlements. They are usually paid on a fee-for-service basis, determined by the time spent on an individual project or by a suggested price set down by their local bar association. Hourly rates range from $50 to $250 or more. Fees can also be determined by the amount of money involved in a particular project. If, for example, your lawyer is able to save you $100,000 with about two hours' work, expect your bill to be more than the usual fee for this amount of his or her time.

It is important to realize that lawyers specialize, even if they don't advertise the fact. A good corporation lawyer may be a whiz at corporate mergers but a wash-out at drawing up a will. When choosing your lawyer, make sure he or she is competent in the area that concerns you.

Before using a lawyer's services, get a fee estimate and set a deadline for completion of the transaction. Remember, too, that lawyers are prohibited by their code of ethics from soliciting business, so the responsibility of initiating contact rests with you.

ACCOUNTANTS

For personal financial planning, you can use accountants in two ways: to perform a mechanical function (e.g., completing your income tax return); or helping you plan for the future.

Planning will require more of your accountant's time, and hence he or she will charge a higher fee. However, if you are self-employed or earning more than $50,000 a year, the fee is probably worthwhile. Accountants' fees normally range from $50 to $250 per hour.

STOCKBROKERS

A stockbroker works for an investment dealer. He or she gets paid a commission for the purchase and sale on your behalf of stocks, bonds, debentures, and short-term money market instruments. Recently, stockbrokers have begun selling movies, mortgages, syndicated oil leases, and other tax shelters.

Today you should expect to pay a stock broker 2% to 3% on the sale and purchase of common stocks. These commission rates are usually a function of the value of the transaction and the price of the individual stock. Commissions are negotiable, but be prepared to pay a fair price, particularly if the broker provides a lot of assistance and/or research back-up. If the broker is merely processing an order, consider asking for a reduced rate or use a discount broker.

On bond purchases brokers are normally paid from the "spread" between the price at which their firm purchased the bond and the price at which they sell it to you.

A number of investment dealers also underwrite securities, and stockbrokers are sometimes accused of promoting only the stocks their own firms have underwritten. Try to determine in advance whether this is the case.

Ask about the firm's research department, areas of specialization, the number of investment options available, and whether or not the individual broker has passed the IDA courses. Make sure, too, that the stockbroker asks you a lot of questions and spends time helping you define your objectives. Find out how successful he or she has been with personal investments. If he or she does not have money in the stock market, you may have chosen the wrong person.

INVESTMENT COUNSELLORS

Some people who are concerned about the lack of objectivity of stockbrokers deal with an investment counselling firm. Investment counsellors do not receive a commission for the sale of securities. Instead, they charge a fee for services usually ranging from ½% to 1% of the money under management and normally require a minimum account of $100,000–$250,000.

Since investment counsellors are paid according to the value of assets under management, they have an interest in increasing your net worth. When choosing a firm, make sure you find out how long the firm has been in business, the turnover rate of accounts, and the firm's success record with investments. Insist on meeting the person who will handle your account and interview him or her in depth about his or her personal background and qualifications.

One advantage in dealing with investment counsellors is that their fees are tax deductible.

REAL ESTATE AGENTS

A home may be the most important purchase you will ever make, so it's worth the effort to do some preliminary research before you contact a real estate agent. Decide upon the area you'd like to live in, find a firm with a number of listings in that area, then choose an agent in that firm who knows the area thoroughly (if you have not already been referred to someone). Ideally, that person should have lived and worked in the area for some time. Meet the agent, tell him or her what you are looking for, and then let him or her go to work for you.

It may take some time to find what you want. A good agent, however, will know what is going on in the neighbourhood, what will come onto the market, and what constitutes a reasonable price. Often the best buys will not even appear on the market because an agent who is familiar with the neighbourhood will know of an upcoming listing beforehand and pick it for his or her client.

The real estate broker receives 5% to 6% of the price of the house, and the agent usually gets 50% of that.

MORTGAGE BROKERS

It is important to obtain a mortgage on the most favourable terms possible. If you have time, shop around at various financial institutions such as trust companies, banks, and insurance companies. If you do not have the time, or if the deal is complicated and difficult to conclude, your real estate agent or lawyer can help you. Lawyers and real estate agents, however, are paid separately for placing mortgages and usually have access to only one or two sources of money.

If you want professional advice from a specialist, consult a mortgage broker. Mortgage brokers deal with a number of different lenders and always have several alternative sources of money available. They can save you a lot of time by getting you the best interest rate, particularly for a second mortgage or a high-ratio mortgage.

If mortgage money is easy to obtain, a mortgage broker will probably be paid by the financial institution doing the lending. If money is hard to come by, you may have to pay him or her. Before you deal with a mortgage broker, make sure you ask how much his or her services will cost. The fee should not be more than ½% to 1½% of the value of the mortgage.

Your mortgage broker also can be useful if you want to invest in a mortgage. Often brokers will divide large commercial mortgages into small units and sell them to individual investors.

BANK MANAGERS

A bank manager can show you how best to use the bank's facilities and help you obtain a loan. People often become intimidated when they borrow money. They feel the bank is doing them a favour. This is not the case. Remember, when you are arranging a loan you are the buyer and the bank is the seller in a highly competitive market. If one bank manager doesn't give you the service or the rate you feel you deserve, go next door. Unless you have let your credit rating deteriorate, you will always find a number of financial institutions happy to accommodate you.

TRUST OFFICERS

Trust officers are employed by trust companies; they usually work in the estate planning area. In most jurisdictions lawyers are required by law to execute wills, but the drafting work can be done by a trust officer. Have him or her draft your will; you'll get the benefit of expert advice and possibly save some money. However, there is a catch: trust companies expect you to name them as the executor or trustee of your estate. Before you even consider a trust will, the value of your estate should be $250,000 to $300,000 and you should need and want the continuous professional management of your estate.

The trust company will not charge you for drafting the will; however, it will levy fees when you die. They vary and can be negotiated. The amount set down by law and applicable to all executors, not just trust companies, is 5% of the total capital, plus an approximate annual fee of up to 1% of the total amount on deposit. Thus, if your estate is $300,000 there is a 5% charge of $15,000 plus an annual fee of about $3,000. When a person outside the trust company is appointed executor and the trust company provides expertise, the trust company charges a fee of approximately 3% of the capital.

FINANCIAL PLANNERS

When the first edition of *It's Your Money* was written, we were one of the few financial planning groups in Canada. Today it seems anyone even remotely connected with giving personal financial planning advice or selling a financial product is calling himself/herself a financial planner. At the date of writing, no government has deemed it necessary to regulate this practice; however, the Canadian Association of Financial Planners (CAFP) is trying to bring some cohesion and definition to this fast-growing industry.

Financial planners are a new breed of advisers who fill a void left by other groups. In the past many people did bits and pieces of financial planning, but until financial planners stepped in, no one was coordinating the whole effort.

Some firms provide only a few services while others have a broad range — from budget and will planning to tax return preparation. They can even help you negotiate how you get paid at work or when to quit your job.

The structure of financial planning firms varies. Some are one-person operations, others employ a number of specialists. Whatever your concerns or requirements, there are several steps involved in choosing a financial planner.

First, you should decide if you even need one. Here is a list of questions compiled by the Canadian Association of Financial Planners to help you determine if you need financial advice.

1. Do you have the time or interest to attend to your personal financial affairs?
2. Are you confused about conflicting financial advice from several sources?
3. Do you feel you are paying too much tax?
4. Are you confused about where to invest your money?
5. Do you feel you can't make ends meet?
6. Do you feel that you can't save any money?
7. Has there been a recent change in your life that could affect your financial future, such as retirement, job loss, an inheritance, an addition to your family, or loss of a spouse?

Second, you should understand the steps in the total financial planning process. The planner should:

1. Clarify your *present situation* through collecting and assessing all relevant financial data such as lists of assets and liabilities, tax returns, records of securities transactions, insurance policies, wills, pension plans, etc.
2. Help you decide where you want to go by identifying both financial and *personal goals and objectives*. The financial planning practitioner helps you clarify financial and personal values and attitudes. These may include providing for your children's education, supporting elderly parents or relieving immediate financial pressure which would help maintain your current lifestyle and provide for retirement. These considerations are as important as what's in your bank account in determining the best financial planning strategy for you.
3. Identify *financial problems* which create barriers to your financial independence. Problem areas can include too little or too much insurance coverage or a high tax burden. Your cash flow may be inadequate, or your current investments may not be winning the battle with inflation. These potential problem areas must be identified before solutions can be found.
4. Provide written *recommendations* and alternative solutions. The length of the recommendations will vary with the complexity of your individual situation, but they always should be structured to meet your needs without undue emphasis on purchasing certain investment products.
5. *Implement* or coordinate the *implementation* of the right strategy to assure that you reach your goals and objectives. A financial planner is only helpful if the recommendations are put into action. The practitioner should assist you either in actually implementing the recommendations or in coordinating the implementation with other knowledgeable professionals.
6. Provide *periodic review* and revision of your plan to assure that you achieve your goals. You should have your financial situation reassessed at least once a year to account for changes in your personal and current economic situations.

Third, you should know the questions to ask the financial planner. The following is excerpted from the CAFP's recently published *Consumer Guide to Financial Planning*.

> Before choosing a financial planner it is essential you meet to determine how well you get along. Ask for a short meeting. Discuss how the planner would work with you. Ask for any material he or she has to review prior to the meeting. Often this will answer many questions and give a basis for comparison

with other planners who have been contacted. Ask about the planner's background. Both the education and experience are important. Ask how long the planner has been counselling clients on total financial plans. Ask what relevant education the planner has. Ask for credentials. The Chartered Financial Planner (CFP) designation is awarded by the Canadian Institute of Financial Planning which has no official connection with the Canadian Association of Financial Planners. While this designation does not guarantee objective advice, it is an indication the individual has successfully completed a study program and passed examinations and is interested in a broad approach to financial affairs. There are many in the industry who have designations such as C.A., L.L.B. and C.L.U. Others have been providing valuable financial planning advice for many years and have no designation. Ask for references. Tell the planner you want to talk with clients whose situations and objectives are similar to yours. The planner also should be able to show you a sample financial plan of someone in circumstances such as yours (actual client information, of course, is held in strictest confidence).

Ask in which areas the planner is knowledgeable. Ideally this should include various areas, such as, but not limited to, investments, insurance, business administration, law, money management and tax strategies. Where service is not provided in house, the planner should have a close working relationship with accountants, lawyers, investment counsellors and other competent professionals. Most financial planners are primarily general planners but often specialize in one or more areas.

Ask if the planner concentrates on a particular type of client. It is not uncommon for a planner to work with a certain profession, income level or age group.

Ask if the planner would work with you directly or if an associate will handle your account. If an associate, ask to meet that person. Make sure he or she is well qualified too. Ask how the planner keeps clients informed such as through newsletters or seminars. Ask how often you can expect to meet.

Ask how the planner selects your investment solutions. He or she should do an independent analysis and not depend only on some other companies' research. The planner's role is to be your guide to financial products, but remember, you should be free to implement your plan with the planner or elsewhere.

Ask how the planner is compensated: by fee, fee and commission, or commission only. Ask how much you will pay for the planner's services and ask if the charge is for the plan only or for ongoing service as well. Hourly rates can range from $50 to $250 per hour. Ask if the planner is a member of the Canadian Association of Financial Planners. If not, why not? Do not hesitate to ask any other questions concerning a planner's methods, techniques or procedures. After all, you are asking that person to shape your financial future.

If you wish to obtain the services of a financial planner, speak to someone who has used one and be referred. If you do not know of any in your area, write the Canadian Association of Financial Planners, 130 Adelaide Street West, Toronto, for a list of financial planners in your area. This list, as well as giving you names, outlines the services provided and method of compensation employed.

Do-it-yourself may be fine for the house and garden, but when it comes to financial and legal matters, the stakes may be too high to risk costly mistakes. Take the time to find and work with skilled professional advisers. Your efforts will be rewarded in better service and greater peace of mind. After all, it's *your* money!

APPENDIX

The ECC Group Personal Financial Profile

SOME SUGGESTIONS FOR COMPLETING THIS PERSONAL FINANCIAL PROFILE

Most people have more assets than they realize. Please complete this profile without making a major project of it. It is not difficult but will require persistence. Do not get bogged down on any one part of it. Skip questions you cannot answer quickly, or are in doubt about. Keep going through the profile

Consult documents such as tax returns, wills, insurance policies, etc.; they are of vital importance as they provide precise and complete information which most people cannot duplicate from memory.

Good Luck!

PERSONAL AND FAMILY DATA

Immediate Family:

Full Name	*Place & Date of Birth*	*Education*	*Occupation*	*Health*	*Social Ins. No.*
You					
Spouse					
Children					

Adopted or Step-Children__________

Citizenship: All are citizens of__________ except__________

Residence: All live at home in__________ except__________

Number of grandchildren__________

Marital Status:__________ Marriage Contract: Yes_____ No_____

Home Address:__________ Phone #__________

Employer:__________ Since__________

Business Address:__________ Phone #__________

Nature of Work:__________

Other Family Members	*Relationship*	*Occupation*	*Address*

CAREER PROFILE

Recent Employers	*Position Description*	*Period Employed*	*Compensation*

1. What are the possibilities of assignment outside of Canada?
2. If so, to what part of the world?
3. For how long?
4. What is corporate strategy on expatriate compensation?

SOURCES OF INFORMATION

Professional Advisers:

	Name	*Address*	*Telephone #*
Lawyer			
Accountant			
Investments			
Bank Manager			
Life Insurance Agent			
General Insurance Agent			
Corporate Staff Employee Benefits Executive Payroll			
Other			

Worksheet 1
PERSONAL BALANCE SHEET

As of: ______________________________

	Ownership				*Projections**	
	You	*Joint*	*Spouse*	*Total*	*Projected Appreciation* (%)	*Projected Yield (yearly income)* (%)
ASSETS						
Liquid:						
Cash, CSBs, Short-term Deposits	______	______	______	______		______
GICs	______	______	______	______		______
Company Savings Plan	______	______	______	______		______
Promissory Notes	______	______	______	______		______
Other	______	______	______	______		______
Subtotal:	______	______	______	______		
Investments:						
Bonds (or Bond Funds)	______	______	______	______	______	______
Canadian Preferred Shares (or Funds)	______	______	______	______	______	______
Other	______	______	______	______	______	______
Cnd. Common Stock (or Common Stock Funds)	______	______	______	______	______	______

Other						
Other Canadian Mutual Funds						
Other Mutual Funds						
Tax Shelters						
Real Estate (other than residential)						
Mortgages						
Business Interests						
Other						
Subtotal:						
Tax Deferral Plans:						
**Pension Contributions						
RRSP, DPSP						
Deferred Compensation						
Other						
Subtotal:						
Fixed:						
Residence						
Seasonal Residence						
Furnishings (cars, etc.)						
Listed Personal Property (art, antiques, etc.)						
Subtotal:						
TOTAL ASSETS:						

Worksheet 1 (continued)
PERSONAL BALANCE SHEET

As of: ____________________

	Ownership				*Projections**	
	You	*Joint*	*Spouse*	*Total*	*Projected Appreciation* (%)	*Projected Yield (yearly income)* (%)
LIABILITIES						
Non-Investment Loans:						
Bank	____	____	____	____		
Mortgage (residential)	____	____	____	____		
Promissory Notes	____	____	____	____		
Other	____	____	____	____		
Subtotal:	____	____	____	____		
Loans (Investment/Business):						
Bank	____	____	____	____		
Other	____	____	____	____		
Subtotal:	____	____	____	____		
TOTAL LIABILITIES:	____	____	____	____		
NET WORTH:	====	====	====	====		

*Complete only if future financial estimates are required.

**Value of your pension contribution plus value of vested pension contributions by employer.

Worksheet 2
YEARLY INCOME AND EXPENDITURE STATEMENT

	You	*Spouse*	*Total*	*Projected % Rate In/(D)**
1. Regular Income:				
Salary	____	____	____	____
2. Less: Source Deductions:				
**Income Tax	____	____	____	
Pension	____	____	____	____
Group Benefits	____	____	____	____
Other	____	____	____	____
Subtotal:	____	____	____	
3. Take-home Pay: (1–2)	____	____	____	
4. Plus: Other Income:				
Bonus	____	____	____	____
Savings Plan	____	____	____	____
Other	____	____	____	____
Interest	____	____	____	
Dividends	____	____	____	
Subtotal:	____	____	____	
5. **Less: Tax on Other Income:	____	____	____	
6. Additional Cash Surplus: (4–5)	____	____	____	
7. Disposable Income: (3 + 6)	____	____	____	
8. Less: Estimated Budgeted Expenditures (from Worksheet 4)	____	____	____	____
Net Discretionary Income (Deficit): (7–8)	====	====	====	

*Complete only if future financial estimates are required.

**Enter approximate figure from Worksheet 3.

Worksheet 3:
DATA FOR ESTIMATED TAX RETURN

Tax Year: ____________________

	You	Spouse	*Projection % Rate**
Personal Information:			
Donations	________		________
Medical Expenses above OHIP	________		________
Employment Income:	________	________	
Taxable Benefits	________	________	________
Other Income:			
UIC Income	________	________	________
Pension or Superannuation	________	________	________
Taxable Canadian Dividends	________	________	
Capital Gains	________	________	
Canadian Interest Income	________	________	
Other Investment Income	________	________	
Other	________	________	________
Deductions:			
RPP	________	________	
RRSP	________	________	
Tuition	________	________	________
Dues	________	________	________
Interest	________	________	
Losses	________	________	________
Other	________	________	________
Other	________	________	________
Exemptions:			
Pension Deduction	________	________	________
Education Deduction	________	________	________
Personal Deduction	________	________	________
Age Deduction	________	________	________
Marriage Deduction	________	________	________
Dependant Deduction	________	________	________
Investment Deduction	________	________	________
Donations	________	________	________
Medical Deductions	________	________	________

Worksheet 4
ESTIMATED AVERAGE BUDGET EXPENDITURES

	Monthly		*Yearly*	
Debt Repayment				
Mortgage(s)	______		______	
Non-investment	______		______	
Other	______		______	
Investment	______		______	
Other	______	______	______	______
Insurance Premiums				
Car, home, property	______		______	
Life, disability, etc.	______		______	______
Home				
Rent	______		______	
Property taxes	______		______	
Household expenses (including heating, electricity, telephone, and Cable TV)	______		______	
Maintenance and domestic help	______		______	
Appliance replacement and decorating	______		______	
Other	______	______	______	______
Food				
Household	______		______	
Lunches	______	______	______	______
Clothing				
Yourself and/or family	______		______	
Laundry and dry cleaning	______	______	______	______
Personal Care				
Hairdresser	______		______	
Cosmetics	______		______	
Other	______	______	______	______
Medical				
Provincial plan	______		______	
Supplementary health plan	______		______	
Other – optician and glasses	______	______	______	______
Transportation				
Car lease payment(s)	______		______	
Gas and oil	______		______	
Car licence	______		______	
Car maintenance	______		______	
Subway, bus, cabs	______	______	______	______

(continued)

Discretionary

Club fees, recreation	______		______	
Entertainment and dining out	______		______	
Vacation, hobbies	______		______	
Special occasions (birthdays, etc.)	______		______	
Donations and gifts	______		______	
Children's education	______		______	
Children's allowances	______		______	
Personal spending money	______		______	
Liquor and Tobacco	______		______	
Other	______	______	______	______
TOTAL		======		======

Worksheet 5
CASHFLOW: SOURCES OF CASH—NEXT 12 MONTHS

NOTES
1. Enter current month under Column 1.
2. Indicate recurring amount with an "X" after the first entry for that amount.

	1	2	3	4	5	6	7	8	9	10	11	12
Month/year												
1. Regular Income												
Salary												
2. Less: Source Deductions												
Income Tax												
Pension												
Group Benefits												
Other												
Other												
Subtotal												
3. Take-home Pay (1 − 2)												
4. Plus: Other Income												
Bonus												
Savings Plan												
Interest												
Dividends												
Other												
Other												
Other												
Subtotal												
5. Less: Tax on other Income												
6. Additional Cash Surplus (4 − 5)												
7. Total all Sources (3 + 6)												

Worksheet 6
CASHFLOW: USES OF CASH—NEXT 12 MONTHS

	1	2	3	4	5	6	7	8	9	10	11	12
Month/Year												
Debt Repayment												
Mortgage(s)												
Non-Investment												
Other												
Investment												
Other												
Insurance Premiums												
Car, home, property												
Life, disability, etc.												
Home												
Rent												
Property taxes												
Household expenses (including heating, electricity, telephone, and Cable TV)												
Maintenance and domestic help												
Appliance replacement and decorating												
Other												
Food												
Household												
Lunches												

Clothing												
Yourself and/or family	____	____	____	____	____	____	____	____	____	____	____	____
Laundry and dry cleaning	____	____	____	____	____	____	____	____	____	____	____	____
Personal Care												
Hairdresser	____	____	____	____	____	____	____	____	____	____	____	____
Cosmetics	____	____	____	____	____	____	____	____	____	____	____	____
Other	____	____	____	____	____	____	____	____	____	____	____	____
Medical												
Provincial plan	____	____	____	____	____	____	____	____	____	____	____	____
Supplementary health plan	____	____	____	____	____	____	____	____	____	____	____	____
Other – optician and glasses	____	____	____	____	____	____	____	____	____	____	____	____
Transportation												
Car lease payment(s)	____	____	____	____	____	____	____	____	____	____	____	____
Gas and oil	____	____	____	____	____	____	____	____	____	____	____	____
Car licence	____	____	____	____	____	____	____	____	____	____	____	____
Car maintenance	____	____	____	____	____	____	____	____	____	____	____	____
Subway, bus, cabs	____	____	____	____	____	____	____	____	____	____	____	____
Discretionary												
Club fees, recreation	____	____	____	____	____	____	____	____	____	____	____	____
Entertainment and dining out	____	____	____	____	____	____	____	____	____	____	____	____
Vacation, hobbies	____	____	____	____	____	____	____	____	____	____	____	____
Special occasions (birthdays, etc.)	____	____	____	____	____	____	____	____	____	____	____	____
Donations and gifts	____	____	____	____	____	____	____	____	____	____	____	____
Children's education	____	____	____	____	____	____	____	____	____	____	____	____
Children's allowances	____	____	____	____	____	____	____	____	____	____	____	____
Personal spending money	____	____	____	____	____	____	____	____	____	____	____	____
Liquor and Tobacco	____	____	____	____	____	____	____	____	____	____	____	____
Other	____	____	____	____	____	____	____	____	____	____	____	____

Worksheet 7
ALLOCATION OF CASH SURPLUS TO SAVINGS AND INVESTMENT

NOTE

1. Enter dollar amounts, then allocate balance of income by putting a percentage in the appropriate row. Percentages must sum to one.

Discretionary Income: ______________ (from Worksheet 2) C.P.I. Projections: ________ %

Acct #	*Less: Allocations to Savings and Investment and Debt Reduction*	*Current*	*Next Year*	*Year 3*	*Year 4*	*Year 5*	*Year 6*	*Year 7*	*Year 8*	*Year 9*	*Year 10*
	Liquid Assets										
1.	Cash, CSBs, Short-term Deposits	____	____	____	____	____	____	____	____	____	____
2.	GICs	____	____	____	____	____	____	____	____	____	____
3.	Company Savings Plan	____	____	____	____	____	____	____	____	____	____
4.	Insurance	____	____	____	____	____	____	____	____	____	____
5.	Other	____	____	____	____	____	____	____	____	____	____
	Investments										
6.	Bonds (or Bond Funds)	____	____	____	____	____	____	____	____	____	____
7.	Canadian Preferred Shares (or Funds)	____	____	____	____	____	____	____	____	____	____
8.	Other	____	____	____	____	____	____	____	____	____	____
9.	Cdn. Common Stock (or Common Stock Funds)	____	____	____	____	____	____	____	____	____	____
10.	Other	____	____	____	____	____	____	____	____	____	____
11.	Other Canadian Mutual Funds	____	____	____	____	____	____	____	____	____	____
12.	Other Mutual Funds	____	____	____	____	____	____	____	____	____	____
13.	Tax Shelters	____	____	____	____	____	____	____	____	____	____
14.	Real Estate (other than residential)	____	____	____	____	____	____	____	____	____	____

15. Mortgages
16. Business Interests
17. Other

Tax Deferral Plans

18. Voluntary Pension Contribution
19. Spousal RRSP
20. RRSP
21. Other

Fixed Assets

22. Residence (purchase or improvement)
23. Seasonal Residence
24. Furnishings
25. Listed Personal Property

Amount to Liabilities

Transfers to (from)

(use Account # from above)

Spouse (income splitting)
Acct #:

Spouse (other —)
Acct #:

Children (income splitting)
Acct #:

Children (other —)
Acct #:

Other Expenditures

MONEY MANAGEMENT

1. How do you take care of household bills? Who pays—you or your spouse?

   Comments:______________________________

2. To what degree are you involved in setting your household budget?

   Comments:______________________________

3. How aware are your spouse and children of family finances?

   Comments:______________________________

4. How would you describe your communication on financial matters? With your spouse? With your children?

   Comments:______________________________

INVESTOR ATTITUDE PROFILE

What are your investment objectives in order of priority? (1, 2, 3)

Preserve Capital __________
Capital Appreciation __________
Generate Income __________

Is income required? Yes______ No______ If yes, yield?__________
Will capital be required? Yes______ No______ If so, when?__________

Do you have enough time to manage your money effectively? Yes______ No______ Your Spouse? Yes______ No______

Do you have the knowledge to manage your money properly? Yes______ No______ Your Spouse? Yes______ No______

Are you interested in learning more about investments? Yes______ No______ Your Spouse? Yes______ No______

What is your desired risk/return ratio?
High______ Medium______ Low______ Combination______

Amount available to be invested:
Tax-sheltered capital (RRSPs, etc.): Lump sum $______ Monthly $______
Non-tax-sheltered capital: Lump sum $______ Monthly $______

What is your experience with and/or attitude toward:
Choosing your own investments?

____

Deciding when to get in and out?

____

Borrowing for investment?

____

Tax shelters?

____

What areas of investment do you prefer?

____

Other comments:

____

____

GOALS AND OBJECTIVES

Career Objectives	You __________
	Spouse __________
	Children __________
Personal Goals	You __________
	Spouse __________
	Children __________
Educational Goals	You __________
	Spouse __________
	Children __________
Financial Objectives	You __________
	Spouse __________
	Children __________
Concerns	__________

Worksheet 8
ESTATE PLANNING

		You	*Spouse*
Wills:	Dated		
Family Trusts:	Dated		
Holding Companies:	Dated		
Buy-Sell Agreements:	Dated		
Marriage Contract:	Dated		
Divorce or Separation Agreements:	Dated		

DESIRED ESTATE DISTRIBUTION

Executor(s) and Trustee(s) ______________________

Contingent Executor(s) and Trustee(s) ______________________

Burial or cremation instructions ______________________

Guardian(s) ______________________

	Value	*Cash/Property*	*Beneficiary*
Plan benefits (RRSPs, IAACs, etc.)			
Specific bequests			
Cash legacies:			
Residue:			
Outright (30-day survival)			
In trust (describe)			
Common disaster provisions (describe)			
Vesting of children's shares (e.g., ½ at age 25, balance at age 30)			

Worksheet 9
ESTATE CAPITAL NEEDS—LIQUIDITY AT DEATH

Liquid Assets Available at Death

Balance Sheet:		
Liquid Assets	______	
Tax deferred accounts	______	
Investments	______	
Other	______	
C(Q)PP (Death Benefit):	______	
Life Insurance:		
Group	______	
Personal	______	
Total Liquid Assets:		____(1)

Less Cash Requirements at Death

Final expenses (funeral, etc.)	______		
Debts	______		
Mortgage	______		
Children's Education	______		
Cash Bequests (personal, charitable, etc.)	______		
Income tax	______		
Capital invested after tax required to produce income (worksheet 10)	______		
Other	______		
Total Cash Requirements at Death:		____(2)	
Cash Surplus (Deficit) at Death: (1–2)			======

Worksheet 10
ESTATE CAPITAL NEEDS—SURVIVOR INCOME

Current Annual Expenditures:		________
Less Reductions for:		
Deceased's living expenses	________	
Mortgage payment	________	
Other	________	
Subtotal		________
Net Adjusted Expenditures:	________	
Spouse's Income:		
Employment	________	
Other	________	
CPP/QPP	________	
Total		________
Net income required		________
Projected after-tax rate of return on estate capital invested:	___ %	
Estimated amount of capital required to produce income	________	

Worksheet 11
INSURANCE INFORMATION

LIFE AND TERM INSURANCE							
Company	*Policy No.*	*Life Insured*	*Beneficiary*	*Face Amount*	*Type*	*Premium*	*Additional Benefits*

Worksheet 12
HOMEOWNER (TENANT) INSURANCE

Insurance	*Limits*	*Last Premium Paid*
Dwelling	______	______
Personal Property	______	______
Personal Liability	______	______

Do you have any scheduled items? For what amount?

Jewellery	$______
Furs	$______
Fine Arts	$______
Camera	$______

Please list location and insurance limits of your:

	Location	*Limits*
Seasonal Dwelling	______	______
Farm	______	______
Watercraft	______	______
Motors	______	______

Rating Information: (Please complete with respect to your home.)

Ground Area Main Floor:	Year Built:
Construction:	# of Stories:
Basement – Is It Finished?	# of Bathrooms:
# Fireplaces:	Where is the Chimney? – Inside or Outside
Type of Garage:	# Cars:
Central Air Conditioning?	Other Features:

What is the Renewal Date of your Policy?______

If your home was built prior to 1955:

1. Is all wiring 100 AMP service?
2. Has plumbing been changed over to copper?
3. Has the roof been replaced or repaired?

Worksheet 13
AUTOMOBILE INSURANCE

Insurance	*Limits*	*Last Paid Premium*
Third Party Liability	________	________________
Collision Deductible	________	________________
Comprehensive Deductible	________	________________
Any Other Coverages	________	________________

Rating Information:

Vehicles	*Year*	*Make*	*Model*	*# Doors*	*Describe Use*
1	_______	_______	_______	_______	_______
2	_______	_______	_______	_______	_______
3	_______	_______	_______	_______	_______

Operators	*Age*	*# Years Licensed*	*# Miles One Way to Work If Driven*
1	______	____________	________________
2	______	____________	________________
3	______	____________	________________

Does new driver have driver training? If so, attach copy of certificate. List *all* accidents and/or violations for *all* drivers, *whether or not demerit points were lost*, over the last four years

What is the Renewal Date of your Policy? __________

Worksheet 14
DISABILITY INSURANCE

Income Required

Current budget expenses		______
Less spouse's take-home pay		(______)
Less reduction in disabled's expenses		(______)
plus cost of special care and/or domestic help		______
Total estimated expenditures		$______
Tax-free benefits available	$______	
Group (employee paid)	______	
Personal	______	
	$______	
Taxable benefits available	$______	
Estimated tax	( )	
Net after-tax benefits	$______	
Total tax-free and after-tax benefits		$______
Net additional after-tax income required		$______

Details of Present Coverage

Company	Contractual Basis	Def. of Disability	Waiting Period	Benefit Period	Benefit Amount *	Comments

Total $______________________

*Indicate tax-free benefits with asterisk (*) i.e., where you pay the premiums, not your employer.

Worksheet 15
DOCUMENTS CHECKLIST

We find that most people tend to keep their important documents at home, at the office or in a safety deposit box at a bank or trust company. Please complete the following checklist:

Item	Location	Submitted	To Be Submitted
1. Tax Returns:			
You	______	______	______
Spouse	______	______	______
2. Wills:			
You	______	______	______
Spouse	______	______	______
3. Trust Agreements	______	______	______
4. Life Insurance Policies	______	______	______
5. General Insurance Policies	______	______	______
6. Annuity Contracts	______	______	______
7. Marriage Contract	______	______	______
8. Divorce/Separation Agreements	______	______	______
9. Business Agreements — Describe:	______	______	______
10. Title Deeds/Mortgages	______	______	______
11. Employee Benefits Summary	______	______	______
12. Others — Describe:	______	______	______
	______	______	______

Worksheet 16
BANKING DATA

Item	*Location*	*Acct/Box/Key Number*
1. Chequing Accounts:		
Personal	____________________	__________
Business	____________________	__________
2. Savings Accounts:		
Personal	____________________	__________
Business	____________________	__________
3. Safety Deposit Box	____________________	__________
4. Safety Deposit Box Key	____________________	__________

FORM OF POWER OF ATTORNEY

THIS GENERAL POWER OF ATTORNEY is given on the . . . . . . , day of . . . . , 1986, by —— of the —— of —— in the —— of —— and Province of Ontario.

I APPOINT —— of the —— in the —— of —— and Province of Ontario, to be my attorney in accordance with the POWERS OF ATTORNEY ACT and to do on my behalf anything that I can lawfully do by an attorney, and particularly the following acts, the enumeration of which is not in any way to limit the general power herein conferred, namely:

(a) To purchase, sell, make, draw, accept, endorse, discount, transfer, renew, negotiate and in every way deal with cheques, bills of exchange, promissory notes, deposit receipts, bonds, debentures, coupons and every kind of negotiable instrument and security;

(b) To subscribe for, accept, purchase, sell, pledge, transfer, surrender, and in every way deal with shares, stocks, bonds, debentures and coupons of every kind and description and to vote and act in respect thereof;

(c) To receive and collect rents, dividends, bonuses, profits, interest, commission, fees, salaries, debts and claims of every kind and to give receipts and discharges therefor and to distrain for rent and interest;

(d) To purchase, sell, rent, exchange, mortgage, charge, lease, surrender, manage, and in every way deal with real estate and any interest;

(e) To take, assume, purchase, discharge, assign, pledge and in every way deal with mortgages of real and personal property and to exercise all powers of sale and other powers therein; and

(f) To conduct any business operations.

In accordance with the POWERS OF ATTORNEY ACT, I declare that this power of attorney may be exercised during any subsequent legal incapacity on my part.

In accordance with the POWERS OF ATTORNEY ACT, I declare that, after due consideration, I am satisfied that the authority conferred on the attorney named in this power of attorney is adequate to provide for the competent and effectual management of all my estate in case I should become a patient in a psychiatric facility and be certified as not competent to manage my estate under The Mental Health Act. I therefore direct that in that event, the attorney named in this power of attorney may retain this power of attorney for the management of my estate by complying with subsection 38(2) of The Mental Health Act and in that case the Public Trustee shall not become committee of my estate as would otherwise be the case under clauses 38(1)(a) and (b) of that Act.

Any power of attorney or other delegation of authority to an agent heretofore given by me is hereby revoked.

____

(Signature of Witness)

____

____

(Name of Witness)

CONSUMER PRICE INDEX
Canada 1961 × 100.00

Year	*Index*	*Increase From Prior Year %*
1961	*100.0	.9
1962	101.2	1.2
1963	103.0	1.7
1964	104.8	1.8
1965	107.4	2.4
1966	111.4	3.7
1967	115.4	3.6
1968	120.1	4.0
1969	125.5	4.6
1970	129.7	3.3
1971	*100.0	2.9
1972	104.8	4.8
1973	112.7	7.5
1974	125.0	10.9
1975	138.5	10.8
1976	149.0	7.5
1977	160.8	8.0
1978	175.2	9.0
1979	191.2	9.1
1980	210.6	10.1
1981	*100.0	10.7
1982	110.8	10.8
1983	117.2	5.8
1984	122.3	4.4
1985	127.2	3.9

Source: Statistics Canada.
*The official time base for the CPI has been converted from 1961 = 100 to 1971 = 100 to 1981 = 100.

INCOME TAX TABLE (1986)[1-2] QUEBEC RESIDENTS

Taxable Income	Income Tax Federal	Income Tax Quebec	Total Tax	Effective Rate	Marginal Rate[3] Federal	Marginal Rate[3] Quebec	Marginal Rate[3] Total
$ 3000	$ 295	$ 429	$ 724	$24.1%	14.2%	16.5%	30.7%
3936	428	584	1012	25.7	14.2	17.5	31.7
4000	437	595	1032	25.8	14.2	17.5	31.7
5000	579	769	1348	27.0	14.2	17.5	31.7
5127	597	792	1389	27.1	14.2	18.4	32.6
5221	610	809	1419	27.2	15.0	18.4	33.4
6000	727	952	1679	28.0	15.0	18.4	33.4
6504	803	1045	1848	28.4	15.0	19.4	34.4
7000	878	1142	2020	28.9	15.0	19.4	34.4
7832	1003	1303	2306	29.4	15.9	19.4	35.3
8000	1029	1336	2365	29.6	15.9	19.4	35.3
8095	1045	1354	2399	29.6	15.9	20.4	36.3
9000	1188	1538	2726	30.3	15.9	20.4	36.3
9935	1336	1729	3065	30.9	15.9	21.3	37.2
10000	1347	1743	3090	30.9	15.9	21.3	37.2
11000	1505	1956	3461	31.5	15.9	21.3	37.2
12000	1664	2170	3834	32.0	15.9	21.3	37.2
13000	1823	2392	4215	32.4	15.9	22.3	38.2
13054	1831	2404	4235	32.4	16.7	22.3	39.0
14000	1989	2615	4604	32.9	16,7	22.3	39.0
14519	2076	2731	4807	33.1	16.7	23.3	40.0
15000	2156	2843	4999	33.3	16.7	23.3	40.0
16000	2323	3076	5399	33.7	16.7	23.3	40.0
17000	2490	3008	5798	34.1	16.7	23.3	40.0
18000	2657	3541	6198	34.4	16.7	23.3	40.0
18275	2703	3605	6308	34.5	19.2	23.3	42.5
18820	2808	3732	6540	34.8	19.2	24.3	43.5
19000	2842	3776	6618	34.8	19.2	24.3	43.5
20000	3034	4018	7052	35.3	19.2	24.3	43.5
21000	3226	4261	7487	35.7	19.2	24.3	43.5
22000	3419	4503	7922	36.0	19.2	24.3	43.5
23000	3611	4746	8357	36.3	19.2	24.2	43.4
23496	3706	4866	8572	36.5	20.9	24.3	45.2
24000	3811	4988	8799	36.7	20.9	24.3	45.2
25000	4020	5231	9251	37.0	20.9	24.3	45.2
26000	4229	5473	9702	37.3	20.9	24.3	45.2
26347	4301	5557	9858	37.4	20.9	25.2	46.1
27000	4437	5722	10159	37.6	20.9	25.2	46.1
28000	4646	5974	10620	37.9	20.9	25.2	46.1
29000	4855	6227	11082	38.2	21.2	25.2	46.4
30000	5067	6479	11546	38.5	22.1	25.2	47.3
31000	5288	6731	12019	38.8	22.1	25.2	47.3
32000	5509	6983	12492	39.0	22.1	25.2	47.3
33000	5731	7235	12966	39.3	22.1	25.2	47.3
34000	5952	7488	13440	39.5	22.1	25.2	47.3

Taxable Income	Income Tax Federal	Income Tax Quebec	Total Tax	Effective Rate	Marginal Rate[3] Federal	Marginal Rate[3] Quebec	Marginal Rate[3] Total
35000	6173	7740	13913	39.8	22.1	25.2	47.3
36000	6394	7992	14386	40.0	22.1	25.2	47.3
36550	6516	8131	14647	40.1	26.6	25.2	51.8
37000	6635	8244	14879	40.2	26.6	25.2	51.8
38000	6901	8496	15397	40.5	26.5	25.2	51.7
39000	7166	8749	15915	40.8	26.6	25.2	51.8
39169	7211	8791	16002	40.9	26.5	26.2	52.7
40000	7432	9009	16441	41.1	26.6	26.2	52.8
41000	7697	9271	16968	41.4	26.6	26.2	52.8
42000	7963	9533	17496	41.7	26.6	26.2	52.8
43000	8228	9795	18023	41.9	26.6	26.2	52.8
44000	8494	10056	18550	42.2	26.6	26.2	52.8
45000	8759	10318	19077	42.4	26.6	26.2	52.8
46000	9025	10580	19605	42.6	26.6	26.2	52.8
47000	9290	10842	20132	42.8	26.6	26.2	52.8
48000	9556	11104	20660	43.0	26.6	26.2	52.8
49000	9821	11366	21187	43.2	26.6	26.2	52.8
50000	10087	11628	21715	43.4	26.6	26.2	52.8
51000	10352	11890	22242	43.6	26.6	26.2	52.8
52000	10618	12152	22770	43.8	26.6	26.2	52.8
53000	10883	12414	23297	44.0	26.6	26.2	52.8
56000	11680	13199	24879	44.4	26.6	26.2	52.8
58000	12211	13723	25934	44.7	26.6	26.2	52.8
60000	12742	14247	26989	45.0	26.7	26.2	52.9
61608	13180	14668	27848	45.2	28.1	27.2	55.3
62000	13290	14774	28064	45.3	28.1	27.2	55.3
62657	13474	14953	28427	45.4	31.8	27.2	59.0
64000	13901	15318	29219	45.7	31.8	27.2	59.0
66000	14537	15861	30398	46.1	31.8	27.2	59.0
68000	15173	16404	31577	46.4	31.8	27.2	59.0
70000	15808	16947	32755	46.8	31.8	27.2	59.0
72000	16444	17490	33934	47.1	31.8	27.2	59.0
74000	17080	18034	35114	47.5	31.8	27.2	59.0
76000	17716	18577	36293	47.8	31.8	27.2	59.0
78000	18352	19120	37472	48.0	31.8	27.2	59.0
80000	18987	19663	38650	48.3	31.8	27.2	59.0
82000	19623	20206	39829	48.6	31.8	27.2	59.0
84000	20259	20750	41009	48.8	31.8	27.2	59.0
86000	20895	21293	42188	49.1	31.8	27.2	59.0
88000	21531	21836	43367	49.3	31.8	27.2	59.0
90000	22166	22379	44545	49.5	31.8	27.2	59.0
92000	22802	22922	45724	49.7	31.8	27.2	59.0
94000	23438	23466	46904	49.9	31.8	27.2	59.0
96000	24074	24009	48083	50.1	31.8	27.2	59.0
98000	24710	24552	49262	50.3	31.8	27.2	59.0

Taxable Income	*Income Tax* Federal	*Income Tax* Quebec	*Total Tax*	*Effective Rate*	*Marginal Rate*[3] Federal	*Marginal Rate*[3] Quebec	*Marginal Rate*[3] Total
100000	25345	25095	50440	50.4	31.8	27.2	59.0
102000	25981	25638	51619	50.6	31.8	27.2	59.0
104000	26617	26182	52799	50.8	31.8	27.2	59.0
106000	27253	26725	53978	50.9	31.8	27.2	59.0
108000	27889	27268	55157	51.1	31.8	27.2	59.0
110000	28524	27811	56335	51.2	31.8	27.2	59.0
112000	29160	28354	57514	51.4	31.8	27.2	59.0
114000	29796	28898	58694	51.5	31.8	27.2	59.0
115000	30114	29169	59283	51.6	31.8	27.2	59.0
116000	30432	29441	59873	51.6	31.8	27.2	59.0
117000	30750	29712	60462	51.7	31.8	27.2	59.0
118000	31068	29984	61052	51.7	31.8	27.2	59.0
119000	31385	30256	61641	51.8	31.8	27.2	59.0
120000	31703	30527	62230	51.9	31.8	27.2	59.0

1. This table reflects the 3% Quebec tax reduction.
2. This table reflects the 2½% surtax on basic federal tax in excess of $6,000 plus the 2½% surtax on basic federal tax in excess of $15,000.
3. The marginal rate applies to each additional $1.00 of income in excess of the taxable income indicated.

INCOME TAX TABLE (1986)[1-2] RESIDENTS OF PROVINCES OTHER THAN QUEBEC

Taxable	*Ont.*[3]		*Nfld.*		*P.E.I.*		*N.S.*		*N.B.*		*Man.*[4]		*Sask.*[5]		*Alta.*[6]		*B.C.*[7]	
Income	*Tax*	%	*Tax*	%	*Tax*	%	*Tax*	%	*Tax*	%	*Tax*	%	*Tax*	%	*Tax*	%	*Tax*	%
$ 4000	$ 785	25.5	$ 837	27.2	$ 798	25.9	$ 819	26.6	$ 827	26.9	$ 806	26.2	$ 591	28.1	$ 525	28.1	$ 772	25.1
5221	1096	27.0	1170	28.8	1115	27.5	1144	28.2	1155	28.4	1126	27.7	933	29.7	868	29.7	1078	26.6
7832	1801	28.5	1922	30.4	1831	29.0	1879	29.7	1897	30.0	1849	29.3	1709	31.4	1645	31.4	1772	28.0
10000	2419	28.5	2581	30.4	2460	29.0	2524	29.7	2548	30.0	2484	29.3	2388	31.4	2314	27.3	2379	28.0
12000	2989	28.5	3189	30.4	3039	29.0	3119	29.7	3149	30.0	3069	29.3	2989	28.5	2860	27.3	2940	28.0
13054	3290	30.0	3509	32.0	3345	30.5	3432	31.3	3465	31.6	3377	30.8	3290	30.0	3147	28.7	3235	29.5
15000	3873	30.0	4132	32.0	3938	30.5	4041	31.3	4080	31.6	3977	30.8	3873	30.0	3706	28.7	3809	29.5
17000	4473	30.0	4772	32.0	4548	30.5	4667	31.3	4712	31.6	4593	30.8	4473	30.0	4280	28.7	4400	29.5
18275	4856	34.5	5180	36.8	4937	35.1	5066	36.0	5115	36.3	4985	35.4	4856	34.5	4646	33.0	4776	33.9
20000	5451	34.5	5815	36.8	5542	35.1	5687	36.0	5742	36.3	5596	35.4	5451	34.5	5215	33.0	5361	33.9
22000	6141	34.5	6551	36.8	6243	35.1	6407	36.0	6469	36.3	6305	35.4	6141	34.5	5875	33.0	6040	33.9
23496	6657	37.5	7101	40.0	6768	38.1	6946	39.1	7012	39.5	6835	38.5	6657	37.5	6369	35.9	6547	36.9
25000[4]	7221	37.5	7703	40.0	7342	38.1	7534	39.1	7606	39.5	7414	41.2	7221	37.5	6908	35.9	7102	36.9
27000	7971	37.5	8503	40.0	8104	38.1	8317	39.1	8396	39.5	8238	41.2	7971	37.5	7626	35.9	7839	36.9
29744	9000	38.8	9600	41.3	9150	39.4	9390	40.4	9480	40.8	9368	42.5	9000	38.8	8610	37.1	8851	38.1
31000	9487	38.8	10118	41.3	9645	39.4	9897	40.4	9992	40.8	9901	42.5	9487	38.8	9077	37.1	9330	38.1
33000	10262	38.8	10943	41.3	10432	39.4	10705	40.4	10807	40.8	10750	42.5	10262	38.8	9819	37.1	10093	38.1
35000	11037	38.8	11768	41.3	11220	39.4	11512	40.4	11622	40.8	11599	42.5	11037	38.8	10562	37.1	10856	38.1
36550	11638	46.5	12408	49.5	11830	47.3	12138	48.5	12254	48.9	12257	50.9	11638	46.5	11137	44.6	11447	45.8
37000	11847	46.5	12630	49.5	12043	47.3	12356	48.5	12474	48.9	12487	50.9	11847	46.5	11337	44.6	11652	45.8
37392[7]	12029	46.5	12825	49.5	12228	47.3	12546	48.5	12665	48.9	12686	50.9	12029	46.5	11512	44.6	11832	47.2
37543[5]	12099	46.5	12899	49.5	12299	47.3	12619	48.5	12739	48.9	12763	50.9	12099	48.3	11579	44.6	11903	47.2
40000	13242	46.5	14115	49.5	13460	47.3	13810	48.5	13941	48.9	14015	50.9	13286	48.3	12674	44.6	13062	47.2
42000	14172	46.5	15105	49.5	14405	47.3	14779	48.5	14919	48.9	15034	50.9	14252	48.3	13565	44.6	14006	47.2
44210[3]	15199	46.9	16199	49.5	15449	47.3	15849	48.5	15999	48.9	16159	50.9	15319	48.3	14549	44.6	15049	47.2

Taxable	Ont.[3]		Nfld.		P.E.I.		N.S.		N.B.		Man.[4]		Sask.[5]		Alta.[6]		B.C.[7]	
Income	Tax	%	Tax	%	Tax	%	Tax	%	Tax	%	Tax	%	Tax	%	Tax	%	Tax	%
46000	16040	46.9	17085	49.5	16295	47.3	16717	48.5	16875	48.9	17071	50.9	16184	48.3	15347	44.6	15893	47.2
48000	16979	47.0	18075	49.5	17240	47.3	17686	48.5	17853	48.9	18090	50.9	17150	48.3	16238	44.6	16837	47.2
50000	17918	47.0	19065	49.5	18185	47.3	18655	48.5	18831	48.9	19109	50.9	18116	48.3	17129	44.6	17780	47.2
52000	18857	47.0	20055	49.5	19130	47.3	19624	48.5	19809	48.9	20128	50.9	19082	48.3	18020	44.6	18724	47.2
54000	19796	47.0	21045	49.5	20075	47.3	20593	48.5	20787	48.9	21146	50.9	20048	48.3	18911	44.6	19668	47.2
56000	20735	47.0	22035	49.5	21020	47.3	21562	48.5	21765	48.9	22165	50.9	21014	48.3	19802	44.6	20611	47.2
58000	21674	47.0	23025	49.5	21965	47.3	22531	48.5	22743	48.9	23184	50.9	21980	48.3	20693	44.6	21555	47.2
60000	22613	47.0	24015	49.5	22910	47.3	23500	48.5	23721	48.9	24203	50.9	22946	48.3	21584	44.5	22499	47.2
60877	23025	48.5	24450	51.0	23325	48.8	23925	50.0	24150	50.4	24650	52.4	23370	49.8	21975	46.1	22912	48.7
62657	23887	54.9	25357	57.8	24192	55.3	24814	56.6	25047	57.1	25583	59.4	24256	56.4	22794	52.2	23779	55.2
65000	25174	54.9	26712	57.8	25487	55.3	26140	56.6	26385	57.1	26975	59.4	25578	56.4	24017	52.2	25072	55.2
70000	27919	54.9	29602	57.8	28249	55.3	28971	56.6	29241	57.1	29947	59.4	28400	56.4	26627	52.2	27830	55.2
75000	30665	54.9	32492	57.8	31012	55.3	31801	56.6	32097	57.1	32919	59.4	31222	56.4	29236	52.2	30589	55.2
80000	33410	54.9	35382	57.8	33774	55.3	34632	56.6	34953	57.1	35890	59.4	34044	56.4	31846	52.2	33347	55.2
85000	36156	54.9	38272	57.8	36537	55.3	37462	56.6	37809	57.1	38862	59.4	36866	56.4	34455	52.2	36106	55.2
90000	38901	54.9	41162	57.8	39299	55.3	40293	56.6	40665	57.1	41833	59.4	39688	56.4	37065	52.2	38865	55.2
95000	41647	54.9	44052	57.8	42062	55.3	43123	56.6	43521	57.1	44805	59.4	42510	56.4	39674	52.2	41623	55.2
100000	44392	54.9	46942	57.8	44824	55.3	45954	56.5	46377	57.1	47777	59.4	45332	56.4	42284	52.2	44382	55.2
110000	49883	54.9	52722	57.8	50349	55.3	51615	56.6	52089	57.1	53720	59.4	50976	56.4	47503	52.2	49899	55.2
120000	55374	54.9	58502	57.8	55874	55.3	57276	56.6	57801	57.1	59663	59.4	56620	56.4	52722	52.2	55416	55.2

1. Following the May 23, 1985 federal budget, this table reflects the 5% surtax on basic federal tax in excess of $6,000 plus the 5% surtax on basic federal tax in excess of $15,000.
2. The marginal rate applies to each $1.00 of income in excess of the taxable income indicated.
3. This table reflects the 3% surtax on basic Ontario tax payable in excess of $5,000 (taxable income greater than $44,210).
4. This table reflects the Manitoba surtax of 20% on basic Manitoba income tax in excess of $2,600 (taxable income greater than $25,000).
5. This table reflects the Saskatchewan surtax of 12% on basic Saskatchewan tax payable in excess of $4,000 (taxable income greater than $37,543).
6. This table reflects the Alberta tax reduction granted to low income taxpayers. The erosion of this tax reduction will cause a slight distortion in the marginal rate for tax brackets below $9,000.
7. This table reflects the British Columbia surtax of 10% on adjusted B.C. tax payable in excess of $3,500 (taxable income greater than $37,392). This table also reflects an 8% surtax for Health Care Maintenance on the total British Columbia tax. The 10% surtax is only applicable to residents of the province.

Glossary

Administrator: An individual or trust company appointed by a proper court to administer the estate of a person who has died without leaving a valid will. A female administrator is an administratrix.

Age of Majority: The age at which an individual can legally act on his or her own behalf. In Canada this age is eighteen.

All Perils: Automobile comprehensive and collision coverage combined, and subject to a common deductible amount.

Alternative Investment Cost: What you might have made if you had done something else with your money. For instance, if you wanted to hold a certain amount in cash, you might have had to choose between holding currency and opening a savings account. If you decided to hold currency, the "alternative investment cost" would be the interest income you gave up by not opening a savings account. Also called "opportunity foregone," "opportunity cost," or "interest foregone."

Amortization: The spreading of an expense (i.e., interest, capital repayment, depreciation) over a period of time.

Annuity: A series of regular periodic payments comprising return of a portion of capital and interest.

Asset: Anything of value that is owned by an individual, corporation, or other business. Includes prepaid expenses and intangibles such as patents and good will, as well as land, buildings, equipment, raw materials, and finished goods.

Association Group Insurance: Insurance available to members of a trade or professional association.

Attribution Rules: If income-producing property is transferred by gift or loan from one spouse to another or to anyone under the age of eighteen, income received by the recipient is taxed as if received by the donor of the property. Also can apply to capital gains in a spouse-to-spouse transfer only.

Beneficiary: One who is to receive the benefits of any type of contract or agreement.

Bequest: A disposition of personal property by will.

Blue Chip Stock: Shares of a large established company with a history of steady dividend payouts and/or growth in profits.

Bona Fide Loan: A genuine loan that is properly documented in writing.

Bond: A debt obligation of a corporation, negotiable in terms of interest and principal and secured by a pledge of assets. For "bonds" of public bodies, see "Debenture."

Bullion: Any metal in mass, especially gold and silver.

Call: An agreement which gives the holder the option to buy specific securities at a given price within a specified period of time.

Canada Pension Plan (CPP): A public contributory pension plan introduced in Canada in 1966; provides death and disability benefits as well as a pension at age sixty-five.

Canada Savings Bond: A bond issued annually by the government of Canada. It differs from other Canadian government bonds in that it can only be purchased by individuals, and can be cashed for its face amount (plus interest, if any) at any time.

Capital: Plant, machinery, raw materials—anything that is used to provide goods and services. Often used to refer to money earmarked for investment.

Capital Cost Allowance: A deduction against income in respect of depreciation against the undepreciated capital cost of an asset. Its purpose is to give tax relief for the decline in value of the asset because of use, wear and tear, and aging.

Capital Gains: The gains realized upon disposition of certain types of assets. Up to $500,000 of lifetime gains is tax exempt; over that amount one-half is taxable as income when received or deemed to have been received on certain gifts or dispositions at death.

Career Average Benefit: A pension benefit formula that defines the pension unit earned in a year in terms of earnings for that year. Total pension at retirement will thus be based on average earnings while a member of the plan.

Cash Surrender Value: The amount an insurance company guarantees to pay if you terminate certain types of life insurance policies.

Central Mortgage and Housing Corporation (CMHC): A federally sponsored agency that acts as guarantor of qualified mortgages for both commercial and residential properties.

Certificate of Deposit (CD): A security issued by a bank stating that it has borrowed money from you and will pay it back with interest at a certain time. CDs pay high interest but usually require deposits of $10,000 or more. (In Canada, more often referred to as a Term Deposit.)

Chequing Account: An account at a bank, trust company, loan association, or credit union against which cheques may be drawn.

Chequing Savings Account: An account at a bank, trust company, loan association, or credit union on which interest is paid and against which cheques may be drawn.

Codicil: An instrument in writing executed by a testator for adding to, altering, explaining, or confirming a will previously made by the testator; executed with the same formalities as a will and having the effect of bringing the date of the will forward to the date of the codicil.

Collateral: Assets pledged as security for a loan. If the borrower defaults on payment, the lender may dispose of the property pledged as security to raise the money to repay the loan.

Commercial Building: A building used for purposes of making money.

Commodity: A tangible thing that can be bought or sold, such as grain or precious metals.

Common Disaster: When both spouses die at the same time or within a short time of each other.

Common Stock: Ownership in a corporation with no preference to income or assets.

Comprehensive: Physical damage insurance on an automobile covering damage from all perils except collision.

Comprehensive Personal Liability Insurance: A form of public liability insurance against occurrences in the home and activities of family members, servants, and pets. (See Homeowner Policy.)

Consumer Loan: A loan to an individual for personal purposes; interest usually is calculated on a different and less favourable basis than on a business or investment loan.

Consumer Price Index: An index compiled by federal authorities showing cost-of-living changes during a specified period of time.

Convertible Bond: Bonds that can be converted into a specified amount of common stock within a specified time period.

Coupon Rate: The stated rate of return for a bond (constant over the life of the bond).

Covered Option: An option written on stock you already own. (See Stock Option.)

Current Service Contribution: Contribution made to a pension plan in the current year.

Daily Interest Accounts: Accounts on which interest is calculated on the daily balance and typically credited monthly. They are available as both chequing and savings accounts.

Death Duties: Generally a synonym for succession duties; occasionally used to refer to all taxes payable at death.

Debenture: "Bonds" of public bodies are really debentures because they are not specifically secured by a pledge of assets.

Debt Ratio: Amount borrowed as a percentage of total capital (debt and equity together).

Deferred Annuity: An annuity under which income payments to the annuitant commence some time after the date it is purchased.

Deferred Compensation: Income paid at some future time, usually upon retirement or termination of employment.

Deferred Profit Sharing Plan (DPSP): A plan that an employer may institute on behalf of employees to allow deferral of personal tax on profit distributions to employees.

Defined Contribution Plan: A "money purchase" pension plan under which employer and employee contributions are fixed; the pension benefit based on annuitizing these contributions.

Demand Loan: A loan on which the lender may demand repayment at any time. Often made interest-free between family members for the purpose of reducing tax on investment income. (See Income Splitting.)

Depletion: Deduction from income of mines and oil and gas wells to recognize that the supply of the resource is limited. Similar in effect to capital cost allowance on physical assets.

Depreciation: An allocation of the cost of replacing fixed assets over a period of time. (See Capital Cost Allowance.)

Devise: A disposition of real estate by will.

Disability Insurance: Insurance that provides for future income payments to a policyholder in the event of disability caused by sickness or injury.

Disposition: Transfer of an asset, usually capital property; can be actual, as in a gift or sale, or "deemed," as in some cases at death.

Dividend: Earnings or profits paid by a corporation to its shareholders. In an insurance policy, a "dividend" is a refund of an overpayment of premiums.

Dollar Averaging: An investment technique of investing uniform sums on a regular basis, thereby lowering average cost of investments because more units will be bought at lower prices.

Dower: The common-law right of a widow to a life estate in one-third of the lands owned by her husband during their marriage, held by him alone, and not previously released by her.

Earnings Per Share: Corporate earnings, less preferred dividends, divided by the number of common shares outstanding.

Employee Benefit: Compensation other than cash received by an employee; usually refers to group insurance, pensions and other broadly based benefits.

Endowment Insurance: Cash value life insurance that pays on death within a stated period of time, or on survival to the end of that stated period of time.

Equity (in property): Rights of ownership.

Escalation Clause: Clause in an agreement providing for the adjustment of a price based on some specific event, usually an increase in relevant costs, e.g., in an office lease.

Estate Planning: The orderly arrangement of one's financial affairs to maximize the value transferred at death to individuals and institutions favoured by the deceased, with minimum loss of value because of taxes and forced liquidation of assets.

Executor: The person named in a will to manage the estate of the deceased according to the terms of the will.

Exemption: Specific deduction allowed taxpayers as a result of their circumstances (e.g., for a child).

Experience: In group insurance, it refers to the relationship of total premiums paid by a group to claims paid out by the insurer. The higher the claims/premium ratio, the poorer the experience.

Final Average Benefit: A defined benefit formula that expresses the pension unit earned in a year in terms of the average earnings over a short period (three to ten years) just before retirement.

Financial Planner: A person who helps you plan your financial future and carry out those plans.

Fixed Income Fund: A fund whose assets are invested in preferred shares, bonds, and mortgages.

Fixed Return Investment: Investment offering constant returns over a period of time (e.g., a mortgage).

Fund Manager: A person who manages the assets of an investment fund.

Gift Tax: A direct tax on the donor of property whose value exceeds certain maximum allowable deductions. No province in Canada levies a gift tax.

Grossed-Up Dividend: Beginning in 1987, dividends paid by a Canadian corporation to an individual are increased by one-third in calculating income tax for tax purposes. Individuals are then allowed a 16.67% dividend tax credit on the grossed-up dividend against total taxes payable. For instance, if you receive a cash dividend of $600, it will be grossed up to $800 for tax purposes and you will receive a $133 credit against federal tax and $26–$38 in provincial tax payable. In 1986, gross up is one-half and tax credit is 22.67%

Group Dental Plan: Group coverage for the payment of dental expenses.

Growth Stock: Stock whose price is expected to increase at an above-average rate (often carrying an above-average risk as well).

Guaranteed Investment Certificate (GIC): Certificates offered by trust companies, banks, and credit unions that guarantee a specified rate of interest for a certain period of time, generally one to five years.

Guardian: A person designated by a testator or by the court to be responsible for the physical care of someone unable to look after himself or herself. Normally appointed for dependent children.

Hedge: A method of protecting against financial loss by investing in assets which will tend to move in opposite directions.

Homeowner Policy: An insurance policy covering residence buildings and contents against fire and a series of other perils such as windstorm, water damage, burglary, robbery, and theft (of contents). The policy includes Comprehensive Personal Liability coverage. (See Comprehensive Personal Liability Insurance.)

Income Averaging Annuity Contract (IAAC): A special type of annuity designed to spread the impact of income tax payable on certain types of taxable lump sum receipts such as taxable capital gains. It was eliminated in the November 1981 Budget.

Income Producing Property: Assets that produce income, such as rent, interest, or dividends.

Income Splitting: The process of spreading income among family members. Most often affects tax on investment income. It usually involves interest-free demand loans from a high-tax-rate breadwinner to a low or nil rate child. In some cases, earned income can be split by employment of family members in a family business.

Incorporation: The legal process of creating a corporation by which an association or group of individuals becomes a legal entity with limited liability.

Indexed Plan: A benefit plan where benefits are related to a recognized index, such as the Consumer Price Index as determined by Statistics Canada.

Indexed Security Investment Plan (ISIP): A registered investment plan which indexes tax on capital and provides considerable scope for tax deferral. Introduced in October 1982 and abolished at the end of 1985.

Inflation: An increase in the general level of prices.

Insurance Deductible: An amount deductible from a claim paid by an insurance company. In effect, the insured "self-insures" for the amount of the deductible.

Interest-Free Loan: A loan for which the lender does not charge interest; most often a demand loan between family members. (See Demand Loan and Income Splitting.)

Inter Vivos: From the Latin for "between living persons," usually refers to a trust established during the lifetime of the person setting up the trust (the settlor), as opposed to a "testamentary" trust in a will that takes effect only at death.

Intestacy Laws: The provincial laws governing distribution of the assets of a person who dies without a will.

Intestate: Not having made and left a valid will. The term also is used to refer to a person who dies without leaving a valid will.

Investment Company: A company whose chief assets are a portfolio of securities.

Investment Counsellor: A person who, for a fee, advises you on what investments to make and makes them for you.

Issue: All persons who have descended from a common ancestor; the more specific term "children" refers to only one generation.

Legacy: A gift by will of money. (See Devise.)

Letters of Administration: A certificate confirming authority to administer an intestate estate, issued to an administrator by the proper court.

Letters Probate: A certificate of authority to administer a particular estate, issued to an executor by a proper court.

Liquidity: Extent to which a person has cash or can procure cash quickly and at relatively little cost or loss, without the sale or mortgaging of assets.

Major Medical Coverage: Insurance against certain medical expenses not covered under government medical coverage. Includes prescription drugs and private-duty nursing care.

Margin: Difference between the value of the stocks purchased and the amount borrowed by the investor from the brokerage firm (i.e., the investor's equity in the stock transaction).

Maturity: The time when the principal amount of a security or loan is due.

Merger: Combining of two or more firms into a single firm with all assets and liabilities of the former firms retained.

Minimum Monthly Balance: The smallest amount in a bank account during the month; the amount on which interest often was payable before the introduction of daily interest accounts.

Money Purchase Plan: A pension plan in which contributions rather than benefits are defined. (See Defined Contribution Plan.)

Mortgage: A claim on property to secure a debt.

Mortgage Broker: A person who helps arrange mortgage financing on a home or other real property, or the buying or selling of a mortgage.

Multi-Account System: The use by an individual of several bank accounts in which each is allocated certain sources or amounts of money.

Multiple Unit Residential Building (MURB): A major tax shelter in Canada since 1974; provides unique tax advantages in that capital cost allowance (depreciation) can be used as a deductible expense to create losses against income other than that from the real estate itself.

Mutual Funds: A portfolio of investment securities held in the name of the fund owned by people who have bought shares in the fund itself; managed by full-time investment specialists.

National Housing Act (NHA): An Act of Parliament under which the government guarantees home mortgages to certain income groups who might otherwise not qualify, and at rates lower than those charged on conventional mortgages.

Net Income: Generally, gross income less expenses incurred to earn income, but before taxes. On a personal tax return net income also assumes deductions for Canada Pension Plan, Unemployment Insurance, RRSPs.

Net Worth: Total assets minus total liabilities.

Non-Cancellable, Guaranteed Renewable: An insurance policy which provides that once the policy is in force the insurance company cannot cancel or alter the contract or refuse to renew it. Usually refers to a type of disability insurance.

Not Sufficient Funds (NSF): A term used in reference to a cheque drawn on a bank account in which the balance is not sufficient to honour it.

Odd Lot: A small quantity of shares (less than 100) that must be exchanged by a special procedure and at higher than normal brokerage costs.

Old Age Security: A non-contributory retirement benefit provided by the federal government to all Canadians age sixty-five or over. This benefit is paid in addition to the Canada Pension Plan.

Option: A right to buy or sell a stated quantity of stock or a commodity at a specific price within a specific time period.

Overdraft: The withdrawal from a bank account of an amount greater than the positive balance in the account. Often used to refer to a negative balance in one's account.

Par Value: Face value of a bond or the par value of a stock used for dividend calculation.

Partnership of Acquests: The regime governing marital property under the Civil Code of the Province of Quebec. It replaced the old community-of-property regime.

Past Service Contribution: Contributions made to a pension fund to provide benefits conferred in recognition of service with the employer when the employee was not a contributor to the pension plan.

Patronage Dividends: Dividends paid to members of a consumer co-operative based on the amount they purchase from the cooperative in a given period.

Payroll Deduction: Payment made on your behalf and automatically deducted from your paycheque by the employer.

Pension Income Deduction: The first $1,000 of income from certain sources is deductible from one's income for tax purposes, at any age when income is from a pension or superannuation fund and from age sixty-five when income is obtained from "private" sources, such as an unregistered annuity or an RRSP.

Perquisites ("perks"): Non-cash compensation to executives: everything from a corner office to a club membership; also includes cars, interest-free loans, counselling, etc.

Personal Net Worth: Total assets minus total liabilities of an individual.

Personal Representative: A general term applicable to a person, including an administrator or executor, having the legal right to represent someone, including a deceased person.

Pooled Fund: Money contributed by different individuals or groups and invested on behalf of all by a fund manager.

Pooled Risk: In group insurance: where claims/premiums experience is averaged to prevent unusually bad experience by a single employer having an adverse effect on future premiums.

Portfolio: The entire asset holdings of an individual or group of individuals.

Preferred Beneficiary: A class of persons who receive special treatment in regard to succession values in life insurance and other property. The term is used in legislation governing life insurance contracts, income tax, and succession duties.

Preferred Shares: Ownership shares which get priority to income or asset distribution but usually forego voting rights.

Present Value: The value today of something (usually money) to be delivered in the future. This recognizes that interest and certain contingencies will make a dollar several years hence worth less than a dollar today.

Price/Earnings Ratio: A measure of stock price (i.e., how "reasonable" it is) that divides earnings per share into the price of the stock.

Principal: The amount or balance outstanding on a loan.

Private Health Insurance: Insurance plans provided by private insurance companies, in contrast to health insurance provided by government or public agencies such as Blue Cross.

Promissory Note: A written promise to pay money or money's worth, usually for money, goods and/or services received.

Public Liability Coverage: Insurance that will pay damages assessed against you as a result of bodily injury, death, or property damage or others (third parties) imputed to have been caused by your negligence.

Public Trustee: The official appointed by the provincial government to supervise the administration of assets owing to a charity, a public trust, or a mentally incompetent person in an institution.

Put: An option to sell a specific quantity of stock at a stated price within a specific time period.

Quebec Pension Plan (QPP): Quebec's version of Canada Pension Plan.

Recaptured Depreciation: The portion of capital cost allowance (depreciation) recovered on sale of depreciable capital when the sale price is greater than the "undepreciated capital cost" (i.e., the original cost minus the amount of depreciation deducted). Recaptured depreciation is fully taxable as income.

Receivables: Amounts payable to a person or corporation for goods and/or services produced, sold, or rendered for which an invoice has been sent.

Receivership: Where control of a corporation is taken over by a trustee (the receiver) to conserve assets until they can be liquidated, or until an arrangement can be made with creditors to continue the business.

Registered Educational Savings Plan (RESP): A plan designed to help an individual save for the purpose of providing for university education. Tuition fees are paid from the plan *if* the child actually attends a university or other approved post-secondary institution; otherwise, contributions are returned without interest.

Registered Pension Plan (RPP): A government-approved pension plan that allows both employee and employer to contribute to retirement savings.

Registered Retirement Savings Plan (RRSP): A government-approved tax-sheltered plan that allows an individual to save for retirement or other purposes with pre-tax dollars.

Remarriage Clause: A clause in a will or other agreement that deals with assets of the deceased in the event of remarriage of the surviving spouse.

Residue: The property that remains after the testator has made provision out of his or her net estate for specific bequests, legacies, or devises. Those who receive the residue are known as residuary beneficiaries.

Retiring Allowance: A taxable payment (subject to some tax deferral related to years of service), usually in the form of a lump sum, made to an individual upon retirement or upon dismissal from a job; a payment in recognition of long service or for loss of employment or loss of office.

Retractable: A share, usually preferred, which can be redeemed at a stipulated date.

Rider: A clause or condition in a contract or policy that may restrict, add to, or more specifically define the terms or benefits.

Right of Survivorship: The right to succeed to the ownership or part ownership of property as the result of the death of an owner or part owner.

Rights: An opportunity for shareholders to acquire shares of the company at below market price (negotiable on the market).

Rollover: The transfer of property from one person or situation to another without triggering tax at the time of transfer; e.g., from an RPP to an RRSP or from one spouse to another.

Rule of 72: A way to determine the effect of compound interest. How long will it take your money to double if you invest it at 8%, keep reinvesting the interest received and earn 8% on all reinvestments? Use the Rule of 72: divide 72 by the rate of interest and you get the number of years it takes to double your capital. 72 divided by 8 is 9; therefore in nine years you'll double your money; in eighteen years you'll quadruple it.

Self-Administered Plan: A plan in which planholders have the right to choose their own investments and administrator.

Self-Insurance: Accepting financial responsibility for the results of insurable hazards, rather than transferring that responsibility to an insurer by taking out an insurance contract and paying premiums to provide such protection.

Selling Short: The sale of borrowed securities in a form of speculation where you expect prices to drop.

Severance Payment: A payment upon departure from a company. Can be paid in the form of ongoing income, a retiring allowance, or termination payment.

Short-Term Deposit: A deposit of money into a bank, trust company, credit union, or savings association for a period of time normally ranging from one to 180 days.

Significant Shareholder: A shareholder who holds, by himself or herself or with his or her family, stock in a company equal to at least 10% of the shares of the company. In some cases referred to as a designated shareholder.

Small Business Deduction: A deduction which creates a preferential rate of tax available to private Canadian-controlled businesses on certain maximum amounts of annual net income, currently $200,000.

Speculation: Commitment of funds for a short time period, and at high risk, in the hope of large returns from price changes.

Spousal RRSP: An RRSP where one spouse makes the contributions and claims the tax deduction, but where title to plan proceeds is in the name of the other spouse, at whose rates income from the plan will be taxed in most cases.

Stock Dividend: A pro rata distribution to stockholders of additional shares of stock in lieu of cash. Now taxable as if received in cash.

Stock Option: The option of purchasing stock (usually from one's employer) at an agreed price.

Stock Split: The division of a company's existing shares into a larger number of shares, to reduce the price per share.

Stop-Order: Designed to limit losses — an order to the broker to buy (if you have sold "short") or sell (if you have bought "long") at a stated "trigger price."

Surrogate Court: The provincial court responsible for the official proving of wills and overseeing the administration of estates (sometimes referred to as the Probate Court).

Syndicate: An association of persons or corporations formed to carry out a common business venture.

Taxable Benefit: An employee benefit or perquisite paid for by an employer on which the employee is taxed; e.g., a company car.

Tax Deductible: Refers to amounts that may be subtracted from one's income for tax purposes.

Tax Deferred: Income or benefits on which payment of taxes may be deferred until some future date.

Tax-Deferred Dividends: Dividends paid from a Canadian corporation on which tax does not have to be paid until some later date.

Tax Haven: A political jurisdiction where no income tax is levied (e.g., Bermuda, Bahamas, Grand Cayman, Channel Islands).

Tax Sheltered: Income that is currently not subject to tax but may be taxed in the future.

Term Insurance: Life insurance that pays if death occurs within a stated period of time. Usually there is no cash value under a term insurance policy.

Termination Payment: A payment made on severance of employment.

Testamentary: Created by will, as in "testamentary trust."

Treasury Stock: Authorized but unissued stock that is still in the treasury of the corporation.

"True" Savings Account: An account without chequing privileges at a bank, trust company, loan association, or credit union on which interest is paid.

Trust: A bequest or devise that puts legal title and control of property in the hands of one party (trustee) for the benefit of another party (beneficiary).

Trust Officer: A person who works in the estate administration department of a trust company.

Trustee: A person who administers assets held in trust for another person.

Underwriter: A person, banker, or group that guarantees to furnish a definite sum of money by a definite date in return for an issue of bonds or stock. In insurance, the one assuming a risk in return for the payment of a premium (i.e., the company), or the person who assesses the risk and establishes premium rates and extent of coverage.

Uninsured Judgment: A judgment of legal liability for damages assessed by a court for an amount not covered by public liability of one kind or another.

Unit Benefit Plan: A type of defined benefit plan under which the pension earned each year is established by formula.

Valuation: Act of establishing the value of a property, whether tangible or intangible.

Variable Return Investment: Investment offering no set rate of return (e.g., common stock).

Vendor-Take-Back (VTB) Mortgage: A mortgage taken by the seller from the buyer, often to facilitate a sale.

Venture Capital: Money invested in higher-risk projects in which an ownership position is taken.

Vesting: The process by which an employee obtains full credit for the employer contributions into a benefit plan (normally a pension plan or a deferred profit sharing plan).

Warrants: The right to purchase stock in a company at a specified price during a specific period of time. Usually offered when market prices of the stock are expected to increase.

Will: A legally enforceable declaration of a person's wishes relating to matters to be dealt with after his or her death, and inoperative until death has occurred. A will is revocable or can be amended by a codicil up to the time of death; it is applicable to the situation that exists at the time of death.

Will Drafting: Determining the intent of the testator and extent of the will, and preparing a rough draft of the will.

Will Execution: The process of making your will valid. Usually involves formalities in regard to signing by the testator and witnessing of that signature.

Whole Life: Also called "straight life" or "ordinary life," insurance that pays whenever death occurs. Whole life insurance has cash values.

Working Capital: Current assets minus current liabilities. A measure of how well an individual or a company can meet current obligations as they come due.

Yield: Investment return measured as a percentage of current market value of the investment. Most often used in reference to bonds or debentures.

Index